I0801561

A Primer for Teaching Digital History

DESIGN PRINCIPLES
FOR TEACHING HISTORY
A series edited by Antoinette Burton

A PRIMER FOR TEACHING DIGITAL HISTORY

Ten Design Principles

Jennifer Guiliano

DUKE UNIVERSITY PRESS
Durham & London
2022

Printed in the United States of America on acid-free paper ∞
Typeset in Garamond Premier Pro by
Westchester Publishing Services

Library of Congress Cataloging-in-Publication Data
Names: Guiliano, Jennifer, author.
Title: A primer for teaching digital history : ten design principles / Jennifer Guiliano.
Other titles: Design principles for teaching history.
Description: Durham : Duke University Press, 2022. | Series: Design principles for teaching history | Includes bibliographical references and index.
Identifiers: LCCN 2021036645 (print)
LCCN 2021036646 (ebook)
ISBN 9781478015055 (hardcover)
ISBN 9781478017684 (paperback)
ISBN 9781478022299 (ebook)
Subjects: LCSH: History—Computer-assisted instruction. | History—Computer network resources. | History—Study and teaching—United States. | History—Methodology. | BISAC: HISTORY / Study & Teaching | EDUCATION / Distance, Open & Online Education
Classification: LCC D16.117 .G58 2022 (print) | LCC D16.117 (ebook) | DDC 907.8/5—dc23/eng/20211019
LC record available at https://lccn.loc.gov/2021036645
LC ebook record available at https://lccn.loc.gov/2021036646

Cover art: Casey Reas, *AYFABTU (Followers 3k)*, 2015. Custom software (color, silent), digital video, computer, screen; dimensions variable, portrait orientation. Image courtesy of the artist.

For the teachers, including my sister Theresa Downing, who spend their lives educating those around them. This book is in recognition of all the hours you spend, the lives you change, and the future you shape. This book is also dedicated to every historian who wants to learn something new. You are amazing for trying, no matter whether or not you succeed. And to Brett, because he wanted a book dedication of his own.

Contents

Acknowledgments ix

Introduction 1

PART I
FOUNDATIONS

One
Sources as Data 19

Two
Learning Outcomes 35

Three
New Forms of Assignments 53

Four
The Basics of Digital Methods 71

PART II
SELECTED METHODS

Five
Digital Source Criticism 85

Six
Text and Network Analysis 97

Seven
Visualization 111

PART III
FORMS OF SCHOLARSHIP

Eight
Digital Archives, Digital Exhibits, and Digital Collections 129

Nine
Storytelling 149

Ten
Crowdsourcing 163

Conclusion: Embracing Digital History 171

Glossary and Resources 179

Notes 201

Bibliography 221

Index 243

Acknowledgments

TEACHING IS HARD. It takes patience, kindness, and a strength of will that requires you to not only master the content but also understand the nuances of how students learn. And it takes someone that understands that teaching and learning is an innately collaborative process. In the classroom, teachers work with the students and their colleagues as much as they check off that they've done what the course requires. When I first began teaching as a twenty-year-old master's degree student in history at Miami University of Ohio, I thought teaching was about students learning all the things. I agonized over how much or how little material to include. I fretted over classroom discussions where we never got to that last thing on my list of things to cover. I thought my success as a teacher was reflected by whether students had earned A's. Now, two decades on, that anxiety has lessened because I'm seeing how the things my students learn are transforming their lives. I'm most proud not of my students who earn A's consistently but of the students who grind day in and day out to move the needle from the C+ to the B, from the D to the C+. I'm gratified by my first-year, first-generation students who work diligently to learn the academic bureaucracy. I'm awed by my returning students who are often balancing full-time course loads with full-time jobs and families. I'm staggered by the vulnerability of my veteran students who don't shy away from talking in the classroom about their wartime experiences. And I am fulfilled as a teacher by watching my students speak up about their experiences with the historical forces of racism, sexism, poverty, and power that shape their lives. Their bravery makes it easier as a teacher to help others understand the significances and consequences of history. This book would not be possible without these students who illustrate the utility of history and its importance in today's global world.

For the last six years, along with my colleague Trevor Muñoz, I have been privileged to codirect the Humanities Intensive Learning and Teaching Institute (HILT). Annually, it brings together over a hundred undergraduate and graduate students, postdoctoral fellows, librarians, faculty, academic staff, and cultural heritage professionals to learn from the best instructors in their respective fields. In the ways that I have learned specific technologies, explored theoretical principles, and built entire research agendas, HILT has been transformative for me as a teacher. Not only are its instructors stellar in their own right as researchers, but they are committed to developing sound, effective pedagogy that is ethical and effective. The conversations I've had with them, the approaches they have taken, and the ways they have crafted their courses are reflected here. I wish to thank Amanda Licastro, Anastasia Salter, Ben Brumfield, Bridget Whearty, Caitlin Pollock, Carolina Villaroel, Catherine DeRose, Catherine Knight Steele, Cheryl Ball, Curtis Fletcher, David McClure, Dean Irvine, Dean Rehberger, Dorothea Salo, Dot Porter, Elijah Meeks, Elli Mylonas, Gabriela Baeza Ventura, Jarah Moesch, Jarom McDonald, Jeremy Boggs, Jeri Wieringa, Jesse Stommel, Jessica Lu, Jim Casey, Julia Flanders, Kam Woods, Katie Rawson, Lee Skallerup-Bessette, Mark Algee-Hewitt, Matt Jockers, Meghan Ferriter, Mia Ridge, micha cárdenas, Michael Meredith, Nicole Coleman, Porter Olsen, Purdom Lindblad, Richard Urban, Sarah Patterson, Scott Enderle, Simon Appleford, Stephen McLaughlin, Tanya Clement, Taylor Arnold, Trevor Muñoz, Virginia Kuhn, and Wayne Graham. Special recognition goes to Brandon Locke, Brandon Walsh, Ethan Reed, and Thomas Padilla, who have modeled year after year how to interweave teaching technology platforms with the ethical and theoretical concerns of content. I extend my deep appreciation for

Lauren Tilton, Roopika Risam, Lee Skallerup-Bessette, and Kalani Craig. Lauren contributed to this book through her keen eye as a feminist scholar of American studies specializing in visual methods. She also did so from France, in the middle of a global pandemic and countrywide lockdown, and with little notice. Lauren, thank you. Roopika participated in any number of frantic text messages and conversations about digital humanities, digital history, and the classroom. Her work to decolonize digital humanities and the classroom is inspiring and has shaped my thinking about the systems of oppression that digital technologies encourage. She's also a patient coeditor of our journal, *Reviews in the Digital Humanities*, who stepped up when I asked for time away to work on revisions to this text. Roopsi, I appreciate you and hope this work speaks to the conversations we've had about student work and pedagogy. As with any book project there is a moment when you realize that you've created your own echo chamber and need outside voices to help you refine your ideas. Lee and Kalani, with no notice and with tremendous workloads of their own, set aside their time to help me address how to communicate the fundamental idea of data to those with little experience. I thank them tremendously for their contributions.

This book has also benefited from the expertise of a number of historians via our discussions about the field of digital history and the practice of teaching. I would like to extend my gratitude to the digital historians who attend the conferences for the Organization for American Historians; the American Historical Association; the American Studies Association; and the Alliance for Digital Humanities Annual Digital Humanities conference. While the contributions are too numerous to itemize, please know that your work at the intersections of technology and history continues to influence my thinking about the classroom. I also want to thank the participants in the "Arguing with Digital History" workshop hosted by the Roy Rosenzweig Center for History and New Media and the "Doing Sport History in the Digital Present" workshop hosted by the North American Society for Sport History. Of particular note are Kalani Craig, Jo Guldi, Micki Kaufman, Sharon Leon, Michelle Moravec, Miriam Posner, Lauren Tilton, William Thomas III, Amanda Regan,

Andrew McGregor, Andrew Linden, Dain TePoel, Mary G. McDonald, Jennifer Sterling, and Murray Phillips. The richness of their intellectual interventions into how digital history exists as both a set of practices and values cannot be understated.

Series editor Antoinette Burton's invitation to write this book serves as a highlight of my career thus far. She has been a role model for me throughout the last ten years not just because she served as a fantastic advisor to one of my closest friends in graduate school; Antoinette has been a prolific author and voice for the place of women in history and in the historical profession. She's built a career being the type of historian and leader I've always hoped to be: kind, direct, and innovative. When she wrote to me to extend the invitation to join this series, I called my friend and told her that I'd done something right in my career if AB trusted me with a book in her series. Antoinette, thank you for patience as I wrote this book and for your trust. Similarly, I'd like to thank those who attended the manuscript workshop at the University of Illinois. Their feedback, along with the feedback from the anonymous reviewers, shaped this book tremendously. All remaining errors or problems are mine.

I'd like to thank Stephanie Rowe, Modupe Labode, Elee Wood, Ray Haberski, Nancy Robertson, Charli Champion-Shaw, and Marianne Wokeck, all colleagues or former colleagues at Indiana University–Purdue University Indianapolis (IUPUI) for their support of this work. They provided encouragement and a needed counterbalance to my desire to say yes to everything. Caitlin Pollock, formerly a digital humanities librarian at IUPUI and digital historian of Ida B. Wells, assisted with this book as it coincided with us coteaching an undergraduate survey. She engaged in substantive discussions with me as we developed our pedagogy and outcomes. I will miss teaching with her in the future as she's just left my office, having told me she's taking a new position elsewhere. Rebecca Shrum deserves special mention for attending all sixteen weeks of my graduate course Digital Public History in the years preceding the writing of this book. She provided extensive feedback on the effectiveness of the course for her as both a student and as a faculty member designing her own digitally inflected modules at the undergraduate level. I am lucky to have her as a colleague. Simon Appleford deserves applause for being a great collaborator and coauthor. A tremendous digital historian in his own right, he willingly let me delay finishing our coauthored textbook to focus on this effort. He also served as a second set of discerning eyes from the proposal through to the final publication-ready manuscript. Many of the exercises spoken of in this text have their root in conversations with him about how best to teach a particular concept. He also answered every late-night text message in which I asked to pick his brain about best practices in digital history teaching. The material on visualization as it relates to space, place, and movement owes its origin to Karen Rodriguez'G, director of undergraduate research at the University of Illinois and a historian of space and identity within the imperial British empire. Karen and I have had too many discussions to count about diaspora, movement, space, identity, and how to represent that information. We've also agonized together over our successes and failures as teachers. It is my hope that the chapter included represents the best of those conversations and successes.

I would be remiss to not thank my family, who I am sure will not read this book. They didn't read my first. I doubt they'll read anything I write, ever. Just to test them, I'll give any one of them who can summarize what it says beyond what is on the book jacket or in a book review a free meal at a local restaurant of their choice once we've ended COVID-19 closures and it is safe to eat out again. Thank you for being there day in and day out no matter what. Thanks for letting me be me.

Introduction

EACH DAY, 2.5 quintillion bytes of data are created. More than 3.7 billion people surf the internet. Sixteen million text messages are sent per minute. Each day, 4.7 trillion photos are stored in the cloud.[1] The deluge of both digitized and born-digital materials is simply unceasing.[2] Full-scale digital repositories allow you to not only access documents on demand but also annotate, analyze, combine, and remix them into new forms of scholarship. Catalogs and search engines assist in uncovering resources. The computer and its associated software can make organizing and producing research more efficient than was previously possible. In parallel, major archives, libraries, and governments have conducted sweeping digitization programs to provide access to their archives, holdings, and analog records.[3] As a result, the opportunities to develop digital history research agendas and teaching pedagogies are flourishing. That flourishing can feel like an overwhelming tide as digital technologies encompass and expand the cultural record. From the digitization of analog physical materials, to the recovery of materials stored on early media formats like floppy disks, to the harvesting of web and social media platforms, historians of the future will certainly have to confront digital sources and the internet when they analyze the past. Professional historians are not alone in engaging with digital technologies and tools. Digital history can put the tools of knowledge creation in the hands of communities so that they can articulate and explore their own histories. One of those communities is our students who are eager to embrace the possibilities of their own history in digital forms. This book serves to assist you in thinking through how the history classroom can serve as a site of knowledge production with and about digital technologies, tools, and approaches.

Depending on which methods and historiographies one elects to draw on, what is digital history and what is possible with digital history methods can vary.[4] Some scholars are attracted to new forms of scholarly publishing, such as websites, podcasts, and multimodal storytelling, and might tie their digital history definition to methods from journalism, new media, and communications. Others are intrigued by the possibilities available through massive digital archives, exhibits, and collections and might define digital history through the lens of digital libraries, archives, and information science. Still more options include statistical models and high-performance computing, which provide a pathway to crunch massive datasets in order to explore humans and their experiences at ever greater scales. These historians may define digital history as intricately tied to computer science, statistics, and mathematics. There are even historians who have embraced digital history to build elaborate video games and digital reproductions that allow us to "play the past."[5] They might define digital history through new media, art, and modeling. Cultural historians Petri Paju, Mila Oiva, and Mats Fridlund define digital history as encompassing "diverse historical practices, such as digitization efforts at archives, libraries and museums, computer-assisted research, web-based teaching and professional and public dissemination of historical knowledge, as well as research on the history of 'the digital,' computers and digital technologies."[6] Hannu Salmi offers a definition of digital history as "an approach to examining and representing the past; it uses new communication technologies and media applications and experiments with computational methods for the analysis, production, and dissemination of historical scholarship."[7] As digital historian Jo Guldi reminds us, "digital history is not so much a field or sub-field . . . as a universal approach to history."[8] For Guldi, digital history is not singular so much as digital histories that are "informed by exchanges, building on works already in progress across the land."[9] This is why most digital history also engages with fields outside history and with the digital humanities generally.

What digital history is and how it is practiced is defined by your historical interests, the audiences you seek to reach, and how you wish to communicate with those audiences. For this reason, digital history definitions are multipart and often demarcate the "how" and "for whom" as much as what digital history is. Digital public historian Sheila Brennan, for example, defines digital history as

> an approach to researching and interpreting the past that relies on computer and communication technologies to help gather, quantify, interpret, and share historical materials and narratives. It empowers individuals and organizations to be active participants in preserving and telling stories from the past, and it unlocks patterns embedded across diverse bodies of sources. Making technology an integral component of the historian's craft opens new ways of analyzing patterns in data and offers means to visualize those patterns, thereby enriching historical research. Moreover, digital history offers multiple pathways for historians to collaborate, publish, and share their work with a wide variety of audiences. Perhaps most important, digital methods help us to access and share marginalized or silenced voices and to incorporate them into our work in ways not possible in print or the space of an exhibition gallery.[10]

How you define digital history is directly impacted by the historical questions and contexts you seek to understand and the audiences you hope to reach. This book will provide overviews of how differing historians articulate and enact their own digital history definitions through classroom pedagogy. Digital history remains tied to the fundamentals of historical scholarship, evidence, and argument, and the historians and projects selected for inclusion in this book represent the variety of approaches to teaching and engaging with digital history. They ask similar questions in the digital space that we do in the analog, but they also represent the questions about access, audience, output, and privacy that you must grapple with as you work with digital technologies and their capabilities. These questions often highlight digital technologies' problematic roots, whether by interrogating power and audience, the ways in which digital technologies enable certain types of historical thinking, or their ties to issues of privacy, data, and security.

Digital history has a long trajectory within the historical discipline. Quantitative history has long leveraged statistical analysis and modeling to allow social and economic historians to create massive databases of historical records.[11] Harriet and Frank Owsley, Merle Curti, William O. Aydelotte, and others in the 1940s and 1950s transformed manuscript records into quantitative data that could be tabulated and sorted via IBM-owned Hollerith machines. This enabled them to provide sophisticated analyses of employment and immigration patterns and of other aggregated trends over time. Economic historians and historians of American slavery spent years enmeshed in a debate over the validity of computational methods for historical scholarship after the publication of the 1974 work *Time on the Cross: The Economics of American Negro Slavery* by Robert Fogel and Stanley Engerman.[12] Digital public history is now almost three decades old. Edward Ayers's award-winning website The Valley of the Shadow, published in 1993, introduced audiences to a digital archive of primary sources drawn from Augusta County, Virginia, and Franklin County, Pennsylvania, during the American Civil War (1861–65). The work of Ayers, William G. Thomas III, Anne Sarah Rubin, Andrew Torget, and others working on the Valley project encouraged generations of historians to consider digitization and hypertext, which allows you to link documents to one another, as an opportunity to reach new audiences.[13] So too did the digital history work facilitated by the American Social History Project, which produced scores of digitized, annotated, and analyzed primary and secondary sources as part of its work in the 1990s on the website History Matters: The U.S. Survey Course on the Web.[14] It hasn't just been scholars employed as full-time historians that have grounded digital history in research and teaching. Much of digital history was created, and continues to be authored by, the archivists, librarians, museum educators, and other cultural heritage professionals who embraced the possibilities of technology for telling stories of the past. Historians rely on their expertise and join them in crafting narratives for specialists and the public alike that highlight the wide variety of possibilities enabled by computers, tablets, smartphones, programming languages, and digital software. They have also been joined by computer programmers, user experience designers, informaticists, and even engineers who contribute to building technologies, providing methods, and challenging how historians conceptualize history and its many varied types of evidence and argument.

The primary connection between analog and digital that grounds this book is the belief that what makes it into our histories is a statement of our values and positions as individuals and as historians. For me, this is an antiracist, feminist, decolonial practice that implements practices from social justice and disability justice, which recognize that selection, bias, issues of institutional support, access to resources and materials, problems of racial hierarchies, the embrace of capitalism, and the consequences of colonialism have long affected and been central in the discipline of history. Digital technologies amplify these concerns. Choosing to use tools like the global positioning system (GPS) ties users to their roots: such devices, created by the military, furthered nation-building in the 1950s. From their inception in the early 2000s, social media tools like Facebook and Twitter have also been tied to surveillance and implicated in violence against colonized peoples. Decisions to create digital archival collections in the midst of the most recent round of anti-Black violence around the globe intersect with concerns about privacy, law, and oppression that analog historians face when they encounter documents of trauma and violence in the physical archive. Choices about appearance and clothing in digital historical re-creations intersect with questions of accuracy and appropriation. The systems of oppression and trauma that dominate the analog world have been amplified in the digital sphere, even as many pretend it is exceptional because anyone can use and post to the internet. These issues are of particular concern for underrepresented and marginalized communities who encounter systemic and highly personalized encounters with digital tools and technologies.[15] These are not US-centric or Europe-centric concerns, as the technologies that are developed in the United States and Europe are often imported to other countries, particularly the global South.[16]

Beginning by highlighting the importance of the creation and analysis of digital archives about the transatlantic slave trade, historian Jennifer Hart argues that African countries and those who study African history face "persistent challenges to processing and preserving archival materials on the continent."[17] Celebrating the ability of digital technologies to bring "new voices and perspectives into the popular and scholarly conversations about the African past," Hart argues that digital history is yet another methodological practice embraced by Africanist scholars who seek to re-think historical practice. She writes, "By engaging in public scholarship, these digital history projects help re-think long-standing concerns among Africanist scholars about the politics of knowledge production and the repatriation of scholarly materials."[18] Elaborating on the links between collaborative projects that are often funded outside the African continent and the lack of resource investment in African countries, Hart cautions that digital history can replicate the extractive processes, biases of funding, and limitations of institution building where centers, institutes, and programs overwhelm concerns of representation, inclusion, and access. Digital history that operates outside of academic contexts is, according to Hart, a vibrant space that problematizes both how the field defines itself and how it is defined by others.

Digital history encourages treating software, platforms, and algorithms as sites of analysis themselves, to challenge these amplified threads. Whether you are encouraging students to explore the logic underlying a freely available tool or asking them to build a digital project from scratch, the thread running through all digital history is a wary eye on the word "digital" and its relationship to historical thinking. This is a necessity because digital history relies on parameters and objects established by nonhistorians. Racism, sexism, and corporate interests are embedded within internet search engines and their functionality just as they are encapsulated in analog archives.[19] Historical misinformation and shoddy citational practices proliferated before the advent of the internet, but the internet enables them to spread at a much more rapid rate and with greater influence, as anyone can retweet, share, or republish. Anyone can say whatever they'd like, however they'd like, on the internet. With the mass digitization of cultural records, materials shared from underrepresented communities and the global South have been made more readily available to academics and their students. Sources divorced from the contexts of their production and the communities they represent are one of the most slippery slopes of digital history research. Students can easily find materials but often are ill-equipped to consider the ethics of their use. This is particularly keen for scholars and students situated in the global North who are disconnected from the scholars, communities, and cultural heritage institutions of the global South.[20] With collaborative digital technologies and partnerships, we can bridge that distance, but as teachers we must do so in a way that is honest to the needs of the communities we wish to engage with. As Indigenous scholar Linda Tuhiwai Smith reminds us, the needs of researchers do not necessarily align to the interests or needs of communities.[21] Digital technologies enable us to have virtual meetings, shared workspaces, and shared projects. One way of ameliorating the disconnect between the source base you hope to use and the community it originates from is through collaborative projects. Partnering with scholars, individual students, classes, and cultural heritage institutions is one way to bridge the disconnect between the positions of privilege many of us occupy and the communities we seek to understand.

It is important to consider as well the "digital divide," which is a blanket term used to refer to the uneven and unequal access to, or use of, digital technologies based on social, economic, geographical, geopolitical, or even cultural criteria. As this text is being written, the global coronavirus pandemic is actively reshaping teachers' sense of those extremes. When I talk with my colleagues about our students, it becomes clear that the problem isn't that students might not have computers or internet access. Instead, it is that their computers are too old, the software too slow, or the connection too poor to give them a consistent, high-quality engagement with virtual learning environments. One student, for example, shared with me that, as the oldest sibling in her family, she had to wait until her three siblings as well as her parents used the family's computer for school and work before she could sign in to our class. The reality for many of our students is that their digital insecurity challenges their ability to contribute to our classes. It is our obligation as educators to recognize that instability and, wherever possible, accommodate students' needs. This may involve setting up loan programs for devices, creating low-bandwidth versions of course content, and providing alternative assignments that scale to the resources available to your students. If you are working within the contexts of communities in the global South, that could also mean recalibrating your projects to be developed on and work with low-bandwidth internet connections and cellphone screens.

Because much of the public gets its historical knowledge from the internet, there is a pressing need to understand how and where digital technologies and historical thinking meet. This book identifies that meeting ground by illustrating how digital history research can be both included in, and at the center of, our teaching practices. Digital history gives historians opportunities to engage in a timely manner. And, as importantly, it provides avenues and opportunities for individuals and communities to tell their own stories, with their own values, and for their own purposes. Audience then is a prime concern of digital history. In this book, the question of audience is woven throughout, including whom history is for, how we write for different audiences, and what obligations we, as historians, have to our audiences. Audience, you'll learn, requires attention not just to what we need as teachers and scholars but also to what our students and digital project users might need as well.

Regardless of how stellar they are or how much they struggle in our classes, students want to hear the histories of their communities. They want to know about their ancestors and how decisions by individuals, communities, and governments in the past shaped their present. While they might seek simple answers on tests, they are most intrigued by history's nuance and complexity. They like the challenge history offers. What decisions might they have made? How might their histories be added to the stories already being told? How might they challenge everything we know about a particular event, period, or interpretation? It is our privilege as teachers to help them seek out those narratives in all their complexities.

This book suggests that in a digital history classroom, the stories we want to tell can fundamentally interrogate not just what histories are told but also how we tell them and who has access to them. Student historians can narrate their own stories and also make them easily available to broader audiences through digital avenues.

At this point, you may be asking yourself whether I am going to prescribe how much of your class should be devoted to developing historical context for the students and how much should be driven by technologies. This book is not a prescriptive textbook that walks you step by step through teaching a digital history course. It does not provide hard and fast rules for the classroom. Instead, this book represents the possibilities enabled by using digital methods and forms of scholarship as they exist in history classrooms today. It highlights for you the variety of strategies and approaches that can lead to digital history outcomes. It shows small slices of digital history scholarship in any given chapter. This means there are ample opportunities for you to look at additional pedagogical examples. To enable this, I've incorporated citations and hyperlinks to digital methods, projects, and portfolios so that you can explore further on your own. I've also included a brief glossary of terms and digital projects at the end of the book to help you as you navigate each chapter.

As we move through the book, you'll be encouraged to make decisions for your course based on your own values, abilities, and course intent. Those decisions will also be shaped by the resources available to you. For that reason, in the glossary, I've indicated which software and tools are free so that it's clear which can be implemented without institutional support. I've also written each chapter to provide varying levels of technical expertise to your approaches for digital history methods and tools. The lines between an example from a collegiate classroom and a high school, or even middle school, classroom are much fuzzier than one might expect. Frequently, the technical capabilities of high school (and even middle school) students are not much less than that of college freshmen. I've seen middle school students building apps while my college students struggle with developing a multimedia-driven website and vice versa. Age has little to do with a student's technical abilities. In fact, one of the most pernicious ideas is that those who are chronologically younger are somehow more technologically fluent than those who are older. You'll notice that, throughout the book, I identify what level a course operates at—middle and high school, college, and so on—along with descriptions of the digital history activities. But I also note how you might scale up or down the historical and technological complexity based on your students' abilities. Don't be afraid to try out any example in a class, regardless of a student's educational level; you'll often be able to nudge it toward a more or less complicated direction based on students' abilities. For that reason, I like to gauge where my students are at through a pre-class survey that asks them what they know how to use versus what they know how to build. I often repeat that survey at the close of class to measure their growth. This allows for customization of the course, so I meet students where they are at and then challenge them, rather than teaching toward either the most or least technologically able.

In large part, digital history is a set of opportunities granted through technical fluency where you'll be continually improving your abilities both as a teacher and as a learner. I like to explain to colleagues the fluency principle as follows: if you are a French historian, you can write histories of France and French-speaking peoples by using documents translated by others. It enables you to work with the sources and offer analyses, but you are limited by your lack of linguistic ability and by what documents others have selected to translate. But, if you are fluent in French, you suddenly have not only more opportunities to identify documents and analyze them yourself, but you can participate more fully in the scholarly community of Francophone studies than you could if you had to rely on translations only. Students and teachers in the digital history classroom are similar. The first time teaching a course, we are often nervous and frequently end up experimenting with different assignments, materials, and outcomes. Over time, as we teach the same subjects for years and mature as teachers, we become more comfortable and dig a little deeper into pedagogy. And, as more historians embrace digital history teaching, we'll see more opportunities to discuss, debate, and revise our teaching. This book recognizes that potentially long arc of digital history adoption and is built to respond to a delayed trajectory. After all, it's rare that we as teachers have time to make rapid changes to our pedagogy. It can take weeks, months, and even years to fully revise assignments and syllabi. Similarly, in a digital history course, you may begin by experimenting with a given method using a readily available tool that doesn't require much underlying knowledge of its functions or customization. But as you master that method, it's likely that you'll desire more control and agency. This book recognizes that wish by providing at least one tool that can be used for any given method without having any additional expertise in programming, mathematics or statistical knowledge, or technical infrastructure. In addition, each chapter provides at least one example of using complicated digital history processes in the classroom that might require you to challenge yourself and your students. As historians, many of us are never truly satisfied with our courses, so revising them to move toward more control in the digital history classroom will feel familiar.

To help demonstrate the varieties of digital history pedagogy available to you, the book is organized in three parts. In part I, we focus exclusively on digital history fundamentals and their relationship to analog historical practice in the classroom. Chapter 1 explores the role of data and the ways in which historical sources can be conceptualized as forms of information that help historians to ask a variety of types of questions. You learn basic terms and processes for identifying data, how to incorporate historical data literacy into your classroom, and how to scaffold data aggregation to align to methodological processes. Chapter 2 explores learning outcomes and a formula that I utilize to develop learning outcomes in the digital history classroom: history, methods, technology. It will help you think about how to balance historical thinking and its fluency with the selection of appropriate methods and tools. The chapter also encourages you to think about how explicit learning outcomes can help your students and colleagues understand how digital history operates similarly or differently from its analog counterparts. Chapter 3 provides a brief overview of three different types of assignment interventions that are possible in the digital history classroom once you have gathered your dataset and determined what learning outcomes you wish to incorporate. The unessay, micro-projects, and comprehensive digital projects are the core assignments that you'll learn about as complementary to, or replacements for, existing analog assignments. In chapter 4, you'll learn a bit about methods and how methods are tied to decisions about your data and your assignments. It primes you to consider how questions of digital methods are extensions of many analog methods that historians have already been using. But it also provides examples of how digital methods that are tied to mathematics, statistics, and computation can introduce new pathways for analysis of historical questions. By the end of part I, then, you'll have a set of tasks for your first syllabus: select your data, identify your learning outcomes, evaluate and incorporate your methods, and determine which tools you wish students to use in the class.

In part II, you'll be provided with a sequence of chapters about digital history methods. Chapter 5 introduces you to digital source criticism and explains the ways in which moving from analog document criticism to digital source criticism can create opportunities for students to understand how digital technologies transform our thinking about sources and their utility. Once students understand how to consider and critique an individual source, be it textual, visual, aural, or some combination of all three, the next step is to consider how that set of materials can be analyzed as an aggregate. In chapter 6, we'll explore text analysis methods that let students explore textual datasets. Ranging from frequency analysis that tells us about individual words, to topic modeling, which suggests themes in document collections, and network analysis methods that help students understand relationships between documents and their contents, chapter 6 suggests that part of what underlies textual analysis is a marriage of math and statistics with historical thinking. Chapter 7 provides an overview of visualization, which is a method for communicating information through visual means. By considering simple charts and graphs, networks and relationship mapping, and cartographic and conceptual mapping, chapter 7 helps you think about how students might leverage datasets to understand space, place, and movement. It will introduce you to common types of visualizations, including graphs, cartographic maps, and historical reproductions (also known as video games and three-dimensional re-creations). The chapter also asks you to consider how gaps in historical information are represented, the ways in which the "visual" component of visualization privileges able-bodied users, and how the design of the visualization must meet your historical question. By the close of part II, you'll be versed in three major methodological processes: digital source criticism, textual analysis, and visualization. You'll have an overview of common methods and examples of robust methodological approaches to your syllabus.

Part III brings us to the question of new forms of historical scholarship in the digital history classroom. In chapter 8, we'll discuss the similarities and differences between digital archives, digital exhibits, and digital collections. You'll be asked to consider how the digital aspect of the historical record aligns to analog archival research practices. The chapter also documents the variety of types of archives and exhibits that might be appropriate for your classroom. Woven throughout are questions about partnerships, student participation, and how to build feedback into your course process. The chapter ends by asking you to think about harm both in the classroom and as part of archival research. Chapter 9 draws your attention to the dominant form of historical communication: the historical narrative. Organized around the concept of storytelling, the chapter explores how to use audiovisual and mixed methods in your classroom. You'll learn about ways to integrate short documentaries, podcasts, and multimodal storytelling into your teaching. The chapter also explores how the desire to tell a story can sidetrack students when they become enamored with digital storytelling tools. The final chapter considers participatory history in the classroom through crowdsourcing. How can students contribute to ongoing digital history projects? What types of crowd-based digital projects might you build your class around? And, as importantly, we'll discuss the ethics of students working publicly. What types of plans do you need in place to address concerns about student contributions to public projects? How might your own wishes for a student's work run contrary to what they wish to do? By the close of part III, you'll be ready to consider what form your students' work will take.

For those who seek guidance on organizing multiple courses, chapter 10 provides that direction. It suggests that your peers should consider choosing the digital methods that most pertain to their own areas of research and that might ignite their interest in building a full digital history curriculum. This will lessen anxiety about the unfamiliarity of digital methods for your colleagues who may be skeptical of digital technologies and approaches. The chapter encourages you to scaffold the curriculum according to methodological complexity and technical expertise. This leads to considerations of independent study as well as ad hoc training as opportunities for yourself, your colleagues, and your students. And, ultimately, the chapter reminds you that the scholarship of teaching and learning offers tremendous opportunities for you to discuss and publish the pedagogy you develop for your digital history classroom and curricula.

For those who are entirely new to digital history, you'll find that reading sequentially through the chapters is likely the most productive use of your time. Concepts introduced in the fundamentals chapters in part I will reappear in parts II and III. By reading in order, you'll be poised to move from developing individual components of sources and assignments to the deployment of a full course. For those with some experience in digital history who feel like they can comfortably define digital history and its concerns, you'll likely find that part II is the best starting point for your reading. Part II offers deep explorations of digital source criticism, textual analysis, and visualization. These chapters can be read individually, with each potentially comprising either a limited module or, if you choose to engage with all of the examples offered, a full multiweek course for your students. Scholars interested in scholarly production and digital public history will find they might wish to concentrate on part III, which explores common digital history outputs: digital archives, digital exhibits, and digital collections; documentaries, podcasts, and multimodal storytelling; and crowdsourcing. These chapters encourage you to think about whom your classroom serves, how students might develop and reach potential audiences, and how their own historical outputs might join ongoing conversations.

As you read, remember that the endnotes and glossary are valuable resources to enrich your reading. I encourage you to follow links to view the digital projects, methods, syllabi, and other materials. That will help you to experience exactly what students would in the digital history classroom if you elected to use the sequence or item under discussion. It's also a way to acknowledge the tremendous wealth of material that underlies our classrooms. Digital historians love to make materials available on the internet, and you should take advantage of that by borrowing, citing, and revising according to your own needs. We ought to recognize that work and actively build on it.

PART I

Foundations

Chapter One

Sources as Data

IN ANY HISTORY COURSE, the first task for most teachers when they start to plan their syllabus is to identify the sources and materials that students might use in the classroom. Digital history courses are no different. The major difference is that the sources we use are called "data," which is a term that encompasses information that a computer can understand. This chapter discusses data, its ethics and complexity, and how it is used in the digital history classroom. Data serves as the backbone of all digital history courses, just as sources function as the grounding material for analog history courses. Data enables us to ask questions of the past. It also serves as a focal point around which you can tailor an entire course from an individual assignment to a complete course arc. Data allows historians to teach a variety of historical thinking skills directly and indirectly through exploration of source identification, analysis, contextualization, and publication.

This chapter will help you think through what data means in history courses. On the one hand, data is about considering its source. Is it a physical object or does it exist only as a digital object? What form does data take? Is it structured like census data or unstructured like prose? What does the data contain? What is missing? But data, as this chapter will illustrate, is also about how it is collated and transformed through your exploration. How do you assemble different pieces of data? How do you identify gaps? Should you organize the data and, if so, in what way? Each of these questions is a potential assignment in digital history courses. As historians, we use various forms of data. It can be quantitative and qualitative data, which requires fluency in methods that work with structured, unstructured, and mixed forms of data. Structured data refers to any data that is organized into the same format and that follows the same logical structure. You commonly encounter structured data in forms, charts, questionnaires, spreadsheets, and logs. Census records, whaling logs, probate inventories, sales records, and address and phone directories are types of structured data that digital historians have leveraged in classrooms. Unstructured data is generally information that doesn't conform to a standard form or that utilizes language rather than numbers. Manuscript collections, photographic and visual archives, audio files, and the like are all considered unstructured data. Much of the work that digital historians do is identifying, formatting, and merging data into a collection of materials that can be used with the software and methods that they wish to work in. Each of these activities can be a key component of work in the digital history classroom. But, first, let me provide an example of how complex digital history data can be.

Imagine for a moment the various pieces of archival information that a historian one hundred years from now might need in order to write a history of the COVID-19 pandemic. Examples of these sets of materials might be medical records; nonconfidential hospital records; local, state, and national records from public health departments; and the hundreds of models and visualizations produced when studying the spread of the disease as well as the various pharmaceutical studies. Another set might be the personal materials related to those who contracted or were impacted by COVID: diaries, creative works, funerary speeches, survey data, and so forth. Still more data might reside with the millions of social media posts from Twitter, Facebook, TikTok, Instagram, and other apps that documented responses to COVID. For each data type, you'd need to ask yourself questions about its provenance, interpretation, and contextualization. This includes questions specific to the data format. For example, how many social media posts were there? Who was posting? What types of languages (visual, aural, and textual) were being used? Who responded? And, as importantly, we'd need to be able to explore both at the level of an individual post but also across the millions of posts to find patterns in the information without discounting the individual contexts of each poster. Now imagine that you need to collect data from every local, state, and national context that experienced COVID-19. For each country, you'd need to deal with issues of data provenance, language, legal use and reuse, as well as limitations on how the data must be stored and accessed. And, as of the writing of this book, the pandemic is ongoing, so you'd need to account for new data that might be brought into the dataset over time: films, movies, music, and physical and digital memorialization might be relevant. Even after we've addressed the contemporary issues around the data, imagine trying to work with the dataset a century in the future. Do you have the right hardware and software to access the information? What rights and responsibilities do you need to be aware of while using the assembled data collection? What information might be missing or no longer relevant? This one example illustrates how complex the picture of what constitutes historical data can be.

Data, for the scientist, consists of facts, measurements, or statistics.[1] Data points are observable and are reproducible (usually). For historians, data can be historical remnants—often held by an archive or library—that we seek out and interpret. It can also be material that we've assembled in the process of our own research. Analog historians often have deep reserves of sources that they've brought together to inform their argument in monographs and articles. A simple digitization workflow might have moved them from the analog sources they identified in their research to digital surrogates stored on computers. For others, we may be gathering digitized sources from libraries, archives, and our own research collections. For digital historians, our sources are not only those digital surrogates but also data that exists only in digital form. Termed "born-digital," these sources exist only as ones and zeros in a computer database or as screenshots within newspaper articles—for example, think of those 2020 US presidential election tweets. Quite frequently, for digital historians, this is also information we create in the process of moving between digital formats. Data is our raw material for historical analysis. It is also the output of our research processes: monographs, articles, digital projects, digital assets, and the like.

As Miriam Posner, who specializes in media studies and information studies, writes, "When you call something data, you imply that it exists in discrete, fungible units; that it is computationally tractable; that its meaningful qualities can be enumerated in a finite list; that someone else performing the same operations on the same data will come up with the same results. This is not how humanists think of the material they work with."[2] The challenge for historians, as Posner continues, is that historical scholarship is about the interpretative acts and framing that inform not only the assembling of data as a collection of materials, but also the interpretative process that marries historiography and theory to the data to form an argument. Jill Walker Rettberg has adapted Donna Haraway's concept of situated knowledges to data.[3] What she and I tell students is that "data is always created in a particular way and presented in a particular way." That situatedness then "prompts us to ask how it's situated."[4]

Sources must be contextualized in terms of their acquisition, analysis, and interpretation in order to render them as meaningful pieces of data. This is the work we've been doing as historians for centuries as we discuss source context and how sources relate to questions of authenticity, power, and identity. For humanists, the cultural complexities of data and information are not new. Anthropologists, historians, linguists, museum curators, and archivists have long probed the contextual subjectivities of knowledge production and representation. From ink and quill maps representing the New World to the carefully stratified layers of an archaeological site, historical data has always been subject to the systems of knowledge that were used to capture, represent, and disseminate it. To those systems of knowledge, historians must now consider how the digital medium captures, represents, and disseminates sources and their arguments. As you may have experienced during the 2020 US presidential election, Twitter had different posting rules than what Facebook allowed. As such, a historian in the future needs to know not only the content of the tweets and Facebook posts but also how the platforms themselves determined what could be posted and by whom. Only by understanding that digital aspect would a historian understand why certain types of content appeared on one platform but not on another.

Data can be about both identification and transformation in the digital history classroom. Digital historian Anelise H. Shrout, for example, draws on her university's special collections and archives as well as the public library to restore nuance to Bates College's history of itself as an abolitionist college in her introductory-level undergraduate course.[5] Using analog business ledgers, invoices, and other documents held by the college's special collections archives and their local public library, students then create digital datasets for use in their research. They access documents that revealed how the cotton trade created wealth for textile mill owner Benjamin Bates, their college's founder. Students learn the historical contexts of the university's founding, including the Atlantic slave trade, the cotton and textile trade network, and the economic history of nineteenth-century Maine. They also learn about analog archival methods that organize the ledgers and invoices. After digitization, the digital dataset that students end up with enables them to ask the following questions: "What does it mean to produce a dataset that represents labor that was violently stolen from people? How do we do that ethically and thoughtfully?" This work also reveals the complicated history of how abolitionism tied itself to cotton harvesting and slavery through wealth accumulation.

Shrout's course is only one such example of how students explore data in various forms. You might consider replicating a similar process but also grounding it with Katherine McKittrick's "Mathematics Black Life," which highlights the way quantification of Black bodies in the slave trade can be read into the responsibilities of Black studies scholars today.[6] McKittrick illustrates how ledgers and economic records concentrate the origins of Black peoples and Blackness as commodities rather than as humans with their own lived experiences. These are histories of Black death, rather than Black life, that students and scholars must grapple with when they study slavery. Students have to consider what it means to ethically engage with these records as they record Black peoples as mathematical certainties. Part of why my students appreciate McKittrick is that they can dig deeply into the ways in which being counted can conflate personal histories, experiences, and nuance into absolute values. Students can bring this thinking to bear against narratives of enslaved peoples and their experiences used in a previous unit. What students appreciate about McKittrick's work is that it illustrates how data is created from lived experiences. It reinforces for them that data is a form of information that communicates to the user.

To help her students understand sources as data, digital historian Lindsey Passenger Wieck uses a tutorial on gathering and curating data in the classroom for her undergraduate upper-level course on the history of San Francisco.[7] After students complete a brief brainstorming exercise on how to gather meaningful information from a 1914 diary excerpt, they then must download an electronic version of the 1907 Crocker-Langley phone directory for San Francisco. Wieck asks students to familiarize themselves with the format of the phone book, select text from the source related to breweries, and create a comma-separated value file to store the data that they extract from the digitized phone book (fig. 1.1). Students learn how to control for issues of punctuation and line breaks in the document before being asked to create header columns to identify the data in each column. What do they do with an entry that continues across lines, columns, or page breaks? How do they handle inconsistent capitalization? What about abbreviations?

Students answer these questions and then amend the data by adding geographical coordinates to each line in the table. By modeling for students how to extract information from digitized sources, Wieck is teaching them two valuable skills (identifying pertinent information and formatting it in a way that is easily used) as well as a digital history method, data cleaning. Students are then assigned to create their own unique query about San Francisco, which reinforces the tutorial steps they've just completed by asking them to apply it to their own interests. These two methods of data identification and formatting—one analog to digital, and one

Breweries ACME BREWING COMPANY, 1401 San- some ALBANY BREWERY i Hagemann Brewing
Co) 409-415. 8th Albion Ale and Porter Brewery, 1009 Golden Gate Av
Broadway Brewing Co. 3173. 19th
Buffalo Brewing Co (.S F Agency) 125 King
California Brewing Co. 111-123 Douglass
Chicago Brewery, 240. 2d
Eagle Brewing Co, 2213 Harrison
Knterprise Brewing Co. 2015-2013 FolSl
>ni HAGEMANN BREWING CO, 409-415
St 11 Htbernla Brewery. 1241-1261 Howard
Jackson Brewing Co. SE cor 11th and
I'Vlsom Milwaukee Brewery of S F. 46S, 10th National Brewing Co, office 7*2 Kulton North Roach Brewery. 428 Chestnut
Philadelphia Brewery. 24o. Id
N..rili Star Brewing Co, 3210-2111 Army
Ruhstnl lei's Kr.wery. 1809 Harrison
I'latieisco Breweries. Ltd, 240. 2,1 Schwars Joseph Brewing Co, 120 '"lust- nut Union Brewing and Malting Co, 18th and
Florida
St Urals Brewing i Pine United Btatea Brewery, 140, Valle) Brewery, Sid Am nr Point Loboa
llcntv 7"- Mission
Wieland John Brewery, 240, 2d Williow Brewery, 240, 2d Wreden Claus Brewing Co. cor Lombard
and Taylor
Wunder Brewing Co, cor Scott and
Lombard

Fig. 1.1. The instructional material from Lindsey Passenger Wieck's course assignment on data gathering highlights the original 1907 Crocker-Langley phone directory for San Francisco as well as an example of what the transcribed information looks like within the student's assignment guidelines. Lindsey Passenger Wieck, "Tutorial—Gathering and Curating Data," accessed June 10, 2020, http://lindseywieck.com/fall_2016_sf/gatheringdatatutorial.html.

entirely reliant on digital surrogates—can be transferred to any tabular data that a student wishes to explore. Data extraction from historical sources is likely one of the most common actions you'll do in the classroom with students.

Part of your approach to sources as data can also be guided study. In her undergraduate introductory course, Posner assigns her students to groups, and each group is given a dataset that she assembled before class begins. Over the weeks of the course, students conduct secondary contextual research on the data they've been provided, analyze the dataset and its attributes, interview relevant professionals and experts about the contexts of the data, and publish a scholarly argument using the data as support. Students in previous classes have explored the history of dance, fashion, superheroes, museums, tenements, the New York Philharmonic, and Japanese art. From course to course, she can vary the datasets to speak to student interests as well as her own.

One dataset that I use frequently in my digital history courses is that of census rolls. I ask my students to extract census information from digitized census rolls, turn them into comma-separated value tables, and then annotate each record with additional information that includes not only geolocation information but also contextual information about the census and the individuals recorded within it. Students often remark during this process that data is about details and standardization at scale. They lament incomplete information, grow frustrated with a lack of access to particular historical sources they might desire, and often spend as much time arguing with each other about selection and standardization principles as they do with learning OpenRefine, a free web-based tool for data manipulation and management that allows them to manipulate the information they've teased from tabular historical sources.[8] When I ask students to combine the data that they've worked with individually with the data that a peer has gathered, we are also able to ask questions about the intent of our data within the research question we have. What data is selected for the final dataset? What format? What additional information needs to be secured? How do we grapple with divergent data collection principles that might make standardization hard?

Pushing students toward moving from sources to data assembly as a task encourages them to think about data curation, which focuses on the protection, amelioration, contextualization, and publication of data for potential users. "The curation of research data—raw and abstracted material created as part of research processes and which may be used again as the input to further research—carries with it the burden of capturing and preserving not only the data itself, but information about the methods by which it was produced," writes Julia Flanders and Trevor Muñoz in their data curation guide for humanists.[9] The guide offers an easy-to-understand series of articles on issues as diverse as what data curation is, what issues researchers confront when curating data, and how data can be represented and aggregated, as well as issues of policy, practice, law, and standards. In my class, we couple the use of the guide with a lesson on version control with the free software GitHub.[10] Originally designed as a repository to store and share computer code, in the last five years, GitHub has become a platform for historians who are interested in sharing source datasets beyond their home computer or institution. These files are simple comma-separated value, text, or image files that they have assembled and posted to the repository. Part of why I like GitHub as a data repository for my course is because it enables my students to work in a controlled environment, and they can share, combine, and recombine datasets as well as publish their process of data curation. The version-control capabilities of the software also allow me to see their work evolve through different drafts.

A growing number of libraries, archives, museums, and cultural heritage organizations are making their analog materials available for download as digital surrogates either through their own website or through data repositories like GitHub. Private companies like JSTOR, Gale Cengage, LexisNexis, and the like provide access to historical data that students can download and use in the classroom. While the nonprofit groups usually do not require you to purchase the data, corporations like Gale Cengage often require financial resources and/or a subscription for access. Both have copyright and permission notations that may restrict what students can do with the data. So that students understand fair use and the legal restrictions around data reuse, make sure to look for these statements so that you can ensure that you and your students are not violating any laws. Students can be asked to analyze these datasets, create annotated libraries, develop bibliographies using the pertinent standards, and leverage digital annotation tools to begin to identify debates in the datasets. Students can also conduct this same exercise multiple times as they refine the scope of the class topic. This subtly (and often not so subtly) reminds them that historical scholarship is an unfinished process that requires continuing attention. This type of digital history is reflective of Benjamin Schmidt's call for historians to reinvigorate historical analysis as a set of three practices: a source criticism that explains what's in the data; a hermeneutics that lets us read data into a meaningful form; and a situated argumentation that ties the data in to questions in their field.[11]

Datasets carry with them the same biases of selection and assemblage that analog archives and collections do, as we will discuss later in this book. They might overrepresent certain individuals, places, or events. They might ignore entire experiences, voices, knowledges, and perspectives. Datasets might also reinscribe systems of privilege and power that overrepresent certain types of human experiences. Catherine D'Ignazio and Lauren F. Klein have helped shape how I address this in my classroom through their work on data feminism and data science.[12] Data feminism is "a way of thinking about data, both their uses and their limits, that is informed by direct experience, by a commitment to action, and by intersectional feminist thought."[13] They argue that it is not enough in our classrooms to merely record the systems of privilege and oppression that are part of our sources. Rather we must actively seek co-liberation, where the outcome is the undoing of the systems themselves and not merely alternative readings of evidence or outcomes. Simply put, they argue that it is not enough to critique sources as data: you must also create alternative sources, datasets, and visualizations to challenge antifeminism, racism, and other forms of systemic oppression.

Building on feminist principles, I'll often ask students to consider the historical, legal, and ethical dimensions of datasets in the history classroom. Students read Katie Rawson and Trevor Muñoz's "Against Cleaning," which argues that data standardization "privileges the structure of a container rather than the data inside it."[14] It encourages them to consider how standards are forms of privilege that elevate certain types of knowing above others. You may find that Ellen Gruber Garvey's excellent "'facts and FACTS': Abolitionists' Database Innovations," which explores *American Slavery as It Is: Testimony of a Thousand Witnesses*, an 1839 publication of the American Anti-Slavery Society, is useful in these discussions. Garvey discusses how abolitionists, well before the advent of the modern computer, had developed a method to convert Southern newspapers into a database of information about the ills of slavery.[15] That information became the compelling evidence that helped abolitionists convince others of the need to abolish slavery. Through Garvey's analysis, students are fascinated by the notion that diaries, novels, and other unstructured forms of information can shape what we consider historical facts. They also are exposed to the idea that facts are not only relative to their interpretation but are also flexible in their exposition. They're also fascinated by the underlying message that data isn't tied to the advent of computers and the internet. When bolstered by a set of activities on unstructured data, students learn that manuscripts and visual sources often have vast amounts of information contained in them that can be highlighted, annotated, and rendered in a variety of ways. For example, students can consider the types of information made available in the North American Slave Narratives collection of Documenting the American South by browsing the individual materials or, as we advance in the course, by downloading the full text of the narratives and analyzing them with textual analysis methods (which we will talk about in chapter 6).[16]

Complementing the question of historical data and ethics is Mimi Onuoha's concept of "missing data sets," which introduces students to historical absence in an easy-to-understand way. Missing datasets are the "blank spots that exist in spaces that are otherwise data-saturated."[17] Data saturation as a conceptual framework can help students think about the issues of quality in relationship to historical data. They encounter a vast world of data every day. But just because data exists does not mean that it is amenable to the needs of the user or the analysis that historians wish to complete. Computer scientists will instruct students that data is considered high quality if it allows the user to correctly represent the real world. But, as students discover, quality is often constrained by the conditions under which the data was captured or generated. So, today, if students want to do geolocation work but the data doesn't record any information that relates to geography, the quality of the data might be considered low. Or, as one colleague noted to me, they were asked by a peer what to do with all the empty cells in their database that correlated to unknown information. Gaps and omissions become more complicated with historical data because the data can be mediated and remediated in multiple ways before we as historians ever get our hands on it in the classroom.

Onuoha eloquently communicates that mediation, including that what is ignored about data and within datasets reveals more than what exists in the dataset. The "hidden social biases and differences"[18] of what is missing are tied to practices of incentivization, quantification, representation, and benefit. Who can afford to make and collect data? Does your life fit into the forms and formats of data that people wish to collect? Does collecting benefit those who are collecting? And, as importantly, does not being represented in the dataset serve as a form of resistance and protection for a vulnerable community or individual? The questions that are raised sound undoubtedly familiar to historians who work in decolonial, postcolonial, and community contexts. Part of why I appreciate Onuoha's work in my classroom is that it complicates our thinking about primary sources by suggesting that the absences of data can also illustrate historical phenomena.

Students arrive in our classes with the assumption that the historical past is, in fact, not fragmentary because much of what they've been exposed to is information on demand and at their fingertips. They also have been encouraged to understand history as a cohesive narrative of forward progress that is ever improving with new and better information. By centering the absence of sources as part of the course, we can begin to explore gaps in historical knowledge. It also allows me to bring students back to D'Ignazio and Klein's notion that part of what makes data science and data ethics central in the classroom is the production of counterdata. Counterdata is the opportunity to quantify and visualize structural oppression.[19] It fits seamlessly in a course on digital history because it aligns to the work we are doing as historians when we revise and iterate arguments not only by accounting for new interpretations but also by introducing new data and forms of argument to challenge our peers. It is a subtle provocation that encourages students to act as historians rather than as passive attendees in a classroom.

Dataset creation can be a long, painstaking, but rewarding process. If you plan to teach topical courses repeatedly, it is worth your time to secure and assemble your own dataset or otherwise assign students to create datasets for classroom use. I share this because often instructors assume that digital datasets somehow are not only complete and accurate but also amenable to the types of analysis you want to do. Get to know the datasets that you are using; there are often assumptions built into them that you or your students may not recognize at the outset. That's part of why I love using census rolls in my classes. We can explore how census categories shifted over time and how the questions we can ask of the historical sources are constrained by the decisions made by census enumerators. A rich vein of discussion that builds on this relates to the US Census for 2020 and the decision by the US Census Bureau to use only "male" and "female" categories for the survey rather than including a more expansive definition of gender that includes nonbinary and gender-nonconforming options. Students often also express frustration with the racial categories used on the census. Inevitably, whether historical rolls or the contemporary questionnaire, students want more data to work with. They want data that is richer, more nuanced, or more complex—it can be granular data that is more detailed, or it can be expansive data that broadens the overall scope of the dataset. I can then ask them to complete an assignment that tells me what level of granularity they think would be necessary to answer the historical questions they have.

When I first began teaching about sources as data in the history classroom, I erred when designing the syllabus by not working with the students to ensure that the dataset we established would work for the variety of types of digital methods that I wanted them to complete. This meant that we had to pause to either augment the dataset we'd established or harness an entirely new dataset that could be used with the specific tool I wanted them to consider. While that was a useful activity in that students learned that data collection and source work is never complete, it often meant that students felt stalled from getting to "the interesting stuff," as one student referred to some of the more advanced methods we'd hoped to use. It also meant I spent a significant amount of time ensuring that students learned the new contextual information they needed to work with the data. That became very overwhelming for them and me as the course rolled along. Data can make or break your classroom pedagogy. I use the axiom "garbage in, garbage out" with my students. This is a saying popularized by data scientists to discuss the importance of data quality. If your data isn't "good" (read: amenable to the types of questions you wish to ask), then the results are likely to be bad (read: not meaningful). It is worth your time and energy to work through your data both at its moment of assemblage and as time passes. New data becomes available every day through digitization initiatives, scholars releasing their personal materials, or community publications. Don't forget to revisit your dataset regularly so that you can continue to enrich it with new materials. Or, if you don't wish to enrich it with new materials, make sure to footnote for your students and peers that you haven't updated your dataset so they are not surprised if they notice that sources that they know about are not incorporated in your dataset.

Given that dataset assembly can be a large part of your course preparation, I want to draw your attention to the dataset's utility as a publication. Datasets count as a professional research publication when they are contextualized with the methods used in their assembly. They can undergo peer review just like articles, monographs, and digital projects. There is tremendous opportunity for historians and their students to publish datasets for use by other scholars and classes. When you couple publication of the dataset with the pedagogical materials you create for use in your classroom, you create a pathway for other historians to follow. I've found great success in trading datasets and the associated learning materials with peers. You get fresh material for your classes while also garnering another set of eyes on your teaching pedagogy. If you can complete formal peer review, you'll also have material that can contribute to your long-term professional development.

In the digital history classroom, data matters. It sets the scope of the course in terms of what historical periods, experiences, and peoples your students will learn about. It also ties into the types of learning outcomes possible in your course. In the next chapter, you'll learn about how digital history learning outcomes differ from analog history learning outcomes.

Chapter Two

Learning Outcomes

CONFESSION: I hate Bloom's Taxonomy. If you haven't heard of it, Bloom's Revised Taxonomy for Learning, Teaching, and Assessing is a widely adopted structure on which most educational curricula are designed.[1] Based on a spectrum, Bloom's utilizes six cognitive levels that become increasingly complex: remembering, understanding, applying, analyzing, evaluating, and creating. Bloom's has been popular for over fifty years. It has been embraced because it allows easy assessment for curriculum review. Best practice mandates that courses should specify which levels and activities it incorporates, select from the corresponding list of verbs to build outcomes, and list those statements on the syllabus. My own university tells us that undergraduate courses most likely focus on remembering, understanding, and applying while graduate courses utilize analyzing, evaluating, and creating more frequently. The problem for digital historians though is that Bloom's Taxonomy doesn't really work for our courses because our learning outcomes move fluidly between cognitive levels. Students rarely are working linearly from least to most cognitively complex activity in a digital history class.[2] I'll talk more about how to manage customized learning outcomes later in the chapter but, for now, we should start by discussing the three types of learning outcomes that should be integrated into a digital history class: historical learning outcomes, methodological application outcomes, and technological proficiency outcomes.

History, method, and technology is a simple three-part formula that lets me set up a structure that I can build learning outcomes around. History represents the historical content and context that students need to learn. It is the dataset that you've established in chapter 1 that speaks to the interests of the course as well as your own sense of the topic of study. It can incorporate primary and secondary source materials and can encompass a variety of data formats that you think you might wish to explore. Method is the analytical process by which students will dig into datasets. Learning outcomes associated with methods tend to rely on evaluation and application. Technological outcomes are about understanding and creating as students move back and forth between the dataset and product. They generally are written about in terms of skills development. Alignment between outcomes and products helps students to learn, practice, and demonstrate their knowledge and abilities. It also encourages students to embrace a learning trajectory over simply getting "good" grades.

A lovely example of this type of explicit utilization of history, method, and technology is the set of learning goals and objectives that Anelise H. Shrout utilizes in her undergraduate introductory course on Bates College's history (mentioned in chapter 1).[3] Shrout bifurcates her learning outcomes into goals that are "higher order ambitions" and objectives that have "specific, measurable competencies." Course goals are to explain how datasets are constructed and how their construction leads to subjective representations of their world; to develop a framework for predicting how different ways of structuring data will help or hinder analyses; to understand how programming languages can be used to manipulate, analyze, and visualize data; to translate learning and working in the class into informed civil action in pursuit of social justice and responsible stewardship of the wider world; and to differentiate among different approaches to the study of data and digital humanities. Her measurable competencies, on the other hand, are to build a dataset that represents both the early financial history of Bates College and the relationship between the college and the American slave economy; to read and write code in the programming language R in order to manipulate, visualize, and analyze data; to create and curate an online presence that presents the work of the class to audiences beyond Bates; to synthesize and take notes on class readings that explore data science, quantitative analysis, digital humanities, and related fields; and to discuss and debate readings with colleagues.

Beginning courses, by definition, introduce students to the fundamentals of digital history concepts and methods. Usually, these courses are tightly controlled and limit students to approaches that do not require coding, programming, or too much under-the-hood poking around. They tend to be titled "introduction to" courses and fulfill general core and survey requirements. Intermediate courses are usually topical courses that are tied to specific methodological approaches. At the intermediate level students generally dig deeply into a handful of methods that allow them to ask directed historical questions. Advanced courses usually give students the latitude to self-select their digital method(s) and generally serve as capstones to their degree. These are independent, research-driven courses that ask students to challenge their abilities or are courses that require significant investment in technical skills development like programming languages. You should consider making sure that if you choose a beginning, intermediate, and advanced structure for your learning outcomes that you are clear about what prerequisite requirements exist for students to join your class. When I am asked to evaluate syllabi for digital history courses, I'm often frustrated by the hidden logics of their learning outcomes. Few syllabi directly tell students how the historical contexts, methods, and technologies match up. Yet studies in teaching effectiveness and student motivation clearly demonstrate that how students do in courses is often tied to their sense that the content and approach to the course are intentional and transparent. When I first started teaching digital history with first-year master's students, my approach could politely be called "what made sense in Jen's head." This meant that students saw each component of the syllabus as distinct from one another. One day, we'd be talking about transforming and encoding census data, and the next we'd be developing a gazetteer of places of origin for workers who labored in the Panama Canal Zone. From there, we'd explore the Mental Health Check records that provided biographical information on workers brought into the Zone. Students thought that the logic of this was temporal and topical. And it was. But it was also cumulative: the syllabus was designed to move students from microhistories that relied on aggregated census information through to place-based histories and then to personal histories of workers. It began with data extraction and then moved students through methods of textual annotation and spatial history. I'd done this intentionally because I wanted students to consider the difficulties of interpreting fragmentary personal histories only after they'd understood the larger structural forces of migration that shaped who was traveling to the Zone as a worker. They then applied this understanding through their cumulative digital project that asked the class to work collectively to develop visualizations and posts about historical thinking in digital public history.

Interestingly, two years later, a student in the course stopped by to tell me that she continues to use the methods of data extraction and analysis we'd studied in her job. She also relayed that she didn't "get" the course organization until much later. As a result, I now try to provide expositions in the syllabus of my history, methods, and technology formula that explain not just what we are doing (assignments, readings, exams, tutorials, etc.) but also why we are doing something in a particular way. Student feedback on this new approach has been positive, and I'm now incorporating it into all of my courses. And, of course, the explicit articulation of course design is one of the rationales for the Primer series that this book is in.

You may find your best strategy for success in your digital history classroom is to set a single limit of one method and one technology when selecting outcomes. For example, in his course about scientific revolutions, Ole Molvig teaches his course thematically rather than chronologically. His students in the introductory undergraduate course develop their own individual timelines using Tiki-Toki, an online web-based timeline tool.[4] They use the timeline technology to reassemble the thematic material given to them in a chronological framework, allowing them to

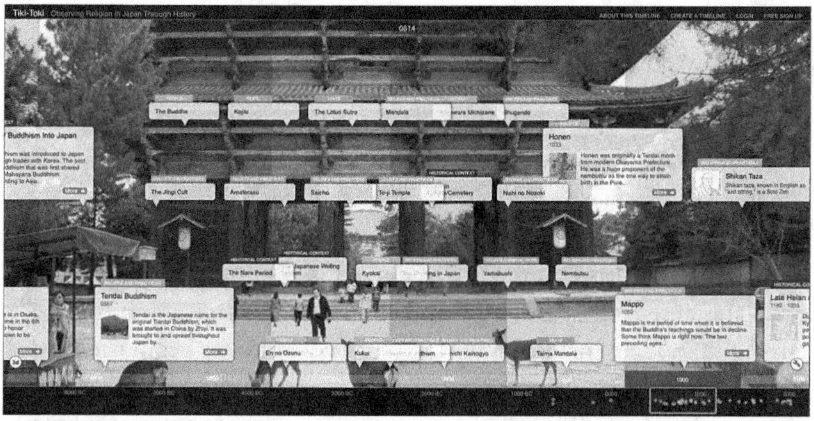

Fig. 2.1. This completed Tiki-Toki timeline was created by Casey Hansen as the final assignment for Brian Lowe's course Religions of Japan. Items are located chronologically on the timeline with associated descriptions, images, and citations, and the project was published using the Tiki-Toki digital tool. Casey Hansen, "Tiki-Toki: Observing Religion in Japan through History," accessed May 11, 2020, http://www.tiki-toki.com/timeline/entry/581067/Observing-Religion-in-Japan-Through-History/.

present an argument about whether the use of the term "revolution" that the course is based on was valid. Students are graded on their timeline as well as a short, written explanation. It then becomes part of their final course paper, which includes content from their timeline. Brian Lowe, in his introductory undergraduate course Religions of Japan, uses a similar exercise where, beginning in week two, students complete four responses per week based on readings and class lectures. Students are graded on their timeline, an in-class presentation, and a final paper that leverages the timeline as a component (fig. 2.1). "Quality points were assigned based on the following criteria: number of entries (at least 60 total for full credit), accuracy, depth (minimum of three substantial sentences), use of media (when appropriate), quality of writing, and citations."[5]

Both examples illustrate one approach to the digital history classroom formula: repetition of technology and method. By having students complete the same assignment mechanics (here, identifying information and placing it onto the timeline) repeatedly, they can focus on learning the historical content rather than having to master progressively more complex technologies as the course moves chronologically through the semester. Change over time is the historical method that students learn, and constructing timelines pushes students to consider how change operates. What motivates change? What stays the same? How do we document the forces of change? How do we document what remains?

Many digital historians use Knight Lab's TimelineJS in their classrooms because it does not require any technical proficiency, but it easily can accommodate the questions listed above. Students begin their timeline by selecting a historical topic with a strong chronological narrative. They fill out a Google spreadsheet template with relevant event information, including dates, titles, and descriptions of events, as well as visual media including photos and videos. TimelineJS can not only leverage social media like Twitter, Flickr, and YouTube; it also ties into Wikipedia, SoundCloud, and any other resource with a URL. This allows students to harness the power of digital assets and combine them with their own narrative viewpoints. Students can either publish their timeline directly from TimelineJS or they can embed it onto any site where they want it to appear. Students learn about how to select historical content to represent change over time within the limits of the TimelineJS tool. How many events are too many? Too few? Which images best express the student's point of view? What context is needed to make the timeline meaningful to their audience? It also allows them to consider change over time as a key factor in historical analysis. They can learn about everything from date standardization and copyright and publication responsibilities to more technical topics like JavaScript Object Notation (JSON) data formats, Cascading Style Sheets (CSS), and JavaScript, which are technologies that allow you to standardize, style, and display information digitally. If these terms are unfamiliar to you, don't forget to consult the glossary.

The Lab for the Education and Advancement in Digital Research (LEADR) at Michigan State University offers another example of how the history, method, and technology formula plays out in learning outcomes. LEADR uses a flipped-classroom environment where students apply what they've read to hands-on research where they can "build, experiment, and play, and then reflect on their experiences."[6] Students are tasked with locating and analyzing primary and secondary sources from digital repositories (information literacy); authoring, publishing, and distributing scholarship on the internet (digital literacy); accessing, refining, manipulating, evaluating, and sharing data (data literacy); and leveraging computational processes to ask and explore historical research questions (computational analysis). Each of these literacies and skills translates into a set of activities built around particular student outcomes. For example, students exploring digital literacy learn to write historical content for the web using HTML and CSS while considering issues of audience, language, structure, multimedia incorporation, and the like. Students exploring data literacy might spend their time transcribing and organizing historical records before conducting analysis looking for patterns. While they are learning the historical context and complexities, the transferable skills of web design and data science can be utilized across other courses and future employment. Part of what I like about the LEADR model is that it is scalable and replicable across different historical subfields. Students can repeat the process in many courses with each increasing the technical difficulty as they progress through the curriculum.

Perhaps historical critique is a central learning outcome for your digital history class. Leah Potter asks her students in her introductory graduate course to read an essay and then complete a written review of a topical digital archive using the guidelines established by the *Journal of American History*.[7] The archive serves as her historical dataset, the method is critical thinking and critique, and the technology is both the archival technology that the digital project is built on as well as the writing software students use to complete their review. This type of exercise marries a reading with a digital exploration. It is quite effective, particularly if you select digital projects discussed within the reading as fodder for the exploration. Most digital historians use some variation of the Digital History Reviews criteria developed by Jeffrey McClurken for digital history critique activities.[8] These criteria provide a set of questions for reviewers around content, design, audience, media, and authorship. It's been my experience with the

Reviews criteria that students aren't well positioned to succeed in the assignment if you use the questions directly from McClurken. For example, the review question "Is the scholarship sound and current?" requires that students be able to draw on a historiographic knowledge base that they may not have. As a result, their attempts to answer this question can often focus on the user experience more than the historical content. Students will often remark that something is aesthetically pleasing rather than noting that the historical content presents a problematic viewpoint or is unsubstantiated with primary sources. I counteract this trend by altering the question to "What scholarship does this point to?" This helps students to identify who the project author is engaging with, and then we can work together to assess whether those connections are sound and current.

We should pause briefly to talk about how to help students draft and revise their work. When I first started to create digital history courses, I failed to leave enough time in the course for students to submit draft work and receive constructive feedback. Part of the problem was that I made turning in drafts optional. What this meant was that in some classes every student would turn in a draft, and I'd allotted too little time to giving feedback. In others, so few students turned in drafts that I couldn't intervene to help those who really needed help to correct mistakes and issues that would have been caught in a draft review. In the case of some students who didn't turn in drafts, they overestimated their technical abilities. This meant last-minute changes to their projects that led to a rushed, lower-quality final submission.

For this reason, when I approach learning outcomes, I include an outcome specifically for reviewing and critique proficiency. I make turning in drafts a requirement and tie it to improving critique skills as one of our learning outcomes. Often, I'll include two different draft stages: one peer-reviewed and one instructor-reviewed, spaced a few weeks apart. In the first, I'll provide a set of simple checkbox questions that list the requirements. This allows students to focus on ensuring they've met the minimum requirements for the assignment. In a digital collection assignment, I'll ask students to review each item in the collection to ensure that the right metadata has been included, that the item was digitized correctly, that the copyright has been cleared, and so forth. The sheet then serves as the basis of the author's to-dos that they need to address before the next round of review. Digital storytelling assignments using Scalar, a multimodal storytelling technology, include peer-review checklists related to storyboarding, artifact identification, node and path drafting, and accessibility. Each item on the list is a key component of the technology and encourages students to follow digital storytelling methodology. The checklists may also be specific to the technology that the student has chosen. I provide a different checklist for TimelineJS assignments than I do for Tiki-Toki assignments because their components are quite distinct from one another even though they both use the same method of change over time. Having a checklist specific to the technology and the underlying method it relies on ensures that your students get clear feedback and can implement recommendations.

I also like to include two open-ended questions on peer-review exercises: What is the main takeaway from this draft for you? What three or more things specifically would you do differently if you were the author? The first question allows the author to understand whether what they think their project goal is matches to what the reviewer thinks the project is about. The second provides concrete things for authors to think about altering or incorporating. I use "do differently" rather than asking about quality because the former allows students to gently point out assumptions or omissions that the author has made while the latter often results in students saying that the draft is fine as is. It also forces the peer reviewer to stretch themselves analytically rather than just saying the draft is sufficient. In one recent peer-review exercise, one student highlighted for another that they'd skewed their selection criteria to include only artifacts about white men. It wasn't something the student had been aware they'd been doing. Another suggested a completely different technology and method to communicate more effectively what the author wanted. I close the exercise by asking students to complete a revision reflection with their next draft. This brief 250-word reflection requires students to state how they addressed concerns that had been raised by their peers. And, as importantly, if they didn't address the issues, they should explain why not.

No matter which types of assignments you are having students peer-review, it is important to explain to them why peer review is required in your course. I like to talk to students about my own experience with peer review and the large number of drafts I'll go through when creating a digital project. This helps them understand not only that feedback is important but also that historical thinking is an iterative process. In fact, one of my favorite digital history activities is group peer review where we work as a team to review and write a letter to the digital history project team that provides concrete suggestions for how to improve the project. I'll often then charge the class with redesigning the project using a different methodological approach and technology. The last time I did this activity in class, it was only after my students had completed the sequence that I revealed that the project we'd rebuilt was one that I'd authored years ago. The point of the exercise was not to have a gotcha moment with the students (although I do enjoy their faces when they've completed undoing years of my work) but to assist them in understanding how to be critical, but kind, reviewers.

Part of why I like to use at least one digital history review assignment as part of my course outcomes is because optional assignments can be built in for students who wish to embrace the computer science and mathematics that frequently underlie digital history projects. Students can be asked to research the algorithms that Tim Sherratt used in the Real Face of White Australia project, which I explore in more detail in chapter 8 on digital archives, to identify what types of computational abilities they would need to develop to duplicate Sherratt's methods, and (if time allows) to attempt to deploy those algorithms on another collection. Similarly, I've given students an assignment that utilizes social media. While most of the students are developing content for Twitter, students who are more technically proficient may be researching how Twitter algorithms work to skew user experiences. This type of extension to a module can encourage students with technical knowledge to expand their understanding. And it subtly adjusts the learning outcome to meet their abilities. Students in my courses who are completing computer science degrees have found these lessons to be a useful counterpoint to the strict curriculum they've received. One student told me after digging into how a particular program was structuring the archive we were exploring in class that he'd never been asked to consider a humanities point of view about the technology he was learning to create in other classes. One of his takeaways was how the classifications we use to structure data privileged using colonialist language around tribal names and identities. An art major, who joined my class because it fit a time in her schedule, was thrilled when she was able to use her advanced design skills to build a functional digital mockup of her course assignment rather than just completing a written proposal as the rest of her classmates had done.

Incorporating customized learning outcomes into your class encourages students to think of themselves as full partners in the course rather than passive attendees. This tone touches on a major topic of discussion among digital historians: the role of collaboration in digital history research. Historians have long incorporated active learning activities into their classrooms in the form of class discussions, debates, think-pair-share activities, and even role-playing that rely on collaboration strategies. Studies have demonstrated that students who are asked to cognitively engage with course materials perform better than those who simply read or listen. They retain information longer, at a better quality, and with clearer ability to recall what they've learned. Digital history courses can be the ultimate form of active learning and collaboration in our classrooms because they decenter the instructor's role as an "authority" by requiring students to work together. They ask students to become active participants in the process of historical research with, and through, digital tools, assets, and platforms.

Thirteen years ago, Robert Stephens and Josh Thumma, then, respectively, an assistant professor and an undergraduate student at Virginia Polytechnic Institute and State University, authored an article in the *History Teacher* entitled "Faculty-Undergraduate Collaboration in Digital History at a Public Research University."[9] Using their collaboratively authored chapter in *The Digital History Reader* as a model, Stephens and Thumma argued that undergraduate students had a "cultural aversion" to collaboration while many professors "feel a certain repugnance toward collaboration of any kind." They lament that historians consider history a "solo sport." They note a lack of structural support for undergraduate research in history classrooms. Mentoring and supervision of students take time away from one's own research. Rising class sizes and the lack of remuneration for faculty limited faculty's willingness to experiment with digital history. Calling their effort a "joint intellectual enterprise," they concluded that the effectiveness of their collaborative work was its ability to "arrive at a better result than either of [them] working alone could have managed."[10] Some of these limitations may sound familiar to you as you consider digital history in your classroom. So too can the "one plus one equals three" type of thinking about working collaboratively. There is a spectrum of possibilities in the digital history classroom that can overcome student and instructor hesitancy by using partnership and collaboration as the glue that holds together your learning outcomes.

I often ask students to begin thinking about collaboration as a learning outcome by reading a series of blogs and articles. Tom Scheinfeldt's 2010 blog post "Stuff Digital Humanists Like"; *A Digital Humanities Manifesto* (both the original and 2.0); the "Manifesto for the Digital Humanities"; and Lisa Spiro's widely recognized "'This Is Why We Fight': Defining the Values of the Digital Humanities" illuminate core values within the field of digital humanities, which is a larger community of scholars in which many digital historians practice.[11] Students are asked to identify and define the values espoused by each document and then draw connections across the documents. They are also asked to specify any barriers they see between digital humanities and digital history. Students find that what motivates the use of collaboration and partnership in the digital humanities and digital history is a lack of something as much as it is an "ethos" of collaboration. Collaboration is a necessity because it is rare for a single individual (be it instructor or student) to have all of the technical and interpretive skills that are needed to reach a learning outcome. We need partners who can provide access to materials. We rely on human and technical resources to get our courses off the ground. And, as teachers, we need our students to collaborate with us so that our classroom is a positive and productive learning environment.

Collaboration is innately participatory and, as a learning outcome, requires students to consider how their own historical thinking builds on those who have written about their topics before them. Peers in the field and within the classroom might have quite different ideas about how to interpret the datasets or construct arguments; students would have to reconcile those differences. A colleague at a research-driven institution waits until the last week of the course to ask students to define digital history for precisely this reason. The fodder for the assignment are the various things they've covered throughout the previous fifteen weeks, including course discussions. Another who leads a small learning community constructs a final project that challenges students to select one digital history method and identify projects that fulfill that method as well as the historical contexts that are revealed through the project. Their final submission is a digital history "state-of-the-method" review that incorporates snippets from the projects they analyzed to enable them to make sense of specific historical fields of study. In making sense of the projects and their relationships to one another, students consider how scholars collaborate through citational politics, quotation, and even interpretation. With students who are less invested in historiographical debates or who might struggle with the advanced language of academic journals and monographs, you might follow the example of one colleague who works with beginning undergraduate students by providing them with a preselected group of digital projects that represents the broad spectrum of possible definitions of digital history that illustrate different levels of collaboration. They work singularly to explore a project and then, with guidance from the instructor, begin to merge definitions with their peers into a coherent sense of what digital history is and the types of collaboration that it requires. He has had great success with this approach because it requires more active participation from students as they engage with each project. I imagine this approach would be quite successful in high school classes because you'd be able to control the breadth of the work you ask students to complete. Instructors could also provide students with a problematic definition that they then argue with throughout the course of their class.

It is important to remember that each learning outcome you select for your course encompasses sets of values and skills that then must be matched to assignments. Electing to define digital history methods as an explicitly public endeavor requires your syllabus to illustrate how students might grapple with audience, user experiences, issues of reception, and incorporation of critique. Each of those components would need its own set of assignments and readings. It also requires students to develop explicit strategies to engage with their selected public audience. It isn't enough to just place something on the web and call it digital history; instead, outcomes must include activities to manage audience development and response.

If you anchor your course in a computational digital history method, you might have to spend time working with students to understand statistical formulas and models used by a given tool. Historian Lincoln A. Mullen developed a work-in-progress textbook, *Computational Historical Thinking*, which focuses entirely on exploratory data analysis, mapping, text analysis, and network analysis with historical data through the programming language R.[12] He provides chapters on individual methods as well as case studies of the use of that method for specific historical research. The dataset you've developed or harnessed can limit your methodological approaches in the classroom. A dataset that is entirely textual won't allow for multimedia methods; a dataset that is entirely driven by visual materials won't be as amenable to textual analysis. And on and on. Your learning outcomes will need to be specific to the methods you intend to work with.

Because digital history can be unfamiliar to students, student advisors, and even your colleagues, you will likely have to respond to a variety of preconceptions about the course and its learning outcomes. One colleague recently noted, "I've had students think that the class would be anything from 'the history of digital things' to 'let's learn Photoshop' to 'I don't know, but it fitted my schedule and met a requirement.'"[13] Others who've taught topical courses have noted that students assumed that all methods would be analog in nature so they wouldn't need to grapple with digital data and methods. For this reason, you should be clear in course descriptions and with your learning outcomes about the types of work that you intend students to complete. Students not expecting to learn a programming language may struggle with the computational angle of a course. Another may find a focus on text encoding and analysis uninteresting and thus be unsatisfied. You should also be aware that student dissatisfaction may be tied to the need for additional technical training like teaching students about directory structures and basic command-line operations to enable the types of datasets and methods you'd like to use in the class. I often include a "basics" subheading in my syllabus under each learning outcome that provides students with access to fundamental concepts and skills they may not have already. This removes the stigma of students needing help by making it openly available without them having to ask. And when coupled with a "further reading" subheading, it can guide students to move from introductory to advanced based on their own interests.

Unlike analog course descriptions, which often reproduce "this course will" statements, you'll likely find that "this course will not" statements are better for managing student expectations. I write these "will not" statements as a draft and then turn them into positive language in my descriptions. "This course will not ask you to learn a programming language" is revised to "This course will ask you to learn to use publicly accessible tools." I'll specify which technologies we will be using as well as what students will need to master. If there is specific existing knowledge either technically or historically that I expect students to have, I spell those out as well. Even if you are incorporating digital history into only a portion of your course, being clear about what students will and won't learn will often lead to greater classroom effectiveness.

Do not hesitate to explore published syllabi to gather ideas about what is possible for digital history outcomes. You will find copious examples of learning outcomes that are tied to types of methods and technologies, including website design, social media usage, podcast development, and type-specific technologies, that you can utilize in your own course. There are several curated syllabi collections you can explore, including the Open Syllabus Project, the Digital Humanities Education group via

Zotero, and City University of New York's Digital Humanities syllabus collection.[14] You'll want to sort through these to find the relevant methods and approaches. These can be rich models of learning outcomes that are easily repurposed for the digital history classroom. Remember to not only contact the instructor to let them know you are using what they've developed but also consider sharing it forward by publishing your own learning outcomes and syllabi. You might also contact the developer of any assignments or activities that you utilize. This makes clear to students and colleagues the value of this type of pedagogical development. This is also one of my favorite parts about professional networking in the digital history community. We often discuss not just our research but also how we're deploying a given learning outcome in our course. Digital historians often exchange lessons, syllabi, rubrics, and models, and you shouldn't shy away from asking for a copy of someone's materials when you run across them. This approach allows you to build a curriculum that takes advantage of your and your colleagues' expertise and also to agree on what other areas of knowledge you need to develop collectively. If you can't find what you need, you can consider reaching out to professional associations like the American Historical Association, the Alliance of Digital Humanities Associations, the Association for Computers in the Humanities, the National Council on Public History, and the Organization of American Historians. You don't have to be a member to ask for help, and many groups will connect you with relevant experts who can assist you. So too should you ask for help via social media. The hashtags #digitalhistory, #digitalhumanities, #publichistory, and #digitalpedagogy are usually used by scholars talking about their research, learning outcomes, methods, and teaching approaches. Don't hesitate to pose the question you have. You may be surprised who can help you!

As we close this chapter, we should briefly go over the role of course evaluations. You might want to build a review form that is specific to your digital history courses, because most course questionnaires don't ask about the digital or technical aspects of courses. They tend to conflate content learning with methods. They also tend to overemphasize the role of "liking" assignments rather than asking students whether the assignments were effective. I like to ask questions on the peer-review form that are generally outside of rubrics like those of Quality Matters (QM), which is a generally accepted certification and review process for university and college courses. In digital history courses you need to evaluate not only the design of the course, which is what QM checks for, but also the implementation of the course. A simple question about the effectiveness of chosen tutorials or activities matching student experiences can be very revealing. In reviewing a course recently, I learned that many students had the same challenge in one module. By adding an additional bridge activity to the module, in the next course where students completed that module, the challenge had mostly disappeared.

If you have access to other experts outside of history who are knowledgeable about digital methods and digital projects, you should ask them if they are willing and able to review the appropriate courses and components. Centers for teaching and learning, digital scholarship centers, and cultural heritage organizations likely have individuals who are well versed in digital methods and technologies. Their perspectives can be quite valuable as they can point you to ways to improve your courses that you may have overlooked. I also encourage you to have a frank and open conversation with colleagues about the review process for your digital history courses. Collegial peer review is a needed counterbalance for women and scholars of color who face challenges with regard to student evaluations. Studies have found that women and scholars of color are systematically scored lower than their white male peers. In digital history courses, these trends continue. One way to counteract this is to incorporate ongoing student feedback that addresses very specific concerns in the digital history classroom. I like to use the pre-test and post-test feedback mechanism where I ask students to provide answers to key questions about their knowledge of the historical content, method, or technology at the outset of a unit. Then, after the unit, we re-measure their knowledge using the same questions. I couple those testing mechanisms with open-ended questions about what worked for the students and what didn't, and then I require them to suggest different approaches that would have worked better for them as learners. These then become fodder that I use to illustrate how

I've incorporated the critique in future course iterations. Another way is to form a digital history working group with peers who are working on similar topics. These individuals can assist with being testers for course content and can be fresh eyes for your course as it progresses over time.

In closing, it's important to remember that you can adapt each aspect of our history, method, and technology formula for designing outcomes to the appropriate educational level of your students. In the next chapter on assignments, we'll discuss common types of assignments in the digital history classroom and how they align to analog models.

Chapter Three

New Forms of Assignments

DIGITAL HISTORY courses move us away from traditional analog assignments of identifications, five-paragraph essays, and research papers toward assignments that take new forms as students utilize different methodologies and technologies. From the timelines that were discussed in chapter 2 to the digital exhibits, archives, and multimedia narratives in chapter 8 of this book, digital history classrooms can introduce a dizzying array of assignment possibilities that can feel quite overwhelming. We don't have the space to cover every type of possible assignment. Instead, in this chapter, we'll explore assignment models that either complement or disrupt analog historical pedagogy by supplanting them with new assignment structures that ask students to utilize digital methods and tools. From digital timelines that extend our analog practice to micro-project visualizations, digital history assignments can shift students toward digital methods.

In 2017, historian of religion Christopher Jones began tweeting up a storm about a new type of assignment in his classroom, the unessay. Jones was drawing on an innovation first promoted by his colleague in the field of religious studies, Emily Suzanne Clark, who herself credited digital humanists Daniel O'Donnell and Ryan Cordell with the idea.[1] Cordell was frustrated with how ineffective digital humanities assignments were in the undergraduate classroom.[2] Students weren't interested in grappling with the question of "what is digital humanities," nor were they invested in the humanities as a genre of study. His students, he wrote, were scarred by their experiences with educational technologies and the rhetoric of digital disruption that they supposedly participated in. All of this collectively amounted to courses where students felt they had little control and saw little opportunity for themselves to participate. Enter the unessay. The unessay asks students to choose their own topics, present them in a compelling format, and undergo evaluation based on how successful their results were.[3] Unessay products can include creative work like digital documentaries, social media essays, and digital visualizations. History Twitter (it's a thing, trust me) lit up with those delighted by Jones's advocacy that enabled students to determine how they would demonstrate their competency. Still others lamented, but what about the final essay? Don't historians need students to understand the five-paragraph convention of essay writing if most of our historical scholarship utilizes an extended form of that as a product? Essay writing matters, but, in the digital age, historical thinking doesn't just appear in written five-paragraph essay forms. It also appears in infographics, maps, digital collections, multimedia essays, and on and on. Each of these is a potential type of assignment that students could complete in a digital history classroom.

Historian Cate Denial uses the unessay assignment in her introductory undergraduate course as a substitution for the final course paper because it enables students to embrace their own interests in topics that might otherwise seem unfamiliar or even alienating.[4] Her students propose their unessay topic, and they establish a set of grading standards by which they will be judged. Grading can include items like use of historical sources, connections to course materials, utilization of citational formats, grammar and style, and the like. She then iterates with the students back and forth until they've finalized both the scope of their unessay and the grading standards. In her words, "students get to set their own bar."[5] That bar also requires them to complete a three-page self-reflection on what they learned, including providing a bibliography that supports their work. Denial's students, like those of O'Donnell, Cordell, and Jones, have produced a wide variety of types of unessays. Some of my favorites include a Monopoly game where the goal is to gain tribal recognition, a cross-stitch sampler of same-sex-loving women from the nineteenth century, a meal investigating the multiethnic origins of southern foodways, an artistic rendering of W. E. B. Du Bois's concept of "double consciousness," and a historical documentary short about the Salish Indians in their homeland in Montana's Bitterroot Valley. Since 2017, the unessay has only expanded in history classrooms. Historian Maureen MacLeod's students in her course on the French Revolution built their own guillotine. Since 2013 Victorianist Lucinda Matthews-Jones has had students in her class about Victorian cities create board games, interactive children's books, and more. These are the results of what she terms "a quiet radical act" in the classroom that dismantles structures that privilege the written word, empowers students in their learning experiences, and allows students to experiment with ways to demonstrate expertise to future employers.[6] Hidden within many of these unessays are digital technologies and methods that can serve as fodder for your classroom. Check out the hashtag #unessay to see what is possible when you incorporate the unessay into your classroom. Importantly, if you are nervous about moving away from formal essay writing, you may wish to consider having students write a formal essay and then have them complete a translation activity where they create a complementary unessay that extends work they've already completed. The benefit to this approach is that you can encourage students to understand different audiences while still serving a thesis, evidence, conclusion-based model.

One step further away from the traditional written paper is the digital micro-project, a riff on the unessay that asks students to apply methods and technologies to prepared datasets in the digital history classroom. A micro-project asks students to complete one aspect or step within a larger digital project, method, or approach. In a course exploring the global history of enslavement, students might begin with a dataset that consists of a couple of dozen primary sources focused on enslaved peoples and their experiences. This might be a reader purchased from a publisher or it can be a dataset you've assembled yourself or with students. From that data, one student completing a micro-project might craft a digital timeline (using TimelineJS or SIMILE), using a published document reader to highlight issues of selection and bias.[7] Another might use the same document set to develop a digital map of the movement (using Google Maps or ArcGIS) of enslaved peoples that renders information about who owned the ships, which countries and groups sponsored the voyage, and other details.[8] Still a third might use text analysis methods (using the programming language R) to generate an index of people, places, things, and topics that helps readers to better understand what the documents contain.[9] A fourth might craft a digital exhibit (using Mukurtu or Clio) of enslavement that brings together materials from outside the class with those they've already explored.[10] Each of these different micro-projects would begin with students selecting and justifying the particular method and technology they wish to use, completing a schedule of due dates for drafting the components that need to be completed, and creating an explicit statement of deliverables. One reason that I appreciate the micro-project in the digital history classroom is that I can elevate the complexity of the project based on the student's demonstrated proficiency, just as Denial, Matthews-Jones, and Jones do in their unessay framework.

Micro-projects are also useful because they can be scaled to be accomplished in the amount of time allotted, which can be anything from a single day of work to multiple weeks, with the outcomes adjusted appropriately. In the digital history classroom, a micro-project can push students toward technical proficiencies. Those can be as varied as demonstrating the ability to publish historical thinking on the web via WordPress or simple HTML pages, through the development of multimodal narrative, or even generating brief documentaries. While I talk to students about the technical aspects of their project, I remind them that the technology is there to assist them in their historical thinking, not fight them. This means that their micro-projects are compelling when they show some combination of the following:

- It is as interesting as its topic and approach allow.
- It is as complete as its topic and approach allow (it doesn't leave the audience thinking that important points are being skipped over or ignored; nor does the topic rely on problematic research or material).
- It demonstrates mastery of primary and/or secondary source analysis as needed (any questions, evidence, conclusions, or arguments you raise are honestly and accurately presented).

In terms of presentation, a micro-project is effective when it shows some combination of these attributes:

- It is readable/watchable/listenable (i.e., the production values are appropriately high and the audience is not distracted by avoidable lapses in presentation).
- It is appropriate (i.e., it uses a format and medium that suit its topic and approach).
- It is attractive (i.e., it is presented in a way that leads the audience to trust the author and their arguments, examples, and conclusions).
- It incorporates the technology and method effectively to reach its intended audience.

The micro-project checkpoint can be embedded at any time in the syllabus. If you organize your course with multiple methods or technologies, the terminus of each method or topical area may be a micro-project that can be graded and will serve as a measure of competency.

Micro-projects may also be staged to result in a course-long digital project. I've found great success with this approach where at the end of each method or technology, students complete the portion of the final project as a micro-project that relates to that stage. Extending our example from the course on global history of enslavement, a student might create four micro-projects: a digital source criticism, a timeline, an interactive map, and then, for their final effort, a published narrative with each of the three components embedded. Students can then develop their final project over time and do so when content, method, and tools are fresh in their mind. Students have reported that they like this approach because it spreads out the work of the class throughout the term rather than concentrating the work at the end when they may have many courses to manage. It also allows me, as the teacher, to intervene if the student clearly didn't learn what they needed to rather than waiting until the end of the course when there may not be time to go back and reassure myself that the student learned what they needed. Stage plus component also makes transparent why we are working on a given method or tool in a specific order.

Micro-projects may also make transparent the relationship between analog historical methods and digital history methods. Trevor Owens asks digital history graduate students to write two project proposals during their course: one that focuses on an analog history project and the other on a digital history project.[11] Students can then elect for the final project to complete the work they outlined in their proposal. The analog project results in a five- to seven-thousand-word article for publication while the digital project results in the project plus a one-thousand-word statement about its goals and relationship to course content. Owens notes for his students that the goal is not to demonstrate technical competence per se but rather to act as a historian in a digital space. He writes, "Examples could include starting and curating a Flickr pool focused on collecting and interrupting representations of the American west[;] in consultation with the DC historical society you might build an Omeka exhibit to complement one of their physical exhibits[; and] you might create an annotated Google MyMap or a set of tours using a mobile app like HistoryPin that gives an interpretive tour of the history of the design of the national mall." By giving students suggestions on what is possible, Owens is enabling them to both have a say in their final project and also scale it to what Owens believes is possible based on the student's capabilities and the time allotted. I can imagine a slight riff on Owens's approach where you constrain both the analog and the digital assignments to utilize the same dataset or archival sources. That would allow for students to complete a written reflection on how the medium of the project shifted their historical thinking and the possibilities of the projects. It would encourage students to understand the relationship and divergence between analog and digital historical practices.

Erin Bush utilizes a similar approach in her advanced undergraduate classroom where she preselects the methods and micro-projects that students will be asked to complete. In a course named Chicago's Criminal Past, Bush's students are guided to use Reclaim Hosting, a web-hosting company run by former academics, to set up WordPress so that they can develop their own course-long projects that result in a website.[12] They begin by exploring Cornell University's 1911 Triangle Factory Fire project as well as learning about the Homicide in Chicago project.[13] They then receive training in finding and evaluating primary and secondary sources online. Students turn in reading notes and participate in an in-class workshop that analyzes primary sources. This correlation of a workshop where they work to develop proficiency with a group assignment to show their development structures the entirety of Bush's syllabus. A workshop on narrative storytelling leads to a TimelineJS and StoryMapJS group assignment where students build a timeline and then tell a story based on Chicago locations (fig. 3.1). Both are free tools available online from the Knight Lab that allow students to construct narratives in either a timeline or map format.[14]

Learning about data use by historians is coupled with downloading and cleaning the Homicide in Chicago database as a group. Understanding maps and their utility aligns to creating a Google Map of the data that they've cleaned in the previous class. This type of sequencing enables students to develop a deep familiarity with the historical context. It also allows them to immediately apply what they have learned through course assignments.

Bush can triage collectively rather than individually when the students complete micro-project work as a group, and that allows her to manage the potential flood of student questions and technical issues. The course's summative assignment is to propose a project that asks students to identify their research question, the primary sources they intend to use to complete the project, and the secondary sources that will support their analysis. Students then can build that final project to reach the final learning

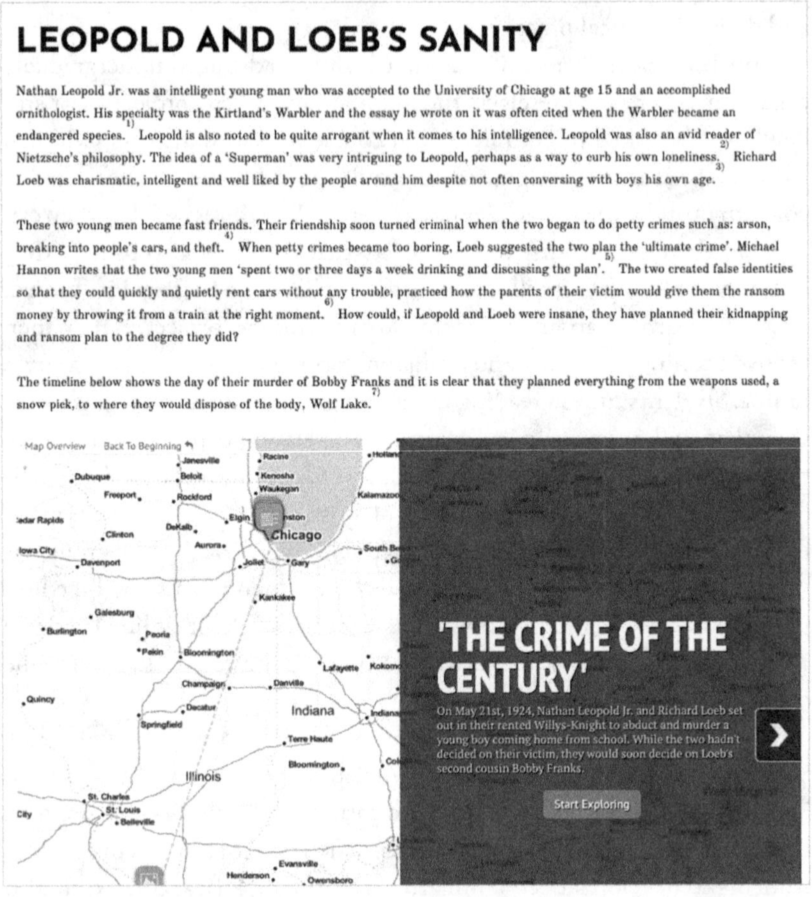

LEOPOLD AND LOEB'S SANITY

Nathan Leopold Jr. was an intelligent young man who was accepted to the University of Chicago at age 15 and an accomplished ornithologist. His specialty was the Kirtland's Warbler and the essay he wrote on it was often cited when the Warbler became an endangered species.[1] Leopold is also noted to be quite arrogant when it comes to his intelligence. Leopold was also an avid reader of Nietzsche's philosophy. The idea of a 'Superman' was very intriguing to Leopold, perhaps as a way to curb his own loneliness.[2] Richard Loeb was charismatic, intelligent and well liked by the people around him despite not often conversing with boys his own age.[3]

These two young men became fast friends. Their friendship soon turned criminal when the two began to do petty crimes such as: arson, breaking into people's cars, and theft.[4] When petty crimes became too boring, Loeb suggested the two plan the 'ultimate crime'. Michael Hannon writes that the two young men 'spent two or three days a week drinking and discussing the plan'.[5] The two created false identities so that they could quickly and quietly rent cars without any trouble, practiced how the parents of their victim would give them the ransom money by throwing it from a train at the right moment.[6] How could, if Leopold and Loeb were insane, they have planned their kidnapping and ransom plan to the degree they did?

The timeline below shows the day of their murder of Bobby Franks and it is clear that they planned everything from the weapons used, a snow pick, to where they would dispose of the body, Wolf Lake.[7]

Fig. 3.1. This WordPress site was developed by a student, Kimberly R. Strong, in Erin Bush's course Chicago's Criminal Past. The student embedded a StoryMapJS timeline that narrates the history of the murder of Bobby Franks within a larger narrative of the insanity pleas made by Nathan Leopold Jr. and Richard Loeb in 1924. Kimberly R. Strong, "Leopold and Loeb," accessed October 12, 2019, http://studentwork.erinbush.org/leopoldloeb/leopold-and-loebs-sanity/.

outcome. And, as many digital historians encourage, they can do that work as a group, which reduces the complexity of classroom management for an instructor. Partner and group work are your friend in the digital history classroom as it encourages students to problem-solve and learn together.

You should not overlook social media as one avenue of technical opportunity for micro-projects. Examples abound of digital historians taking advantage of forms of new media in the classroom. Social media platforms like Twitter, Instagram, and Tumblr have all served as the backbone of micro-projects. These assignments might ask students to follow a particular hashtag or thread, engage in a question-and-answer with a historian or institution about a topic through text or image, or even follow a history conference. Classes might explore newspapers in a country to identify what historical topics are being discussed in public. This would allow students two different types of work: they could read these posts to learn about and follow contemporary debates about history, or they could use this material as the basis for a Wakelet essay.[15] Students can then organize content drawn from various social media platforms as well as online primary and secondary sources to craft a narrative essay about contemporary challenges to history. I could easily imagine students in my African American history courses, for example, embracing Wakelet to create an analysis of contemporary discussions around the building of, protests about, and removal of Confederate memorial statues.

Some digital historians prefer to front-load their courses with learning historical content, method, and tools to create space at the close of the syllabus for students to select their own course-completion project. A digital project at the end of a course is usually a culminating assignment that asks students to craft their own historical analysis by articulating the complete cycle of history, method, and technology. Public historian Rebecca Wingo, for example, asks her students in a graduate course about Cincinnati's West End to complete the course by designing an Omeka exhibit using items gathered previously in the course.[16] Omeka, a free technology that you can create digital exhibits with, allows students in Wingo's course to demonstrate their knowledge about Dublin Core archive standards—a controlled vocabulary used to describe sources, the history of African Americans in Cincinnati, and best practices in community and public history. To demonstrate the importance of the final exhibit, students present it to the community members whose objects they have digitized.

It helps when thinking about culminating digital projects for students to work backward from the total amount of time available to what's possible. If the project is forty hours and students think it'll take them half that time to become proficient technically, then that project likely isn't feasible when they account for all project steps in draft and final form. For this reason, I also like to ask permission from students in courses to keep their final projects on file as examples for subsequent classes. Informally, you might use email or, like one colleague did, a digital deed of gift, a form students fill out that specifies how long you can use their work, whether you can use their name or list the project anonymously, and other details about reuse. It is enlightening for students to see work completed by their peers under the same conditions that they themselves are being asked to work in. It also helps me, as a teacher, be realistic with how much time I have to assist students who want to work with technologies that I might not be familiar with. You might replicate this process yourself for syllabus planning where you work backward from course outcomes to assignments as well.

If you anticipate teaching the same course over time, you might consider a project-based approach that builds from semester to semester. Jeffrey McClurken and Ellen Holmes Pearson co-taught a course over multiple semesters titled Century America, which looked at the Great War (1914–18) and the Spanish Influenza epidemic (1918–19); students from seventeen public liberal arts colleges collaborated on the project.[17] Using local archives and special collections, different students enrolled each semester in the courses and documented life at their college and in the surrounding communities. Course assignments on what is digital history, the basics of WordPress for blogging, and archival methods, as well as assignments on reviewing digital history projects, provided students with an overview of what was possible in their own research. From there, students in each course crafted project contracts that included a mission statement, a list of tools they planned to use, and a schedule of milestones. Midway through the course, students were asked to give weekly updates to monitor project progress. They closed out the course with an eight- to ten-minute public presentation and a reflection on the project and how it met or did not meet the project goals as outlined in their contracts. Their result then was a digital history project built with a specific tool that enabled them to contribute new knowledge about the period from 1914 to 1918 in their local community. These contributions were gathered after all students and all classes across the years were complete and made available as a project set illustrating all of the potential avenues for new historical thinking about the war and its effects.

Part of what is lovely about McClurken and Pearson's approach to a multicourse digital project is that students are asked to consider their community as stakeholders in their historical research. Working with the community enables students to see an immediate relevancy to their work that may be missing from digital projects where the primary audience is their instructor. It also allows us to think about how digital project work that is going to be made available publicly is tied to questions about student work and privacy. What information about themselves are students comfortable with sharing publicly? How will they handle positive and negative feedback? What happens if a digital project "goes viral"? And, just as importantly, what recourse do students have if their anticipated audience doesn't respond to the digital work? These questions are not just for students but also for you as an instructor. It is important, particularly when we are partnering with community groups or utilizing community-based sources, to consider the security and privacy of our historical subjects and their descendants. Students should be asked to discuss what constitutes data privacy and how to respect community knowledge. They should also be asked to grapple with how community needs may diverge from those of students.

When I first began asking students to contribute to digital projects, author digital history publicly, or engage with digital historians via social media, it didn't necessarily occur to me that there could be consequences for myself, and my students, related to audience. Consequences can be as minor as an angry email or tweet from a community member or as dire as legal cease and desists and the complete sundering of a partnership. I was focused on helping students develop strategies to recruit users, garner attention, and ensure they received appropriate credit. Now, as a more experienced instructor, I am more cautious about asking students to develop or participate in public digital history projects. At a minimum, digital projects last longer than the course of a single digital history course. Users can grow frustrated by a lack of updated content, a lack of timely response to questions or concerns, or even by a project not having updated its technical platform to account for new capabilities. While it is useful for students to see these types of critiques and demands for attention, it also places a burden on them to remain engaged after a course has ended. This is one of the unique challenges of digital history both in research and teaching. A journal article or monograph may be fodder for dialogue among scholars, but the actual article or monograph does not alter in response to requests and demands by its audience. Once it has been published, it exists as a moment in time. Digital history projects, however, carry with them assumptions that they will always be responsive to new data, methods, or audiences. You should ensure that classroom projects clearly articulate any limitations. If content will not be updated, say so. If you don't intend to update the technology, note that. If students will only be responsive during a certain semester, provide that info. And, as importantly, if you aren't monitoring the project continuously, state when you will.

Digital projects also can convey a sense of authority that may be false simply because they exist on the internet. Students often trust digital projects and datasets that conform to their beliefs about appearance and utility. Rather than seeking to answer the question of quality of the data or whether the project aligns to best practices in method and research, students (and their teachers) are often swayed by digital projects that "look good," "seem slick," and "speak to them." Drawn from our exercises in digital review, the "speak to them" students are often referring to the emotive experience of things like aesthetic decisions of color, font, and project style, but also to difficulty in information organization. One student notably hated a well-regarded project because it took too many clicks for him to enable the interactive visualization embedded within the project site. If we enjoy the experience of the project, we often are permissive about issues around quality or argument. Students tend to rate a project as valid regardless of whether the underlying exposition of method and research adheres to disciplinary standard. Projects that have excellent reliability in their method and analysis but do not "speak" to a student often are poorly reviewed.

Digital projects, particularly those published with the .edu domain or another university-sponsored URL, are also susceptible to transferrable authority where students assume that since the project is tied to a college or university it must be reputable and meet scholarly standards. You may face this as you ask students to utilize the open web to discover digital projects as models for their own work. It will be key to provide them with questions that they should ask to evaluate the legitimacy of the project. A few simple ones I use in my classrooms include a clear statement on project purpose, identifiable contact information with full names, the inclusion of a bibliography or references section that guided the development of the digital project, and a statement on permissions, copyright, and use. Projects without this type of information may not need to be discarded, but students should be more wary of them because they do not espouse an ethic of collaboration and care that encourages dialogue with their users. This links easily to our digital review assignments to reassure students that part of our positionality in the course is critical inquiry and not merely consumption of digital content.

Part of incorporating digital project work into your classroom will require that you consider the ethics of student work and labor as your own form of collaboration. Many digital historians prefer to have students join their own digital research projects because it allows the instructor to demonstrate deep fluency in the historical content and the methods that are being used. Generally, this pathway is useful because you can develop elaborate training materials that you can utilize from course to course that will take advantage of technical infrastructure that you maintain yourself. A colleague in my department has used Omeka+Curatescape repeatedly over the last seven years in three differently titled courses: Introduction to Public History (an undergraduate lower-level course), Introduction to Public History (a first-semester course for master's students in public history), and The Nature of History (a required course for history majors). Another utilizes a multisite installation of WordPress that allows him to use one infrastructure for every course he teaches. Students in each course get access to their course's WordPress site and can build and publish content related to the course. The instructor, though, only has to maintain a single WordPress infrastructure. This is a common approach in many digital history classrooms because it helps lessen some of the detailed work that you'll need to have in place to activate students as digital historians. It's important though that you consider how students fit into your digital research project beyond the classroom. You'll want to ensure that you've reviewed your school's relevant policies on the use of student work. Many of my peers have been shocked to learn that student work is copyrighted to the students themselves. Ethically, students should always receive credit for their contributions to research. They should be clearly named as project contributors, complete use agreements where they note how their contributions may be used by faculty, and receive a citation for the elements of the project they contributed. One colleague uses the metric that students should be getting more of a benefit than the instructor and it should be more effort for the instructor than if the instructor were doing the project alone or with expert colleagues. Students should always be given the option before the course starts to reserve their work as their own and waive contributing to the larger research effort. This waiver can include having students publish their work not to the main digital project but to a closed, password-protected repository. I encourage you to make yourselves familiar with "A Student Collaborators' Bill of Rights," a larger initiative within digital humanities that encourages ethical mentorship, teaching, and research.[18] It offers a useful model of how to develop these processes with your students.

One benefit to limiting students' project work to contributions to your own personal digital history research is that you'll also be able to manage your own need to stay fluent in methodological and technological changes. Version updates for technology in particular can throw a wrench into tutorials that teach students certain methods of analysis. Building time into your own schedule to re-confirm that the technology and associated tutorial still work in the days, not weeks, leading up to the lesson is key to having a successful course. When I first started integrating tutorials into my classes, I'd spend weeks prior to the course working through the tutorials and preparing to teach. Then, without warning one semester, the program we were using was updated the week before I was teaching with it. The entire tutorial I'd assigned to students was no longer functional. Because the tutorial didn't work, I had to scramble for an alternative way to teach the method of spatial analysis I'd planned on. My colleague once developed a university-wide program around the multimedia tool Scalar only to find out, between one week and the next, there had been a version update. She had to redevelop all teaching materials and retrain her student assistants on the new interface with almost no notice. It was either that or scrap multimedia narration as a method until she had time to choose a new tool to take Scalar's place. The lesson: set aside time in the days immediately prior to teaching a method and associated technology to ensure that if the teaching materials and tutorials need updating, you have the time to do so.

Version updates can be particularly frustrating to you as a teacher. Interface updates to the public-facing aspects of a tool can make or break a digital project for your students. From one day to the next, your audience's experience can shift tremendously. Menus may move, the aesthetics may change, or information may disappear or appear in different places than it did previously. By asking students to complete digital project reviews as we move through the semester, I am sensitizing them to the questions of audience experience that all projects should answer to be successful. Behind the scenes, those changes may play out for students by making it nearly impossible to complete the work that they had anticipated. What do you do when students can't complete what is assigned?

Fear of failure in a digital history course can be real and substantial on the part of the instructors and the students. For students, the social and personal pressures to excel can lead to anxiety when they cannot master a technology on the first try. Some students suggest that "failing" in front of their peers equates to a personal weakness. In my course, before we begin our first set of technical tasks, we talk about what failure means. For the students, it is important to hear from me that they will not master every task the first (or even the fifth) time. I provide them with an example of how I failed in learning a specific technology and how it has taken me years to master its use. I also talk to them about how nervous it can make me when I try something publicly that doesn't work. It is key to provide them with language they can use that doesn't use the word "fail" so that they can admit that what they are doing isn't working. One colleague brackets these conversations with students by using the concept of iterative or recursive development. Another grounds it by talking about struggle being useful intellectually. Students in my classes are asked to talk in terms of what they are struggling with or what they are trying to improve. Often, I'll ask them to write reflections on their use of a technology that asks them to highlight what it was they struggled with or why a given technology didn't work. They provide screenshots of what they did accomplish along with a reflection about how they attempted to solve their problem. Common responses include a problem with the instructions they've received, an attempt to complete an assignment when rushed/tired/distracted, a technical failure like a web-based tool being slow or "janky," or even something as simple as "I realized I never pushed submit" (which happens more frequently than you might think).

Students can be enticed to become proficient in seeking answers from message boards, technical guides, and tutorials using bonus points attached to assignments that don't include step-by-step directions. Hashtags for methods or tools, as well as technical forums, can also guide students to resources as they attempt to problem-solve. Part of the goal of this is to empower students to problem-solve and then talk across the spectrum of student experiences. It also reflects the reality for most technical work where internet forums and published documentation provide solutions rather than formal training. This is how most digital historians develop their competencies in new methods and tools. If multiple students simply did not complete an assignment, I'll task them as a group to work together to do the assignment. Or, if a student is struggling immediately,

I'll often stop the exercise and partner students together to work through the assignment. This allows students to serve as sounding boards for one another rather than having a student not complete the assignment. If everyone is struggling, we'll often do an entire assignment as a group and then students are tasked with working through it a second time as their homework. In a digital history classroom, repetition can be a useful classroom management strategy. We will complete tutorials as a group using the provided dataset first, and then students are tasked to complete the assignment a second time with the unique dataset they've generated in previous exercises. It may take students more attempts to understand a given method, the tool I've chosen that fits the method, and its use beyond simple step-by-step instructions. That is perfectly acceptable as the goal is not who moves the fastest through the assignment but who engages the most constructively with the concepts and functions that underlie the tool and its method. For the digital portion of the course, this type of problem-solving is essential as students are encouraged to take charge of their own learning.

Students in my courses appreciate watching me fail at a technical task or admitting that a method challenges me intellectually. My not having an answer delights them. This type of technical triage gives us opportunities to talk about the ephemerality of digital resources, software, and platforms. Just as enjoyable to them is being recognized as experts in particular technologies or approaches themselves. They appreciate the ability to either problem-solve or to reflect on why things didn't work. For students who enter the classroom with existing capabilities, I generally provide a note in my syllabus or at the beginning of a unit for a student who might have existing technical skills that they want to take advantage of.[19] I also keep a live version of the course syllabus for my own purposes. It serves as a for-next-time file that includes brief bullet-point notes on specific things I need to do differently next time, copies of student feedback about a particular assignment that I link to the micro-project in the schedule, details on other assignments I come across when teaching that might be useful later, and notes on how to improve the course generally. This allows me to sit down after the course is over, reflect, and revise (when I have time) so that my next course addresses the weakness of the previous version. Don't be afraid to experiment with different types of micro-projects or digital projects in your classroom. If you are honest with your students about the fact that you're trying a new technology or assignment, they will think of themselves as partners in the course who can provide useful feedback.

If learning outcomes are our goals and digital projects are our outcomes, the question we are left with in part I is how we move from the outcomes we've selected to the digital projects that students will complete. The answer to that lies in the subject of the next chapter: methods.

Chapter Four

The Basics of Digital Methods

WHEN I START thinking about digital methods in my history classroom, I like to remind myself that being a responsible teacher and researcher is making apparent what I know and what I don't. If there is any area of digital history where that becomes most apparent, it is when I teach and talk about digital methods. Just as there are dozens, if not hundreds, of potential methods that historians can utilize in analog history, there are dozens, if not hundreds, of digital methods available that can complement or contradict our historical thinking. Digital methods are not oppositional to analog. Rather, many analog methods are the basis of digital methods that we'll talk about. My starting point for thinking about digital methods then is to always be honest with myself and my students about where methods come from, what they are intended for, and how they can be used (and misused) by historians. If we are borrowing methods from anthropology, archaeology, geography, linguistics, feminist studies, and so forth, we should identify those methodological processes and the scholars who developed the methods. What is the method? What was it originally intended for? Why is that method useful to you? What are the limits of the method? And, finally, how do the types of questions historians ask challenge or add to the method? These are the questions that you should answer when you begin to select methods for your classroom.

Part of what digital history has done is peel back the structure of historical thinking to highlight the processes and decision making that we call "methods." Methods are techniques and heuristics used to analyze our sources. In most analog monographs, discussions of methods, or the process of arriving at one's conclusions, are relegated to footnotes or brief discussions. Rarely in contemporary monographs (or even articles) is there a systematic recounting of all approaches and methods taken up in the author's analysis. Part of this is a result of limitations related to length (printed works have gotten shorter and shorter), but it is also related to questions about the acceptability of the methods being deployed. Take, for example, oral history. When oral history methods were being codified and professionalized after 1940, it was quite common to have extensive discussions about both the oral history methods used by scholars and the implications in their publications. Analog works published between the 1940s and the 1970s were filled with expansive discussions of oral history methods. Yet now, because oral history is seen as being an accepted method in historical scholarship with clearly articulated standards and procedures, there are far fewer expositions needed for the result of oral history to be accepted as legitimate. Digital history, because it is perceived as an emerging field with "new" methods, requires methodological exposition for it to be accepted as valid by our peers. Just as every historian is not fluent in every analog method, so too is every digital historian not fluent in every digital method. The result is that methodological exposition acts as a statement of advocacy that can address questions and concerns about the validity of our conclusions. By elucidating our methods, we are reassuring our peers that we followed best practices and standards but also that we have treated our sources appropriately with respect to accepted historical practices in our analysis.

Excitingly, and overwhelmingly, there are untold numbers of methods available to you as a digital history teacher that you can bring into the classroom. Generally, any analog method in history has a correspondence or equivalent in the digital historical domain. By simply adding the word "digital" before the analog method, you can discover methodological possibilities for your classroom. Oral history methods, for example, which used to rely on pen and paper, have moved into digital forms of media. As historians moved from reel-to-reel technologies to cassette technologies and into digital audio recordings, their methods shifted as well. Each form of media brought with them their own standards as well as structures of access that would guide later use. The Oral History in the Digital Age project at Michigan State University provides an excellent introduction for students on how different forms of digital media have altered oral history methods.[1] Ethnography, as another example, has an intersecting method of digital ethnography. Digital ethnographers use methods of kinship, relational analysis, and cultural and linguistic custom analysis, as well as techniques of observation and interview. But digital ethnographic methods also contend with the complications associated with the digital sphere. As a result, students utilizing digital ethnographic methods will need to understand software; digital capture and recording tools; digital publishing systems like blogs, websites, and content management systems; forums and social media spaces; and on and on. What the addition of "digital" to any given method gives you is not just an additional set of questions related to the digital forms and medium. It also can broaden the methodological playbook available to you by introducing new techniques that you may not have been able to use in analog form.

How do you know which digital methods answer which types of historical questions? Generally, I recommend that historians working in the classroom start by drawing from pedagogical materials provided by peers when they are exploring which methods they might use. The *Programming Historian* (PH), which is an open educational resource that offers tutorials specifically for use with historical content, is one such repository of peer-reviewed tutorials created by and for historians around specific methods.[2] Let's illustrate the use of *PH* by briefly discussing histories of migration. Historians interested in migration have long used pen and paper or even basic computer programs like tables and databases to identify and track the movement of individuals and goods. With the introduction of digital methods, though, migration historians have new options for analyzing movement. Digital historian Adam Crymble began his work with two simple questions: "For every 1,000 migrants who moved to London in the 1770s–80s, how many would we expect to come from each English county? For every 1,000 tons of coffee exported from Colombia in 1950, how much would we expect to go to each of the Western Hemisphere's 21 independent countries?" While Crymble could hand-count every migrant in his dataset and tally them, his analog process would not demonstrate patterns of movement. With digital history methods, however, Crymble can use mathematical modeling related to distribution and probability theory to understand migration and trade.[3] Regression analysis is a set of statistical processes for estimating the relationship between a dependent variable and one or more independent variables. Probability theory considers the probability of an outcome, given a set of variables. Combined, these two processes let historians understand and model the push, pull, and economic factors that motivate migration. Crymble provides a summary in his tutorial in *PH*: "Given a number of influencing forces (distance, cost of living) affecting migration or movement of a large number of entities of the same type (people, coffee beans, widgets) between a set number of points (39 counties and London or Colombia and various countries), the model can suggest the most probable distribution of those people, coffee beans, or widgets. It operates on the principle that if you know the volume of movement, and you know the factors influencing it, you can predict with reasonable accuracy the outcome of even complex movement within a confined system."[4] Students can follow Crymble's tutorial to reach several outcomes. They can learn about the characteristics of the datasets and the basics of the mathematical concepts of regression analysis and probability theory, as well as how to decide on the variables that need to be used (here population at origin, distance from London, price of wheat, average wages at origin, and trajectory of wages). For every variable, students also create a weight that tells us how important that variable is relative to the others. Perhaps distance matters more than wages? Perhaps wheat prices? Each is a decision that must be recorded as it will impact the results of the model. To this point, we see three different methods operating—one archival in the assemblage of the dataset and two mathematical (regression modeling and probability theory)—but part of what this process requires is historical interpretation. Crymble tells students in the next step that the modeling was a case study that sought to interpret lower-class migration in the eighteenth century. The model demonstrated that certain parts of England were "either over- or under-sending lower class migrants to London." But it was only by the coauthors drawing on their contextual knowledge that they were able to conclude what caused those variations: in one area it was rapid industrialization that limited migration while in another it was the loss of work that encouraged migration to London. Additionally, the method of regression modeling showed that there were unexpected patterns of migration from Northumberland, with more female migrants than they would have expected to see based on average migration. That, as Crymble writes, is the beauty of this method: it can reveal anomalies that encourage—even require—further investigation and analysis. While terms like "regression analysis" and "probability theory" may seem outside your comfort zone, the underlying historical questions about migration aren't.

PH organizes its tutorials around five different stages of research: acquire, transform, analyze, present, and sustain. For each research stage, you are given access to methods that enable you to complete the needed processes. Some methods are tools that guide you from start to finish in conducting analysis. Others point you to programming languages that guide you to follow a prescribed set of steps to conduct an analysis. Each tutorial specifies the types of sources and data that must be worked with and provide examples of the types of historical questions that may be asked. An entire digital history class could be constructed just using *PH* tutorials and their provided datasets as illustrations of methods. Part of why I like *PH* is that it also lets you sort by difficulty. By difficulty, they are referring to one's technical capabilities, but it also serves as a fabulous shorthand for methodological difficulty. Crymble's exposition and tutorial are listed as difficult. But you can find new digital methods that are easily introduced into your classroom that don't require understanding programming languages or mathematical and statistical concepts.

And again, because every tutorial includes examples and the audience is specifically historians, *PH* calls out the types of questions that any given method can answer. Digital methods encourage you to explore with your own dataset. This is because the process of decision making that is incorporated into the method will lead to differing conclusions. It is only when you make those decisions for yourself that you can reach results that might help you in crafting historical meaning.

Analog methods, digital methods, and the tutorials that accompany them have their own important place in the classroom. When I introduce methods in my classes, I like to tell students that methods are the pathways we build between the historical questions we have and the answers we seek. Methods don't lead us to predetermined answers. Instead, every decision we make opens and closes new pathways. The more proficient we are in a given method, the easier our work is. The more complex our methods, the longer it may take us to understand it and develop our historical understandings. Students tend to relate our initial conversations about digital history methods to the show-your-work principle in math. In math, to show one's work is to reveal step-by-step each decision you made that led to your conclusion. In analog history, we show some of our methodological work in our writing, citations, and footnotes. But most decisions are implied within our writing. In digital history, methods are the step-by-step decisions we make (or fail to make) that guide us to our conclusions.

If I was forced to choose only one assignment tied to methods to build into a digital history course for the rest of my career, it would be the research notebook that lays bare what students do in their work as historians. Rather than focusing exclusively on conclusions, a digital history research notebook asks students to reveal how they reached their argument's conclusions. It is entirely about methods. What evidence was kept? What evidence was discarded? What transformations did the evidence undergo? Did you introduce new evidence? The digital history research notebook is an assignment that encourages techniques and heuristics to be laid bare to the reader.

Digital history notebooks, like lab notebooks, can include computer code, links to relevant material, and even programs that can be re-run to illustrate how what was inputted was transformed into an output. My first experience with digital lab notebooks was through information scientists and computer scientists who presented at workshops and conferences in the digital humanities. Rather than providing narrative essays of their methods, they would provide attendees with access to their Jupyter lab notebook.[5] Jupyter notebooks are an open-source web application that allows anyone to create and share documents that contain over forty different programming languages with live code, equations, visualizations using built-in tools, and narrative text. It enabled us to poke under the hood of the presenters' work to understand how their computational methods had led to their results. It also offered an opportunity to ask questions, make copies so that we could utilize their methods for our own work, and address any methodological errors we identified.

Shawn Graham and Rob Blades use this organizing structure in their Crafting Digital History course for advanced undergraduates.[6] They argue that a digital historian needs a digital research notebook or space because it serves as a "scratch pad / fail log and code repository so that we remember what we were doing, or (more importantly) what we did—that is to say, the actual commands we typed, the sequence of manipulations or data moves." It also allows students to solicit help by asking about "the why" of what you've done, keep a registry of things you've come across on the web, and attach screenshots, videos, and even bibliographic programs that contextualize their work. Graham and Blades ask students to use GitHub for the course, where they've shared their research notebook template. It includes six primary modules for the course: why open access research, finding data, fixing data, analysis, visualization, and final thoughts. Most modules are built around a concept that includes key readings that have been hyperlinked. Students "fork" the notebook on GitHub, which basically allows them to make a complete copy of all readings, assignments, exercises, and the syllabus itself in their own repository. Students then work weekly to complete an assignment titled the "fail log," which asks them to "document their worries, post questions, and reflect on their weekly learning." They must include a link to at least three annotations written about the assigned material and a reflection on how those annotations

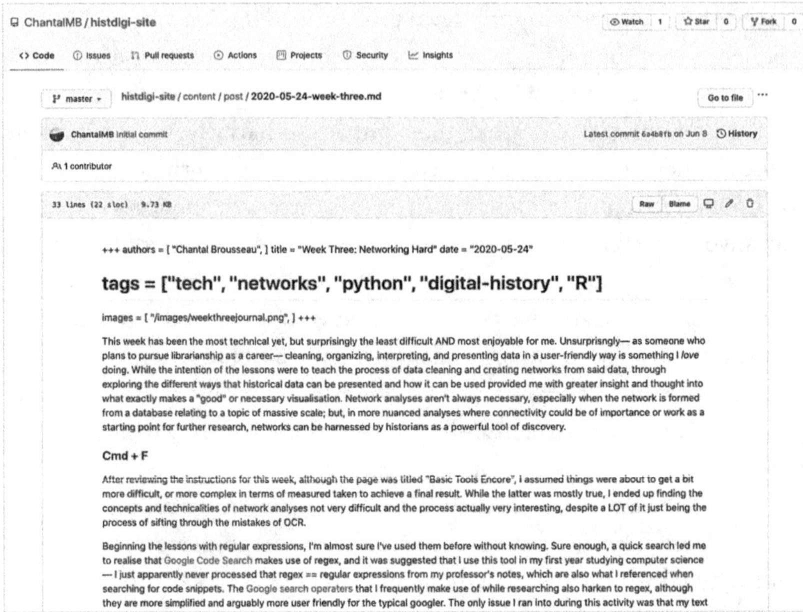
ChantalMB / histdigi-site

Watch 1 | Star 0 | Fork 0

Code | Issues | Pull requests | Actions | Projects | Security | Insights

master | histdigi-site / content / post / **2020-05-24-week-three.md** | Go to file

ChantalMB Initial commit | Latest commit 6a4b8fb on Jun 8 | History

1 contributor

33 lines (22 sloc) 9.73 KB | Raw | Blame

+++ authors = ["Chantal Brousseau",] title = "Week Three: Networking Hard" date = "2020-05-24"

tags = ["tech", "networks", "python", "digital-history", "R"]

images = ["/images/weekthreejournal.png",] +++

This week has been the most technical yet, but surprisingly the least difficult AND most enjoyable for me. Unsurprisngly— as someone who plans to pursue librarianship as a career— cleaning, organizing, interpreting, and presenting data in a user-friendly way is something I *love* doing. While the intention of the lessons were to teach the process of data cleaning and creating networks from said data, through exploring the different ways that historical data can be presented and how it can be used provided me with greater insight and thought into what exactly makes a "good" or necessary visualisation. Network analyses aren't always necessary, especially when the network is formed from a database relating to a topic of massive scale; but, in more nuanced analyses where connectivity could be of importance or work as a starting point for further research, networks can be harnessed by historians as a powerful tool of discovery.

Cmd + F

After reviewing the instructions for this week, although the page was titled "Basic Tools Encore", I assumed things were about to get a bit more difficult, or more complex in terms of measured taken to achieve a final result. While the latter was mostly true, I ended up finding the concepts and technicalities of network analyses not very difficult and the process actually very interesting, despite a LOT of it just being the process of sifting through the mistakes of OCR.

Beginning the lessons with regular expressions, I'm almost sure I've used them before without knowing. Sure enough, a quick search led me to realise that Google Code Search makes use of regex, and it was suggested that I use this tool in my first year studying computer science —I just apparently never processed that regex == regular expressions from my professor's notes, which are also what I referenced when searching for code snippets. The Google search operaters that I frequently make use of while researching also harken to regex, although they are more simplified and arguably more user friendly for the typical googler. The only issue I ran into during this activity was that my text

Fig. 4.1. This markdown file created by a student, Chantal Broussard, uses the GitHub platform and serves as an example of the "reflection" assignment that Shawn Graham asks his students to complete weekly. Students write about their experiences in working with the particular tools and ideas, in this case developing their expertise in the Python programming language to build network graphs. Chantal Broussard, "2020-05-24-week-three.md," accessed July 17, 2020, https://github.com/ChantalMB/histdigi-site/blob/master/content/post/2020-05-24-week-three.md (site discontinued; additional examples are at https://hist-digitized.netlify.app/).

contributed to the student's learning (fig. 4.1). Graham reviews each student's log and offers individual and communal feedback.

The second part of each module is a set of technical exercises that asks students to complete progressively more difficult assignments. Some of the technical exercises are built around DH Box, a freely available digital environment that allows you to have a pre-equipped research space. It includes common tools and programming languages used in digital humanities methods, including IPython, RStudio, Omeka, MALLET, and the

Natural Language Toolkit—some of which are discussed in the methods chapters in part II.[7] These are various technologies and programming languages that allow students to explore a given method. Others link to external tutorials that the students are asked to complete. Students attach their work to their individual repository, which enables Graham to not only confirm completion of the assignment but also assist the student if they are having technical issues. After completing all modules in the course, students are poised either to craft a new work of digital history using data and results from one of the technical exercises or to contribute to an existing project by applying one of the methods they've learned about.[8] Part of what I like about this approach is that it encourages students to embrace what they've learned. I also appreciate Graham's guidance to students. He provides "to know if you're 'done,' ask yourself" questions to help students know whether they've completed their work.

Lauren Tilton and Taylor Arnold use a similar approach in their workshops on image analysis.[9] Students, which include faculty, cultural heritage professionals, and staff, learn methods related to color analysis, object detection, facial recognition, image similarity, and image clustering through deployment of a Jupyter notebook that provides Python programming language for each method. Students learn the basics of Python as well as how each method constructs what we can learn from image corpora. In the face-detection lesson, for example, students were able to identify faces in still images from two episodes of the sitcom *Bewitched*. Students learn not only where the face is in the image but also who the face belongs to. By the end of the course, students can begin to apply the Distant Viewing Toolkit, the Python packages the course is built on, in their own still- or moving-image corpus.[10] By combining the conceptual material with programs, code repositories, and datasets, students can easily begin working at their own pace. And, as Tilton and Arnold have shared, students often come back to the workshop notebook repeatedly to refresh their knowledge as time passes.

For those who think a research-driven notebook approach is too complex for their digital history class, you might consider providing students with HTML, WordPress, Scalar, or other digital templates that contain all relevant course materials to walk them through methods associated with web publishing and digital storytelling. Students can then edit and customize the templates as they make their way through the course. It eases the learning curve for students who aren't technically proficient while also allowing us to still achieve our goal of showing not just what our conclusions are but how we arrived at those conclusions. This second approach is limited in that if you intend students to work with technical programs, they won't be able to include executable programs inside their sites. If you are wary of developing your own templates, you might consider using Digital Mappa in your course.[11] It is an open-source set of tools that are integrated together (commonly referred to as a "workbench") to help you annotate and mark up images and texts, create links between items and annotations, and publish work as a single publication. Built by the Center for the History of Print and Digital Culture, you can create a course publication for students where they serve as creators building out your syllabus through their own work.

The question of the depth of methodological knowledge needed to understand a digital historian's conclusion was discussed recently at a meeting of digital historians as it relates to our own scholarship and that of graduate students we are educating.[12] Should a digital history project be required to provide a methodological overview that details the various methods, the underlying archival data, and the transformations that were required to conduct analysis? What type of audience should that methodology address? A digital historian? A historian with little experience in digital methods? And, as importantly, should we be requiring digital historical representations to reveal any methods that they are using that impact the interface, organization, and utility of its contents? Digital historians have often divorced the methods of a project from its scholarly conclusions, either via the publication of a separate methodological article or via deployment of a methodology section. Yet, by relegating methods to a separate scholarly product, there is concern that we are losing an opportunity to educate and proliferate digital history methods to our non-digital colleagues. One corollary for this chapter is the question of how deeply students need to engage prior to deploying a particular method. There is no universal rule or recommendation for this question. In part, this is because historians are seen as consumers of these methods rather than as actively engaged in their development. It is also because many of us are squeamish about partnering history with units on mathematical and statistical probabilities and computational reasoning. "I thought I was taking a history class," one student wrote to me, "not a math class." In that same class, a student who loved math told the class that this was the first time he'd thought a history class could intersect with his business major.

We'll discuss the issue of logics in chapter 6 on textual analysis in part II, but for now as we close our consideration of methods, we should pause to note that iteration, revision, and a keen eye will likely be needed no matter which methods you select for your course. New digital methods, tools, technologies, and issues arise frequently. Ten years ago, it was not common to see digital history courses explore three-dimensional representation both because the cost of three-dimensional scanning technology was expensive and because there were few historians familiar with three-dimensional methods. Now, dozens of courses include three-dimensional visualization methods as part of their courses. Similarly, methods of game design are much more common now in history classrooms than they were even five years ago. This is a result of tools that have made the design aspects of video games more accessible to students, and there also is a broader community of historians talking about the appropriate methods for historical re-creations. If these trends signal how quickly the field is moving, they also suggest the many different pathways into digital history and its methods even now.

As we end part I then, you should feel confident in the basics of a digital history course. You should have a sense of sources as data, types of learning outcomes, opportunities for new forms of assignments, and the basics of digital methods. In part II, we're going to explore commonly used methodological approaches in the digital history classroom. As I mentioned, there are so many methods to choose from. I've selected those that are most effective in a variety of types of learning environments. So let us begin with digital source criticism, which every history classroom can incorporate.

PART II

Selected Methods

Chapter Five

Digital Source Criticism

IN THE FIRST few weeks of most introductory history courses, a lesson teaches students the who, what, when, where, and significance question process that guides historical source criticism. Usually, this occurs by the teacher providing documents and students working iteratively over the course of the class to "read" the source and apply their contextual knowledge. These are the famous (or in some case infamous) short identifications that appear on many exams in history classrooms. Students are generally prompted to identify who is involved, what happened, when approximately it happened, where it happened, how/why it happened, and what is significant about it. Students learn that significance is not only about the identification they are completing but also about relationships between that identification and larger course themes and content. The starting point for digital history pedagogy is this same process: source criticism.

Using sources as the starting point for my digital history pedagogy helps me highlight for students the conflicts and tensions that historians face when they conduct archival research. Fundamentally, historical sources are embedded in social and cultural systems, rife with biases and challenges of authority, subjectivity, access, and control. In the late twentieth century, digital historians promoted the notion that sources as information and knowledge should be open access and widely circulated for the public good. It is a priority for us to think about how what constitutes historical evidence has shifted because of the digital age.[1] Today, we are more skeptical of what happens when you publish sources on the open web. In some instances, access to new sources, whether born-digital or digitized, constitutes a public good. In others, born-digital and digitized sources can be problematic documents that encourage continuing trauma and violence. When I think about evidence and source criticism as the starting point for digital history classes, I'm cognizant of the challenge that postcolonial digital humanist Roopika Risam offers to us. We should encourage students to "avail themselves to the transformative possibilities of technology while calling attention to the ways that [Indigenous, immigrant, and Global South knowledges] resist easy answers or simple solutions to the ongoing effects of colonialism and neo-colonialism on the production of knowledge."[2] Key to highlighting the transformative nature of digital sources and evidence is asking students to understand themselves as historical subjects and as part of the cultural record. Students are often shocked to be asked to consider that they are becoming the next generation's dataset through surveillance software, e-records, social media, and personal fitness devices. An icebreaker assignment is to ask them to track all the data they produce or interact with in a given amount of time. Each student uses a spreadsheet to record the time, location, and information recorded anytime they use anything electronic. Students record card swipes in the campus center and each time they use their laptops, cellphones, and personal fitness devices. They also record internet searches, use of campus learning management systems, and even things like surveillance cameras and home Wi-Fi. From their spreadsheets, we categorize their entries into types of information recorded and then talk about what historical equivalents exist and how a historian one hundred years in the future might use their personal data. Students can then extend this into publishing an essay about how data impacts their daily life, who profits from their data, and how data matters for historical thinking of the future.

The wealth of digitized sources that exist on the internet offers us opportunities to allow students to seek out primary sources that speak to their own interests and to course topics. As we know, finding sources is an activity that historians spend lots of time on. When seeking out this material, it is most useful to have students start with government-supported repositories and/or major collecting institutions across the world. The British Library, Bibliothèque Nationale de France, the National Library of Australia via its Trove repository, the National Archives of India, and others, including many university libraries and archives, all have digital sources available for download and use in the classroom.[3] Digital aggregators including the Digital Public Library of America (DPLA) enable you to easily surf over twenty-three million images, texts, videos, and sound files drawn from member institutions.[4] The utility of DPLA is enhanced by its exhibitions function, which lets you view topical digital exhibitions of material drawn from DPLA holding institutions. These topic collections make it easy to develop assignments that help students to undertake source criticism exercises on documents related to the same topic. The Smithsonian Institution museums have a similar platform, the Learning Lab, which provides access to millions of digitized and born-digital sources.[5]

Source criticism exercises in digital history classrooms can start in the analog physical space. Many students have never been to an archive and may need guidance to understand how physical documents relate to historical thinking. I like to provide students with an assignment guide that asks them to highlight, underline, color-code, circle, and star the key information in a copy of a physical document that will enable them to answer questions I provide. I often print out copies of documents and have students mark them up with colored pencils or markers. I pair students together to share their annotations; each pair reports back to the full class, where we then annotate a poster-sized version of the document. This low-tech version of a source criticism exercise is a great way to ease students into working with historical sources. It allows them to focus exclusively on the skill of source criticism without also asking them to figure out how digitization and digital tools complicate things.

Many historians and their students encounter digital sources after the process of that transformation. We are consumers of digital data, rather than the producers. But, if you are doing digital source criticism at its fullest, you'll also need to work with students to consider the steps involved in source transformation. Those steps can be quite varied. An archive that wants to make every item in its analog collection available will generally identify which collection they will digitize; evaluate the existing collections structure, arrangement, and descriptions down to the item level to identify if it needs revisions; determine the copyright or other restrictions that might exist in relationship to items and the collection; and then proceed with the digitization workflows. Digitization involves direct digital capture with a high-resolution scanner, camera, or other digital device. Technicians will control for issues of quality including standardization of lighting or sound, sizing, and image density. They'll also address issues of formats, providing descriptive information about the digitization tools and process and file naming. The workflow might also include post-processing steps like captioning, translation, transcription, and development of lower-resolution surrogates for use on the internet versus the high-resolution versions that the archive will maintain for preservation. Each action within the digitization workflow constitutes a decision that will be recorded and attached to the final digital surrogate as evidence of its mediated state. You might bring in a partner from your local library's special collections or archives to demonstrate for students their digitization workflow and how it informs the digital surrogate. If that isn't possible, you can always have students analyze the publicly available information from an archive or library. What are they digitizing? How? What impact did the decisions made in the digitization workflow have on the utility of the source? What does the display interface look like and how does it function? How does that interface limit or expand possibilities of identification and analysis? I like to choose two or three archives that have digital surrogates of the same document in this type of exercise.

Students can then compare and contrast the archives' approach to the analog object. It also begins to make them conscious of how display interfaces in their web browser will allow or limit the viewing of certain types of information. With students, it is important that they understand the basics of this workflow so that they can understand how these processes impact the final surrogate and its utility.

If working with the wide world of internet-available sources isn't of interest, you might consider identifying an analog source from your own research and turning it into a digital surrogate for students' use in your classroom. Many historians have begun to embrace Tropy, a free software for managing your research documents that enables you to organize and describe photos taken of analog materials.[6] Part of what is great about Tropy is that you can not only include information and annotation on each individual photo but also group documents into collections and share them with others. Tropy is a convenient way to share documents with different groups of students or to have students share their materials with you as their teacher if the course includes an archival research component.

Tropy was developed as a partnership between the Roy Rosenzweig Center for History and New Media and the Luxembourg Centre for Contemporary and Digital History (C^2DH). C^2DH recently released Ranke.2, a teaching platform that offers opportunities for students to conduct source criticism, as another avenue for incorporating source criticism into your digital history class.[7] Ranke.2 provides lessons, handouts, and exemplars of what might be incorporated in an exercise about digital history source criticism. Lessons are available in English, French, and German and are organized according to module length. A small module can take fewer than fifteen minutes and serve as a basic introduction to a topic related to source criticism. The medium-sized module consists of a series of assignments that take up to ninety minutes and can be completed individually or in a group. A large module, which requires at least a full day, helps students to complete filtering digital source criticism through the lens of creating a digital history project. Possible projects include a website, a podcast, a digital exhibit, or a photographic collection with annotation. Currently, there are six modules available for classroom use that begin with digital source criticism; more lessons are under development. Part of why I like Ranke.2 and think it could be useful to you as you begin thinking about history fundamentals in the digital history classroom is that it also offers a useful set of questions that illustrate how analog source criticism meets digital source criticism. As they write:

> Students will learn
> 1 How digitisation and the web have changed the nature of historical research.
> 2 How digital objects are created (retro-digitised, born-digital, converted documents).
> 3 What changes when an analogue source is turned into a digital representation.
> 4 How to question the concept of the "original."
> 5 How information is added to a digital object (metadata).
> 6 How data is published online and made searchable.
> 7 What the impact of search engines is on finding and selecting sources.
> 8 How to apply a number of digital tools to data.
> 9 The difference between conducting research in an archive and online.
> 10 The properties of different types of data (text, images, objects, audio-visual).[8]

Trevor Owens provides a slightly different angle on these questions in an article on digital sources and digital archives.[9] His digital source criticism questions are broken out into digitized primary sources and born-digital sources. As a reminder, born-digital sources are assets that are created and exist only in a digital realm. For the former, he asks why the source was digitized, was the digitization of "significant quality" for the purpose, and how did you find the source and does that process of identification affect what can be written about the source? In the latter category, the questions relate to what is lost. That loss is represented by what is missing from the source when the user experiences it in the digital interface as well as what is missing from the source because of the decisions of how it was produced and presented. For example, websites often go through many iterations. The current view of a website on your browser is only one version. Any user will gain or lose material based on the browser and version of the content being called up. Many historians use the Wayback Machine, a born-digital archive of the internet, for this reason.[10] The Wayback Machine lets you enter any website address and, if it was "crawled" by Wayback, view it on a given date from previous years. Email that was sent during the late 1990s utilizes completely different technologies and appears quite differently to users than the browser-based email interfaces we use today. Owens also points to issues around source identification through search engines and questions about born-digital source creation and management that can impact the type of criticism that can be constructed.

There are independent digital tools out there to facilitate source criticism exercises using the types of questions that Owens poses. Hypothes.is is a digital annotation tool that you can use to comment on or annotate anything on the web.[11] Students can do all the same annotation actions they would on the physical document, but they can also share those annotations to the full class immediately. If you are part of a school that uses a learning management software (LMS) like Canvas, Blackboard, or Moodle, you should look at installing Hypothes.is on your course LMS site. By adding the Hypothes.is app to your course, you and your students can annotate PDF documents, websites, and anything else posted to the web. The app also integrates with your gradebook so that you can create annotation assignments where students submit their annotations for feedback and grading. I have found that these assignments allow me to check their ability to identify key information in situ while also giving students the ability to see the variety of ways they approach the same document. The app can also guide students in organizing information so that those who haven't been taught notetaking and annotation previously can develop those skills. I also frequently assign students to turn their annotations into a prose statement. Such statements are a great opportunity to begin teaching students about historical writing and what the conventions of our discipline are. They turn in the written prose, and it is peer-reviewed. Studies have found that peer review encourages not only student participation but also a greater sense of the classroom as a community. This sense of community is particularly important if you are teaching your course online, where students can feel disconnected simply because of a lack of social contact with their instructor and peers. It asks students to learn how to provide written and verbal feedback that is productive and positive in nature. It can also help them understand professional norms about critique.

A great example of how peer review can be facilitated as part of digital source criticism exercises is the work that Russian historian John Randolph does with his undergraduate history students at the University of Illinois through SourceLab. SourceLab is a digital documentary publishing initiative that trains students how to create freely available digital documentary editions of individual historical artifacts suggested by other scholars, partners, and members of the general public. In SourceLab courses, students are provided with just one single digital surrogate of a historical source that needs contextual information. A digital surrogate is the reproduction that results from the photographing or two- or three-dimensional scanning of a physical object. Over the course of their class, students work together in small teams to research source provenance, complete any transcription or translations, and write a short publication that includes historical analysis.[12] Undergraduate history majors and graduate students serve as editors, providing them with skills in editorial review, publishing, and team management that are valuable for their careers. Part of what students learn about is the process of digitization, the affordances of digital surrogates, and how to create and amend metadata, which is the descriptive data that is attached to every object. Student work on topics as varied as Arctic expeditions, World War II films, the Second Anglo-Afghan War, and menstrual hygiene have been published publicly at the end of each class via Scalar, a multimodal publishing platform that we'll explore more in a later chapter (fig. 5.1).

Visual materials also work well in digital source criticism exercises. Historian Antonis Hadjikyriacou works with his advanced undergraduate students in an Ottoman History course to demonstrate how to focus on spatial documents. Using the tool Recogito, which lets users identify and mark places referred to in historical maps, texts, and tables, students

Fig. 5.1. The students Austin R. Justice, Artur Stasiek, and Archana Upadhyay completed their digital source criticism with the publication of a discussion of "Stamping It Out," an 1880 illustration drawn by John Gordon Thompson about the Second Anglo-Afghan War. Using the Scalar digital tool, students provided access to the original illustration (*right*) as well as annotation in the form of overlays to the illustration (*right*) and textual explanation (*top left*). Austin R. Justice, Artur Stasiek, and Archana Upadhyay, "Stamping It Out (1880): Imagining the Second Anglo-Afghan War," accessed October 3, 2019, https://iopn.library.illinois.edu/scalar/stamping-it-out/online-edition?path=introduction.

annotate "Ottoman travelogues and contemporary histories; records of the assets of the pious endowments (vakıfs) belonging to the founder of a powerful family of Ottoman statesmen (Köprülü Mehmet pasha); and readers' letters to Kadınlar Dünaysı (Womens' world), one of the first Ottoman women's magazines."[13] They were tasked then with compiling this place-based information with the existing reference gazetteers that the tool has preloaded. The exercise helps students to consider how authority is conferred in terms of place and educates them on the locations outside the "imperial" center that were being corresponded with. Digital history shines in this type of application because the tool enables the type of historical knowledge production that historians have been doing in analog form with students for decades. By doing it digitally, though, Recogito allows for an efficiency and ease of this process that normally only happens well after an in-person course ends, if at all.

I should pause here to note that these types of annotation and source criticism exercises are not limited to primary sources. Secondary source materials can be treated similarly. While you may gravitate toward monographs and articles as your form of secondary source material for your history courses, digital assets including websites, digital projects, photographic materials, videos, audio files, and others are possible avenues for critique. Part of the brilliance of Hypothes.is is that you can use it on anything published on the internet if they allow third-party cookies in their browser. In beginning history courses, I might share very specific questions that students need to answer when conducting this exercise. At advanced levels, I'll often ask students to use Hypothes.is to reverse-engineer a critique by exploring a recent digital history project review and its associated digital project. Students notate not just the project itself but also the review. They then visually link the two together by developing a project map, which is an exercise that involves students diagramming key concepts, structures, and evidence. This type of exercise allows students to not only have their own user experience with the project but also position themselves to ask the following: did this review see the same things I did? What did they critique that I did not? What might have been added to the review? In classes where the first learning outcome is teaching the nature of history and the work historians do, this type of activity can ask students to grapple with narrative form, function, and content all within a single assignment. In advanced courses, the exercise also provides students with the opportunity to learn about professional norms related to critique and publication. When students begin layering critiques from differing journals, they begin to understand how particular analytical lenses are tied to sub-disciplinary interests and how those lenses shape the types of critique that projects face.

Our goal with digital source criticism is for students to understand that many of the same concerns that historians have of analog sources are transferred to the digital space. Whether it is the overamplification of certain voices, narratives, and geographies, questions of selection and bias in archival construction, or archival omissions, starting with source criticism provides students with a firm basis to move into asking questions about the digital aspects of sources and their criticism. It reminds students that research in history is fundamentally a source-driven exercise. It also primes them to consider how individual sources act in concert with one another through source collections. Importantly, though, part of what digital history provides you in the classroom is the opportunity to explore sources with new methods. In the next chapter, we'll discuss how textual analysis methods can be deployed after students have learned to analyze individual sources.

Chapter Six

Text and Network Analysis

IF INDIVIDUAL SOURCE criticism is the starting point for many digital history classrooms, the next nearest methodological stopping point is textual analysis and its related method of network analysis. Text analysis is a way of extracting grammatical, semantic, or structural information from words or collections of words, which we refer to as a corpora.[1] It is a set of methods drawn from linguistics, computer science, statistics, sociology, literary and book history, and library science. You can do things like graph the use of a word or phrase over time, count words and phrases, or look for correlation between words. Text analysis is highly flexible and will let you automate the extraction of information about people, places, events, and the like. While text analysis has been dominated by literary historians, linguists, and digital humanists, it offers methodological possibilities for the digital history classroom for three primary reasons: text documents are widely available as plain-text files that make them amenable to analysis; a wide variety of free programs and tutorials that already exist can be easily incorporated into your syllabus; and text documents can easily be used with a variety of text analysis methods, which makes them highly flexible for experimenting with processes.

Corpus analysis fits under the umbrella of textual analysis and lets us make comparisons between large volumes of texts. A quick aside on "large" or its nearest cousin "big data": what constitutes large scale or big data is often in the eye of the beholder. Computer scientists would tell you that large scale and big data means that your dataset is too large to be processed on a personal computer. Digital humanists would tell you that "big data" isn't a measure of the amount but rather its complexity. For digital historians, we tend to use "large" or "big" when we mean any dataset that can't be read by an individual in a single (or even year-long) sitting. So don't let "large" or "big" scare you away. It's all relative to your perspective.

The simplest starting point for students when it comes to text analysis methods is frequency analysis. How often does a given word appear in any given corpora? Voyant Tools, a free cloud-based service, enables students to count words and develop visualizations that can demonstrate the frequency of a word's use.[2] Students can upload a text or use an existing textual collection to investigate a corpora. While students don't find word clouds or frequency analysis that exciting, they do find the other built-in tools interesting. For example, students studying the US Civil War (1861–65) might study public sermons after Abraham Lincoln's death by following the published work in Lincoln Logarithms, a project of Emory University's Digital Scholarship Commons (fig. 6.1).[3]

They might compare and contrast the sermon of Reverend Pliny White of Coventry, Vermont, with that of Reverend Charles Lowe of Charlestown, South Carolina. They will learn that while they were delivered on the same day, their content varied greatly. White's sermon emphasized Lincoln's contribution to ending slavery through the Emancipation Proclamation while Lowe's discussed the need for unity in the country. From there, students can extend their use of the sermons to map relationships between each, extract proper terms and map them geospatially, and identify keywords. They can then construct lists of individuals mentioned in the sermons, record any location mentioned on a map, and sort documents topically by keywords. You may find the included tutorials particularly useful for students as it not only walks them through the included tools but also highlights how the chosen tool is problematic methodologi-

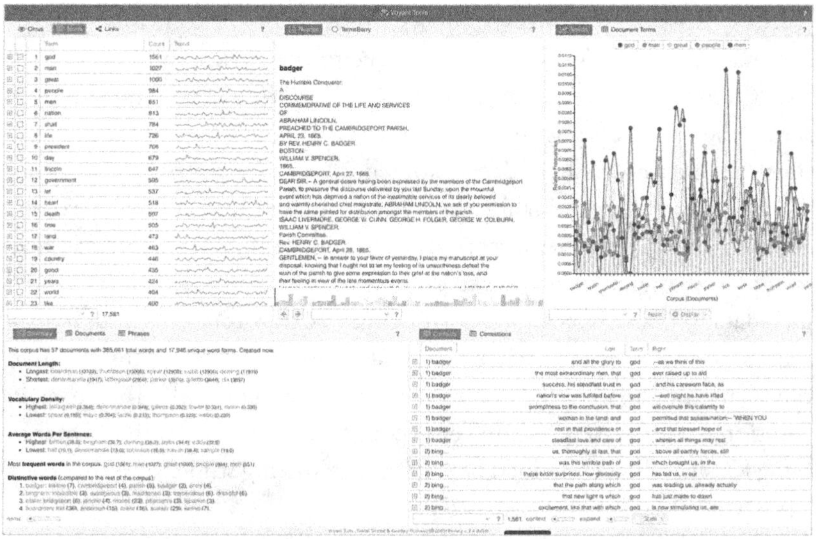

Fig. 6.1. Using the Lincoln Logarithms sermon dataset, students completed a number of text analysis activities using the Voyant Tools interface. In this view, students can see count and trends of particular words (*upper left*), a transcription of the documents (*upper center*), and the corpus plotted by frequency (*upper right*). A summary of the entire corpus (*bottom left*) and a list of contexts (*bottom right*) complete this view. Stéfan Sinclair and Geoffrey Rockwell, "Voyant Tools," accessed November 4, 2020, https://voyant-tools.org/?corpus=b9a23575c1892d9580eee791be595873.

cally in its approach. Students don't have to understand the underlying math. Instead, the developers explain how the tool might guide you to erroneous conclusions if you don't understand the method the tool relies on.

I've recently begun using "Everything on Paper Will Be Used against Me": Quantifying Kissinger, a digital project authored by political historian Micki Kaufman that asks students to consider how text analysis methods can challenge how historians encounter archives and their contents. Quantifying Kissinger applies "'big data' computational text analysis techniques to research the Digital National Security Archive (DNSA)'s Kissinger Collections, comprising approximately 17,500 meeting memoranda ('memcons') and teleconference transcripts ('telcons') detailing

[Henry] Kissinger's correspondence during the period 1969–1977."[4] Kaufman argues that the search interface to the DNSA collection is obstructionist to historical research because it does not facilitate analysis across the entire corpus. Basically, you can see only one document at a time. Yet, as scholars have demonstrated, to understand political history you need to understand many genres of document in relationship to one another. To construct her historical argument, Kaufman needs the archive to supply all digital surrogates to the analog documents and all associated metadata. She also needs each document to be transformed through optical character recognition (OCR) technology into a de facto transcript that can be used to analyze the contents of the document itself. Therefore, in addition to showcasing the power of computational text mining, Quantifying Kissinger has the added benefit of introducing students to the issues that OCR raises.

OCR is the process of converting images of handwritten or typed text into machine-readable text. Digital historians rely on OCR to create plain-text documents that are based on original analog or digital images as well as born-digital images. It basically transforms physical materials into digital texts that you can then use as your dataset. The pros of OCR are that it allows you to skip having to individually transcribe every document that you've scanned or photographed and it can handle volumes of material much more rapidly than you can as an individual researcher. The cons are that OCR isn't correct 100 percent of the time and the number of errors can render the results close to useless. While re-keying—where a user manually views the document in one window while typing the words into another—can be an antidote to this issue, it is also highly laborious. OCR can offer students the opportunity to experiment with different tools that all are built to create machine-readable text even as they embrace the limits of the tools themselves. Tesseract, OCRopus, and ABBYY FineReader all enable students to input image files and to output machine-readable text.[5] Yet each one produces different results using the same exact corpus of materials.

Kaufman's method is often referred to as "distant reading" (in the case of textual material) and "distant viewing" (in the case of photography and moving images). This method, adopted from literary history and linguistics, lets Kaufman consider all documents in parallel to one another and at the same time. The analog equivalent, as I explain to students, is not reading every book on one's bookshelf one right after the other. Rather, it would be reading everything in your library at the same time, at the same speed, and with the same attention and focus. Kaufman's work is useful fodder in the classroom for this conversation because she uses a multiplicity of textual methods within the same project: word counts and frequencies, topic models that group terms together to allow her to identify common themes, influence mapping that allows her to align individuals to particular types of language that Kissinger uses, and sentiment maps that allow us to see how what Kissinger said suggested particular mindsets related to feelings of sadness, anxiety, and other emotions. All are methods drawn from and validated by the field of linguistics. Kaufman's driving motivation though is her effort to better understand what the declassified archive contains and how that archive can help us understand Kissinger's actions during this pivotal period in American history.

Students can easily break into groups, research one of the methods Kaufman utilizes in her argument, and then develop their own application of the method to a different corpus of material. This allows them to consider how much you need to know about a text to utilize in your own historical research. I like to pair Kaufman with one of the most successful examples of textual analysis that you can use in the digital history classroom, digital humanist Robert K. Nelson's project Mining the *Dispatch*.[6] It lets students uncover and explore the myriad ways in which Richmond, Virginia, and its citizens experienced the US Civil War. Part of why I like to utilize Mining the *Dispatch* in my unit on textual analysis methods is because Nelson directly addresses the relationship of textual analysis methods to analog historical provocations. In 1865, Civil War journalist George Alfred Townsend declared that Richmond, Virginia, the Confederate capital, remained a "mystery" to most northerners. One hundred and twenty-five years later, the historian Kenneth Noe echoed this sentiment by noting that Richmond and its citizens had largely been ignored in histories of the Civil War. Nelson is attempting to speak to both specialists in topic modeling and historians focused on the Civil War. His "introduction" is particularly valuable because he demonstrates how his intervention into the Civil War is expressed through a particular method. He delineates the possibilities and limitations of the method. He concludes that topic modeling historical newspapers can "reveal patterns that we can't, patterns that surprise us and that prompt interesting and useful research questions."[7]

Using the *Daily Dispatch*, Nelson formulated a series of queries about Richmond through topic modeling. "Topic modeling," Nelson writes, "uses statistical techniques to categorize individual texts and, perhaps more importantly, to discover categories, topics, and patterns that we might not be aware of in those texts."[8] It's a form of linguistic analysis that looks for patterns and themes across a corpus. Using algorithms designed for topic modeling, Nelson and his team were able to identify statistically significant peaks in how the Union army presented enslaved peoples with the opportunities to seek freedom by escaping behind Northern army lines. These were specific historical moments when the army intentionally appealed to enslaved people to leave Southern territories and seek respite in Northern-controlled areas. After these peaks were identified, Nelson and his team then married topic modeling to close reading of the *Dispatch* newspapers on those days. This allowed him to map the proximity of the Union army to the Confederate capital of Richmond to understand whether Union enticements were weaker or stronger based on proximity to Southern military lines. Graphing newspaper content in this way helped to bring these historical moments into stark relief, while the larger project provides a model of how topic modeling could be used on historical newspapers of this period.[9]

Rebecca Sutton Koeser's "Trusting Others to 'Do the Math'" frames our conversation of what exactly historians need to understand to utilize topic modeling, which is highly reliant on mathematical concepts and algorithms.[10] Koeser asks, "When scholars use software to complete or share their research at any point in the process, how reasonable is it for them to ignore the complexity and the various points at which they must trust others to 'do the math'? How much do scholars need to understand the technological tools they use, and what role do the creators of that software play in the resulting scholarship?"[11] These questions are useful for students as they help them understand the layers of mediation that we encounter by using tools and platforms. By mediation, I mean not only how the creators have instilled practices, approaches, and values into their tools but also how those decisions frame realities for users and lead them to certain types of knowledge. I also like to point students toward digital historian Benjamin M. Schmidt's "Words Alone: Dismantling Topic Models in the Humanities."[12] Schmidt deftly lays out the assumptions that underlie topic modeling as a method of textual analysis. Topic modeling, we learn, assumes that topics are both coherent (read: have things in common simply because they are published alongside each other) and stable (read: that its meaning is consistent across documents simply because they are in the same corpus). Schmidt goes on to use his own work exploring digitized ship logs to illustrate how topic modeling suffers when the corpora contains both unstructured information (prose words) and structured information (geographical information). Students learn that the most frequent words (that is, the words that make up the most statistically significant topic model) are in fact the least meaningful to a historian. Rather, it is only the expert eye of the scholar who is intimately familiar with shipping during that period who can discern that the least frequent topics contained the most impactful whaling routes. By wrapping these various digital projects together, students are forced to consider what constitutes meaningful historical conclusions. Can it simply be a list of topic models? Simple graphs of a word over time? We return again and again to the question of exactly what one's audience needs to know to trust the conclusions reached. In the digital history classroom, this type of direct exposition of a project, its audience, questions, and conclusions offers students the opportunity to explore issues of language selection, clarity, and audience response.

Frequency analysis and topic modeling are not the only textual analysis methods that digital historians can utilize in their classroom. Digital historians Andrew J. Torget and Caleb McDaniel utilize ads about runaway slaves as the primary dataset for their undergraduate digital history courses at Rice University and the University of North Texas. In two classes on different campuses, students identify, transcribe, and analyze nineteenth-century slave ads from Texas newspapers. As part of their work, students create text files of the newspaper ads to form the textual corpora that they will work with. They learn how to work with Python, a programming language, to write regular expressions that allow them to extract information from the digitized materials. Regular expressions are strings of text that describe a pattern used to search within any given set of characters. One you are likely familiar with is "find and replace," which is a regular expression that allows you to first identify any given word and then replace it with another. Students use regular expressions to find every instance of an ad seeking an enslaved person and then to extract that ad into a new corpus that is only ads from the newspapers rather than the entire newspaper.

Once students have their ad corpora, they then are asked to experiment with topic modeling and named entity recognition (NER), which is a computational way to identify proper nouns. Students use MALLET, a Java-based package for statistical natural language processing, to classify, cluster, topic-model, extract information, and conduct other machine-learning applications to text.[13] MALLET is a command-line tool that supports a variety of textual analysis methods and was what Nelson used to do his textual analysis for Mining the *Dispatch*. Command-line tools bypass the graphical user interface of the computer so that students can directly command the computer to do things using only a string of text commands. With knowledge of the command line, students can view, handle, and manipulate any file on their computer, including executable files like MALLET.

An aside about using command-line-based programs in the digital history classroom. While it may feel uncomfortable to ask students to use the command-line interface rather than the graphical browser that lets them simply point and click, mastery of the command line has a long-term benefit for them as researchers. With knowledge of the command line, students can more quickly navigate files and folders, read and edit files, as well as move, copy, and delete files. When I've taught command-line activities in my classroom, students get excited once they've learned the basics about scripting. Scripting allows students to write a set of commands that unspool automatically. For example, students can identify all files in a specified directory, automatically open those files in a specified program, and then command the computer to re-save those files in a different format and in a different directory. Students can also automatically sort files based on characteristics, rename those files, and deposit them in a new folder. Any action that you would undertake in a graphical interface using your mouse can be turned into a command-line action and script. It's also useful to give students a sense of how far computers have come in terms of the visual interface.

After they have assembled their plain-text corpora, students are also introduced to NER, which allows information within a textual corpus to be identified and classified into predetermined categories including, but not limited to, names of persons, organizations, locations, dates, quantities, and percentages. NER is incredibly useful for historians because they can then automate the creation of indices, gazetteers, and the like. We'll talk more about NER in our exploration of spatial humanities in chapter 7, but, for now, why NER matters is that it allows students to move from identification and annotation of people, places, and so forth by hand (or with Hypothes.is) to computer-assisted identification and annotation. In her class on the historical experiences of enslaved persons in the United States, Sharon Leon asks undergraduate students to experiment with NER by first reading the *Narrative of the Life of Frederick Douglass* as well as selected entries from Documenting the American South's North American Slave Narratives.[14] Students are then tasked with contributing to a Google Doc where they list every person, place, and event chapter by chapter. I can imagine complementing this assignment with a group exploration of NER where we compare and contrast the results of the Stanford Named Entity Recognizer, which is Java-based software, with the list that students completed by hand.[15] Part of what this illustrates for students is that sometimes computer software may be more laborious than just using an analog method.

Returning to our example from Torget and McDaniel, the end results of the students' work are not the individual components that result from the topic models and the NER list. Instead, the final product of their text analysis methods is a public-facing website that includes links to their various digital tools and their outputs, their digital methods, and the conclusions they reached about runaway slave ads based on their work.[16] By confining the students' data work to a preselected database (the Portal to Texas History) as well as a particular form of data (advertisements), students delve deeply into a single historical period while experimenting with a number of digital methods. This approach allows for a measure of fluency on behalf of the instructors since it draws on McDaniel and Torget's disciplinary expertise in slavery and the American West. They can aid students in their analysis and provide needed guidance as students grapple with unfamiliar historical contexts and methods simultaneously. By selecting just one single digitized dataset, they can move relatively swiftly from questions of how the data was collected, digitized, and contextualized to experimentation with the different types of text analysis methods for answering historical questions. It also provides an opportunity to discuss with students how scholars are challenging using the language of "runaway" in their scholarship to better reflect enslaved peoples' perspectives.

When students have mastered textual analysis, you'll find that they get very excited to work with network analysis. Network analysis is the use of mathematical graphs that connect entities to one another and render those relationships visually. Imagine those chain letters you might have participated in as a child. Network analysis allows you to map how that letter moves, who it is sent to and from, how many times, and in what form. In my classes, I begin exploring networks by asking students to read two chapters from *Exploring Big Historical Data: The Historian's Macroscope.* A freely available online textbook written by Shawn Graham, Ian Milligan, and Scott Weingart, *Macroscope* focuses on how historians can use big data in their research. It includes chapters that focus on the fundamentals of networks and that provide examples of how networks have been used in historical scholarship.[17] Trade networks, kinship networks, correspondence networks, genealogical networks, political networks, and even citational networks are all examples students are exposed to through this reading. You can complement these examples with ones from the Center for History and Economics at Harvard University, which offers eleven different digital history projects focusing on networks that cover issues of empire, economy, marriage, the Atlantic World, suburbia, and trade.[18]

An alternative starting point is the seven-part series of blog posts written by early modern historian Scott Weingart on networks. He walks students through the basics of network analysis and its implementation, and they can follow along to learn how to use Twitter data to conduct citational networks using the Sci2 tool.[19] At the close of the series, students experiment with the tool using a sample dataset. Given the growing importance of social media to the future historical record, students really love the opportunity to consider social media as a historical network. Elizabeth Dale conducts a similar sequence in her introduction to digital history course where students learn the basics of networks and then experiment with Segrada, an open-source tool for graphing networks, and Palladio, which helps you not only graph relationships but also map, list, and visualize data.[20] Students can upload their own data to both and immediately begin to see relationships within the corpus.

Digital historian Jason Heppler uses Shin-Kap Han's "The Other Ride of Paul Revere: The Brokerage Role in the Making of the American Revolution," which considers the men involved in brokerages as central to the revolution; Weingart's blog series; the network analysis–based digital project Mapping the Republic of Letters; and Caroline Winterer's "Where Is America in the Republic of Letters?" to introduce students to network analysis within the context of the American Revolution.[21] After having used instructor-provided data to graph a network in Palladio, students are asked to write a reflection piece on how "network visualizations might help historical research. What can networks show us that we would otherwise have trouble seeing? How can networks accurately capture the complexity of the past?"[22] You could easily integrate the Magazine of Early American Datasets made available by the McNeill Center for Early American Studies as fodder for student assignments.[23] By moving between practice and reflection, this type of study of movement guides students to consider what types of information are needed for networks to be useful as a method of historical scholarship.

I also appreciate network analysis in the classroom because it can pull students into conversations and debates that analog historians are having. In a class about medieval history, for example, students might be asked to read Jean-Paul Rehr's article on the "Great Inquisition" of 1245–46.[24] In it, he argues that historians have been biased toward sampling the records of the Inquisition (MS 609 of the Bibliothèque Municipale de Toulouse) rather than exploring it as a complete corpus. Using network analysis methods, Rehr graphs the network of accusations documented in MS 609 after tagging every individual person by their role and activity. These then can be visualized as simple accusations (this person accused that one) as well as weighted accusations (the number of times the accusation was recorded in the manuscript). Rehr's analysis reveals three patterns: the number of people implicated by inquisitors in the villages of Le Mas and Saint-Martin is greater than previous historical scholarship reveals; there is a small, subgroup of people who are "strongly incriminated," regardless of where the accusation originates; and accusations are overwhelmingly concentrated inward toward other villagers rather than toward those outside the villages.[25] He then goes on to show how previous scholars have overemphasized particular families and their influence, as well as how his analysis modified existing historiography around the question of how widespread the Cathar counter-Church movement between Toulouse and Carcassonne was.

The utility of this example in your classroom is that it can illustrate how students can move between analog and digital methods. Almost every example in this chapter is possible only through inquiry at the level of the individual document and through exploring the entire corpus. Students learn that as they move through the methodological process they must explicate not just what they did, but how what they did introduced questions or concerns about the conclusion that they reached. Returning to our research notebooks from chapter 4 on the basics of digital methods, this movement between analog close reading and digital textual analysis forms a useful example for students of how tracking one's research methods can serve as fodder for larger historical writings. Rehr hasn't built some elaborate digital project. Instead, he uses the digital edition of MS 609 that is available to him and leverages it through network analysis tools to craft alternative meanings about the manuscript and the larger context of its creation. An additional reason to utilize Rehr's article or one like it is that it mirrors the micro-project steps we discussed in part I that you might build into your classroom. Each graph included in the article could form the basis for a single assignment.

As you work with text analysis and network analysis tools as methods, you'll have to continually remind students that the graphs they make or are viewing are only as good as the underlying data that is input into the tool. Quality data leads to quality graphs. Poor-quality data leads not only to poor graphs but also to potentially erroneous or misleading conclusions. Datasets should, at minimum, be easily identified according to the criteria of their creation. Where does the data come from? Who created the data and what processes did they use? Can I review the digital dataset against either its original analog or against other digital datasets that interrelate? Is the logic behind the data assemblage clear and transparent? Does the dataset include a statement about what it does not contain?

As we close, a final note about textual analysis methods. Every text analysis method we've learned about in this chapter relies in some way on math, logic, and statistics. From counting words, to the statistical models for sampling and parsing, and to the math that underlies how a computer recognizes the difference between handwriting and the page when running an OCR program, part of what textual analysis methods bring to the digital history classroom is an opportunity to talk with students about how the "hard" sciences play out in the history classroom. Students receive many messages today about the viability of history and humanities disciplines for careers, yet part of what text analysis methods illustrate is a way to merge disciplinary interests together into a holistic view of information and knowledge. Just as there is a place for historians to bring math, logic, and statistics into our classrooms, there is also a place for historians to enter math, statistics, and computer science classrooms. When I close our unit on textual analysis methods, I like to ask students to reflect on the take-aways from these methods for history and for these other disciplines. Students note that the processes we use in digital history of experimentation and exploration are not as far apart from the methods they are learning in their laboratory and applied classes in science as they may have been led to believe. For me, this is one of the important aspects of textual analysis in the classroom: it demonstrates how history is relevant to other disciplines as much as how those disciplinary methods are relevant for us—a high-stakes question in the context of what the twenty-first-century liberal arts degree should look like.

We'll now turn our attention to a variety of visualization methods that students greatly enjoy. Visualization ties to this chapter on text analysis, as many of the outputs of text analysis are rendered as visual diagrams, charts, graphs, and networks.

Chapter Seven

Visualization

CLOSE YOUR EYES and imagine every photograph taken between 1935 and 1945 by the United States Farm Security Administration and Office of War Information. Can you see the 170,000 photographs? Now sort through those photographs and find me all of the images taken by Esther Bubley. How many are there? Describe them for me. But, first, place them all in the order they were taken. Now imagine sorting those 170,000 photos to account not just for the photographer but also the location, the date, and the descriptive information included with the photo. But, wait, maybe I want to see all the photos taken in just 1935. Can you show me those? When I talk about visualization with my students, I love to start with this type of imagination exercise, which is based on a digital project, Photogrammar.[1] It is a visualization project developed by historians Laura Wexler and Lauren Tilton and mathematician Taylor Arnold that uses a collection from the US Library of Congress as its dataset. Using the robust metadata created by the library, Photogrammar enables students to create a dynamic cartographic map that lets them sort by year, photographer, location, and more. Each variable they choose then limits their screen view to only those photographs that qualify. They "see" each photograph plotted on the map. Bubley, they learn, took thirty-seven photographs in Marion County, where their school is located. All are images taken at the local Greyhound station. Students can also browse photographs by subject, showing, for example, only photographs pertaining to agricultural work or commercial life. They can also explore a county-level view that plots the photos longitudinally, via classification, via photographer, and with a reel strip that presents the photos in the order that they were taken.

Generically, visualization refers to any technique that communicates information through visual means. Photogrammar is one example of how multiple types of visualization can be layered together to present information—and to show how information is organized and presented. In the case of Photogrammar, students are viewing original photographs, a map, and three types of graphs. In the digital history classroom, visualization is a slippery term that can be used to refer to maps, graphs, and charts. It can also be used to refer to metaphorical rendering of space, thematic representations of space, and any combination of information and visual representation. It also refers to some of the work discussed in the previous chapter. In your classroom, you'll need to think carefully about how you define visualization and its scope, as the definition you choose will constrain what you have your students learn.

First, some basics about visualizations. Common visualizations in analog historical scholarship include time-series data, which records variables as they change over time; histograms, which chart frequencies and distributions; scatter-plot matrices, which represent relationships between variables; and maps, which render information either spatially or geographically. Maps can include subforms like choropleths, graduated symbols, cartograms, or geographical maps. Digital historians, particularly those who experiment with network analysis, also utilize node visualizations, dendrograms, tree diagrams, and other forms of hierarchical graphing.[2] Additionally, visualization methods are also used in the context of historical reconstruction and reproduction, most notably in two- and three-dimensional visualization for things like video games, immersive experiences, and photogrammetry. In this chapter, we'll sample briefly from each of these methods. We'll also discuss how the visual component of visualization methods will need to be responsive to issues of user accessibility.

You might want to consider beginning your work with students around visualization by following the material outlined in *Exploring Big Historical Data: The Historian's Macroscope*, which I mentioned briefly in the last chapter.[3] Developed with integrated tutorials, *Macroscope* helps students learn how to gather data and format it, learn text analysis methods, as well as receive a gentle overview of types of visualizations and how historians have used them in their own analyses. I can easily imagine a syllabus that asks students to read the section related to visualization and then experiment with creating each type of visualization covered in the textbook. You can complement the textbook by asking students to seek out bad visualizations of historical information. In this assignment, students are tasked with exploring the world around them, identifying a historical visualization, and then presenting it in class. From charts used in newspapers to graphs in television documentaries to dynamic maps available on social media, students quickly realize that most visualizations about historical topics aren't actually designed by historians. Instead, the visualizations they encounter are most frequently created by graphic designers, journalists, advertisers, information specialists, and cultural heritage staffers, including librarians and museum professionals. By asking students to analyze and redesign the "bad" visualization, students have to first identify where the underlying data is from, what decisions were made in developing the visualization, and issues around its purpose. The redesign portion of the assignment pressures students to think about the ways in which historical thinking by historians can differ from generic information communication. It can also encourage them to develop creative skills around information design. Students in my classes have completed the assignment by turning in analog redesigns where they create transparencies that overlay one another, full digital redesign using popular visualization tools, and even an anti-visualization inspired by pop-up videos where the student annotated the existing visualization with commentary written over it. The assignment can also encourage students to discover the analog roots of digital visualizations. Students have discovered that digital visualizations can merely be remakes of existing analog versions. These can be direct recapitulations, or they can embrace additional aspects that fully utilize the digital tool.

A lovely example of this relationship between analog and digital ties to one of the most frequently used examples in visualization units. Almost sixty years after the defeat of the Grand Army in their 1812 campaign against Russia, retired French civil engineer Charles Joseph Minard developed an analog visualization of "tactical errors, hasty decisions, exhausting foot marches, fruitless battles, and a brutally severe climate."[4] The Minard map is frequently referred to as the "best graphic ever produced."[5] Revered by both statisticians and data visualization specialists, the 1869 map was first celebrated by Edward Tufte in *The Visual Display of Quantitative Information*.[6] Minard's map united geographic places related to cities and battles with the movement of troops, weather, and outcomes. The graphic continually narrows through time as the number of troops who perished is expressed as an ever-reducing trend line. Historians who work in quantitative methodologies embrace Minard's map as just one example of how quantitative data can be interlaced to construct a historical narrative of a sequence of events. I adopted the use of Minard's map after reading John Theibault's article on visualization and historical arguments.[7] In it, he writes that the key dimensions of a visualization are its density and its transparency. Density refers to the amount of information communicated, while transparency is the ease of that information being understood by the user.

Using Minard's map in the classroom enables students to consider not only which information is communicated and how it is displayed, but also how static representations serve as a form of information. Minard's use of line thickness and branching provide not just details about historical action but also nuance to the larger narrative about troop movement during the battle. Students in my classroom are generally very comfortable with Minard's graphic because its underlying axis is longitude coupled with chronology. They understand the scale of the map: temperature (the Réaumur scale), time (month by month over the course of a year), and geography (latitude and longitude). Interestingly, though, I have found that while they learn about "the troop" as an aggregate, the scales of the map can't accommodate what they want to know: troop experiences, details on troop composition, and even individual stories of heroics and brushes with death. In digital history courses, Minard's map illustrates how visualizations can allow you to create layers that reflect many axes and factors, but it's insufficient on its own. By considering the map along with Theibault's article, I can ask students to consider the lines between interpretation, communication, and information. What makes a visualization useful? How do we know what the information is? Where has it come from? What messages is it communicating? And how does the data that we have access to structure what is possible in a visualization?

The relationship between communicating information and interpreting it is the subject of all history. Visualization can be especially useful for dramatizing this relationship in the digital history classroom. In 2017 undergraduate history students in E. Thomas Ewing's Introduction to Data in Social Contexts course used data from the Medical Heritage Library to create a visualization to identify, reveal, explain, and interpret patterns of human behavior, identity, and interactions. Studying tuberculosis in California, Jack Fleisher, Jae Ha, and Joey Hammel used digitized records from the State Board of Health to illustrate how tuberculosis patients moving to California impacted death rates.[8] Using digital visualization tools, students first reproduced the existing charts. This amounted to communicating existing information. Then after they'd mastered the individual charts, they could compare data across areas of the state as well as the cities of Los Angeles and San Francisco to begin interpreting the data available to them. This transition from simple communication of information to active interpretation inspired them to appreciate both the greater density (the amount of information communicated) and the transparency (ease of understanding) that visualization can offer. Students identified that "the high rates of tuberculosis deaths in San Francisco were mainly due to immigration from states east of California, while the high rates of tuberculosis deaths in Los Angeles were mainly due to journals like *The Land of Sunshine,* promising healing powers of the California Sun to sick tuberculosis patients."[9] There are many ways that you could embed such an approach in a digital history course—for example, students could begin with state-level records and move toward visualizations that allow for ever larger comparisons, or they could marry state-level records to individual counties or cities.

The best exercises let students move from communication to interpretation and push the capacity of visualization to the next level. In the case of Ewing's students, they developed aggregated data visualizations (the cities) along with annotations that led to individual records. If you were engaged in a similar project, you could ask students a series of questions that push them from the original dataset into new information gathering: What types of records exist at the state and local levels that can tell us more about these victims? Is it possible to use coroners' records, obituaries, and oral histories to learn more about these individuals' lives? Do diaries or other personal records exist that could tell us more about their daily lives? Students might then create a database of coroners' records, use text analysis methods like named entity recognition to mark up the appropriate information, and create medical biographies of the victims. Each of these could link to the main visualization. This ability to move between scales where you can click to select or delimit is one of the main advantages of digital visualization methods that are considered either dynamic or interactive. Dynamic visualizations are preset visualizations that are made available to the user based on queries the historian thinks that users might want to see. Interactive visualizations, on the other hand, allow the user to select multiple variables and adjust the visualizations accordingly. Hyperlinking as well as faceting, where you are able to subselect criteria within your data and have the visualization dynamically respond, enable digital historians to immediately call forth the information they desire without having to redesign or redraw the visualization. Both interactive and dynamic visualizations contrast with static visualizations, which can be developed digitally (e.g., designed using digital tools and software) but do not result in anything other than a one-dimensional representation. TAPoR3, a digital research environment for analyzing texts, now includes a directory of more than one hundred digital tools for use by digital historians.[10] By sorting through drop-down functionality, you can delimit your exploration of the tool directory by type of activity. It is a useful place to start when trying to identify tools that you might wish to use for visualization as well as other digital history–related methods.

Many digital historians use Tableau, a free visualization software that gives a one-year license to Tableau Desktop to a student at any academic institution, including primary and secondary schools. Tableau is built with a drag-and-drop interface that lets me quickly teach students how to create one hundred different types of visualizations. Histograms, chloropleths, cartograms, network diagrams, radial graphs, and timelines are all possible assignments for students. Part of why I like Tableau is that it uses spreadsheets as its main form of data organization and that it enables students to split, combine, or recombine different datasets together. They can also annotate and share their visualizations. Digital historian Sarah J. Purcell, working with digital arts specialist Katherine Walden, teaches Tableau to her undergraduate digital history students at Grinnell College.[11] Students explore the 1870 Federal Census of Grinnell Township to learn the differences between dimensions (data fields that cannot be aggregated) and measures (data fields that can be aggregated) as they visualize the distribution of occupations by gender and role. Students are then encouraged to experiment with other queries and styles of visualization. As you introduce students to tools like Tableau, they should keep in mind the historical questions that they wish to answer. Students often are enamored of visualization because it can render information symbolically in appealing ways. But visualization can also fail to meet the needs of digital historians when the information is rendered for visualization's sake rather than as part of a method of analysis. In effect, they forget their historical question and instead just make lots of pretty visualizations. Visualizations can require exposition in the form of a supporting narrative, methodological exposition, or annotated argument to make conclusions apparent.[12]

Digital visualization is particularly important as it is uniquely amenable to the methods of transnational, global, and cultural histories of movement and exchange that seek to embrace both conceptual and literal representation. Since the 1980s, the influence of geography on historical thinking has only grown as tools that geographers use to render space and place visually have become easier to use by nonspecialists.[13] In 1999, students at Horace Mann Middle School in San Francisco, California, were introduced to digital history via a web resource their teacher had built about a fourteenth-century Muslim Berber Moroccan traveler, Ibn Baṭṭūṭah.[14] Using Baṭṭūṭah's travel account, their teacher Nick Bartel leveraged the ability of the internet to embed images and maps to trace the traveler's movement as he completed his pilgrimage to Mecca. Students were asked to map the voyage to contemporary nations, find additional supporting materials, construct their own travel brochures and postcards, and apply their knowledge of the challenges Baṭṭūṭah confronted to send a letter back in time to warn other travelers. The project then formed the backbone of students' work to understand the Middle East, travel, and place more generally. Travelogues, like those that Bartel used, offer opportunities in digital history classrooms to consider movement and exchange as historical forces and maps form the primary medium of communication.

Maps feature so frequently in digital history classrooms for three reasons. First, there are a wide variety of easy-to-use mapping tools available; second, change over time as a method is one of the easiest methods for students to understand and thus adding time-based information to their dataset becomes a simple intermediate step as they develop historical queries; and third, maps are seductive to students. According to my students, visualizations, particularly interactive maps or graphs, are "fun" and "engaging." They provide a sense of immediate gratification as students can point and click or simply enter latitude and longitude coordinates to place information on the map. They know they have been successful because the information is immediately rendered in place. They also can usually spot egregious errors in their mapping, as one student did recently when there was a pin dropped in the middle of an ocean instead of in the right location.

Maps must be carefully constructed to account for these issues as students can quickly become overwhelmed by colors, lines, and dot sizes and ignore the nuanced decisions that should be considered when rendering information visually. You may find it beneficial to concretize for students the history of maps as a genre of scholarship by asking them to read Susan Schulten's "Capturing the Past through Maps."[15] She provides an excellent overview of the history of cartography and how maps function to represent spatial, territorial, and geographical information. Her companion site, Mappingthenation.com, offers students the opportunity to view every map she utilized, including all metadata.[16] I like Mappingthenation.com because students can view the maps not just by chapter but also by creator, which allows them to consider how an individual creator shapes the map.

A parallel approach is to ask students to spend time exploring the Slave Revolt in Jamaica, 1760–1761, project.[17] Developed by historian Vincent Brown, the project presents an animated thematic map of the enslaved insurrection or, as Brown calls it, "a cartographic narrative." The underlying dataset includes maps produced by the British empire, diaries, private correspondence, periodicals, and military and administrative records, as well as selected secondary sources that document the roughly 1,500 enslaved peoples who staged a revolt against Britain. Part of why students like Brown's project is that he is quite explicit with how mapping answers the historical questions he has: Was the revolt a unified and coordinated affair, or was it instead a series of opportunistic riots? What in fact did the rebels hope to achieve? Was there ever a real danger to the British empire in America, or was the threat blown out of proportion by panicked whites? If the insurrection was as well planned as the colonists feared, why didn't it succeed? Brown and the team at Axis Maps articulate a clear method of how mapping functions to answer these questions. They used Leaflet, a free JavaScript library for mapping, which allows users to build a map that is mobile-application friendly.[18] Part of why many digital historians have turned to Leaflet is that it is HTML5 and CSS3 compliant (meaning it meets the current standards for web development) and has extensive plug-ins that can add functionality like animation.[19] It also doesn't require the purchase of expensive geographical information software or installation on your own servers to render the map and make it available online.

So how did Leaflet work for Brown? Historical maps were combined and adapted to create two base maps. Base maps are the visual representations upon which all information will be placed. Each historical map was georeferenced with latitude and longitude so that information from a locational database could be plotted on the base map. The locational database

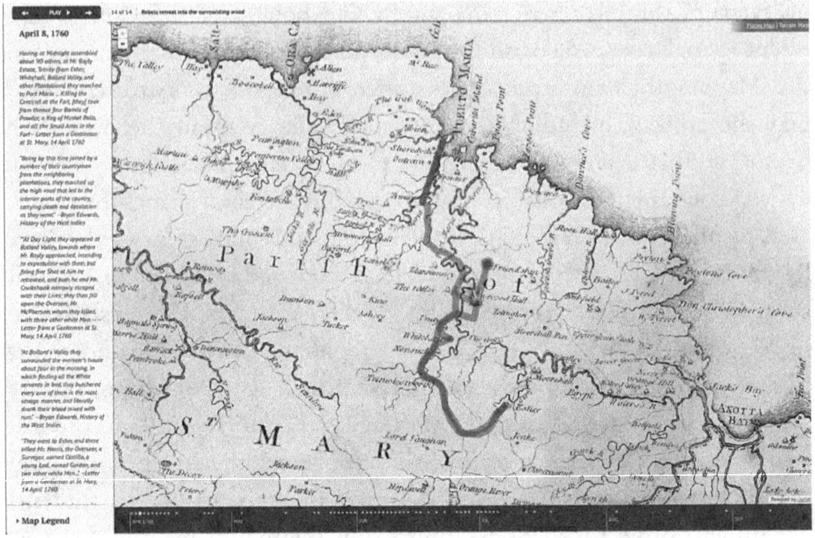

Fig. 7.1. This map is paused on the date April 8, 1760, illustrating the movement of rebels retreating into the surrounding woods during the Slave Revolt of 1760–61 in Jamaica. Built as an animated, thematic map in Leaflet by historian Vincent Brown, this map serves as an example of the type of annotated analysis that students can develop in a visualization unit by marrying change over time and spatial analysis. Slave Revolt in Jamaica, 1760–1761, accessed June 28, 2020, http://revolt.axismaps.com/.

comprised a chronological database of locations drawn from the historical documents. This included descriptions of positions, movements, and fighting units. Brown also recorded any quantitative information that could be gleaned from the documents, including records of numbers captured or killed in action. From that database, Brown created a legend to represent visually information that was in the records (fig. 7.1). Rebels, militia, army, navy, maroons, conspiracy, and slave courts each received a unique color to let users see exactly who was fighting where and when. The size of force was represented with a person symbol where each symbol equated to one hundred persons. Grayed-out fuzzy circles represented "uncertainty" where gaps in the historical record or conflicting reports were evident.

Students viewing the interactive map can, by triggering the play function on the map, watch the insurrection "occur" through a time-lapse rendering.

They can see how the topography shaped the rebellion and how what is referred to as a singular uprising was in fact a string of three uprisings that each required British military response. As an instructor, I appreciate that Brown clearly lays out the method of mapping and the decisions he made regarding information representation. Not only is this type of methodological exposition exactly what we ask students to do with their research notebooks, but it is also an excellent jumping-off point to discuss the ways in which maps can reveal or obscure historical information.

Maps, as digital historian Lara Putnam cautions us, can lead students to ignore place-based histories and the contextual knowledge gained only by researching in the location being studied.[20] As historians of the Black diaspora continually tell us, what constitutes space, place, and movement has significant overlap with the questions of who can move, how, and to what ends. Maps can elide local contexts by operating at a representational level that is too abstract. In her curatorial statement on diaspora as a concept in digital pedagogy, historian Jessica Marie Johnson writes, "Non-linear thinking is especially important to those doing work on diaspora and the digital lends itself well to elucidating this. Non-linearity captures elements of fluidity, dispersal, mobility, and resilience/resistance, alongside violence and the embodiment of violence (structural, personal, and intimate); force (involuntariness) and non-consent on macro as well as micro levels; loss and hauntings (echoes); and the themes of heartbreak, absence, and silence that appear and reappear in diaspora work."[21] Brown's project runs counter to this by intentionally recording uncertainty as a variable. By raising uncertainty to its own variable, students not only learn that records of rebel movements are visible only when recorded by the counterinsurgency (here the British empire and its records), but also learn that the numbers themselves were the "products of aspiration, fear, and rumor."[22]

Encouraging students to be aware of what is unknowable via any tool or method is one way of addressing historical gaps, omissions, or conflict in students' visualizations. I tend to talk to students about this in terms of "limitations": what are the limitations of our dataset when we are attempting to represent information spatially or geographically? Undergraduate students at Boğaziçi University followed a method similar to

Brown's where they used textual materials as the backbone of their mapping exercises. In a class on Ottoman history, students were asked to map spatial relationships from a set of Ottoman historical documents including travelogues, records of endowments, and readers' letters to one of the first women's magazines in the empire. Students completed exercises to identify places in their documents, annotate the places in relation to time, and conduct assessments related to language and transcription. Antonis Hadjikyriacou writes that his students not only learned the fundamentals of spatial history, gazetteers as authorities, and Ottoman history but also were able to grapple with the challenges of verifying the veracity of historical information through internet research and reconciliation.[23] Their research helped them to provide a list of additional place-names to add to the gazetteers used by their spatial mapping tool to render coordinates.

Recogito, which I mentioned in the last chapter, served as the spatial tool that Hadjikyriacou and his students used. Recogito allows anyone to create their own account and get started working with maps of their choosing. The ten-minute getting-started tutorial is perfectly scaled for you and your students to experiment with this approach in the classroom. Upload your texts and documents and you can offer students their own lesson on the history of place. You should also check out the Pelagios Network, which is the institutional home for Recogito. It is an excellent resource for you as you look for examples of spatial history, as is the Europeana Network Association, an online community of scholars working with digital cultural heritage.[24] They provide extensive case studies with methodological expositions that can serve as fodder for your syllabus.

Colleagues working with biographical and literary materials have found similar success by limiting their inquiries to a particular individual, topic, location, or body of work. Tyechia Thompson, for example, uses the work of James Baldwin to geolocate the "buildings/monuments, restaurants/cafes, arrondissements/areas/street names, and residences in Paris that appear in his novels, collections of essays and short stories published during his lifetime."[25] Her method is similar to Google Lit Trips, a project that uses immersive 3D technology to allow K–12 students to virtually travel with characters from common literary texts taught in their schools.[26] World literature and history students at Kadena High School in Okinawa, Japan, developed a trip for three different literary works, each concerned with World War II. Most of the Google Lit Trips feature English-language texts, authors, and selection criteria; you might develop a project with your students that work in non-English languages, with non-Western authors, that would diversify the canon of what is available for K–12 students in their literary tours.

Students' enthusiasm for mapping in the classroom is exceeded only by their interest in three-dimensional methods and representations. Simulation and virtual reality have emerged in the last decade or so as a form of historical knowledge that students are primed to enjoy, thanks to video games. I like to start my students with visual scholar Victoria Szabo's definition of three-dimensional visualization. "Three-dimensional visualizations can be used for creating models," she writes, "supplementing maps, developing games, printing objects, developing virtual environments, enhancing telecommunications, and housing simulations. They can be used to support retrospective and prospective analysis, exploration of counterfactuals, and representation of hybrid or alternate realities, particularly when they combine objects in 3D contexts."[27] Students then proceed with exploration of a variety of three-dimensional reproductions as well as a visit to our local library with its three-dimensional scanning center.

Examples abound of digital three-dimensional representation for your class. Diane Favro and her colleagues at the University of California at Los Angeles developed the Digital Karnak project to highlight how the temple of Amun-Ra at Karnak transformed from a local shrine to the national center of power in Egypt.[28] Using three-dimensional modeling techniques, they developed a simulation that allows students to view the temple over time from its first days of construction to its destruction. This helps the students to learn about daily life within the temple as well as issues around construction, political reigns, and space. Here movement is not only change over time but also the movement of bodies within a delimited space. VSim, the tool behind Digital Karnak, is being used to develop other historical reconstructions: the Roman Forum, the Pantheon, the Basilica of Santa Maria Maggiore, Santiago de Compostela, and the

World's Columbian Exposition of 1893 are all currently under development. Students interested in trade, diplomacy, and environmental history may be interested in the Virtual Angkor project, which uses simulation to expose students to how Angkor Wat functioned as a site of trade in Cambodia even as it dealt with water precarity.[29] The project provides 360-degree views of the reconstruction coupled with teaching modules, static images for use by students, and an extensive bibliography that can bolster project use in the classroom. It's important to pause here to note that three-dimensional simulation is a time-intensive and painstaking process. Students can explore, read about, and critique these models but usually will not have the opportunity to construct anything in the class that comes near this type of scale of simulation in a single class.

Currently, most digital history courses include a limited view of 3D digitization and visualization as part of their methodological explorations. S. Colin Rose asks students to watch the National Gallery of London's YouTube video on the destruction of the church of San Pier Maggiore.[30] They support their critical exploration with John Bonnett's article "Following in Rabelais' Footsteps: Immersive History and the *3D Virtual Buildings Project*" and Caterina Balletti and Francesco Guerra's "Historical Maps for 3D Digital City's History."[31] Together, they illustrate how three-dimensional visualizations can be used to re-create lost or altered city landscapes as spaces of movement and change. Those with interests in hidden, lost, or counterfactual narratives of movement may also want to consider three-dimensional visualization as a space of creative analysis for students. I can readily imagine students researching the lost or destroyed landscapes to create alternative histories of the sites they move through daily. It also opens up opportunities for students to consider how anthropology, archaeology, and material culture relate to the work historians do.

For all of these examples, it is important that you ground students with a discussion of how visualization methods relate to audiences. I usually begin this conversation by asking students a series of questions about how they've learned history: Where did they get their historical information (electronic textbooks, Wikipedia, blogs, games, etc.)? What technologies do they use every day? What are good and bad examples of history that have been published using that particular technology? And, importantly, if historical scholarship hasn't been used with that platform or technology, why not? The student answers in this exercise are illuminating. Podcasts, video games, Wikipedia, websites, Twitter, Facebook, Instagram, and Snapchat all appear on their list of common technologies they've encountered history on. Yet, when I ask students to identify whether they would use those technologies to write or publish their own digital history project, they quickly begin to refine their answers. Wikipedia is "boring" and only used for "writing papers." "Nobody under the age of 40 uses twitter." Facebook is for "grandparents," "wedding and baby announcements," and "history that old people care about." Video games and immersive reality though are "cool," "interesting," and "fun," particularly when they incorporate competitive gaming.

I utilize this questionnaire along with an open-ended question about what users need to experience the visualization as the student intends. Almost always, students neglect to mention visual, aural, or cognitive abilities that users must have. Students need to understand in a unit on visualization that audiences are not mirrors of themselves. Audience considerations in digital history can be quite complex when accounting for the spectrum of users' abilities. Inaccessible design choices like a lack of descriptive information about photos, a lack of audio or video transcriptions, and even choices in project architecture and aesthetic elements can limit the user. A simple exercise I use in my classroom when we begin our conversations on audience and accessibility in relation to visualization is to ask students to navigate a digital history visualization without using a mouse or touchpad.

Most students are unaware that they can use a keyboard to navigate a webpage. Even more are shocked to hear a screen reader "read" a digital map or visualization they've created and embedded into a project. The internet provides an important resource for those with disabilities. This is particularly pertinent as visualizations can be limited in their use by blind, low-vision, or cognitively delayed users as their logic can be hidden behind buttons that must be clicked, timelines that must be adjusted, or behaviors that must be triggered. How does someone know what to do with your visualization? What type of framing should your visualization include? What alternative forms of information need to be provided? I point students to the World Wide Web Consortium standards on web accessibility and the Web Accessibility Evaluation Tool (WAVE).[32] One student, in this portion of the course, realized that their own color-blindness limited their ability to understand a time-lapse map of migration. Another noted that the lack of "how to use this visualization" instructions meant that users would never know how to engage with their complex network analysis. Students then were prompted to create "alt" titles and descriptions so that someone who is blind or had low vision can still experience the product. Also, if their visualization includes audio materials or cues, students are asked to create transcripts so that hearing-challenged users can still experience the audio-visual asset. Not only do these steps increase the usability of a site for someone who has hearing or visual difficulties, but these additional tasks increase the identifiability of one's visualization. Search engines, for example, can crawl transcripts and produce results with greater confidence than if they are relying only on a brief description of a visualization, video, or audio file.

As we close this chapter, you'll notice that we've not discussed in greater detail the relationship between visualization technologies and games. I've reserved that discussion for chapter 9 on digital storytelling. For now, what I'll leave you with is the importance of discussing with your students the purpose that visualization serves. Every type of visualization has its utility. Only by asking students to consider the historical questions they wish to answer can they accurately identify what type of visualization will best serve their interests. For this reason, I encourage you to incorporate models in your syllabus that help students to see what is possible. You should also survey your local landscape to see what visualization resources are available. Your local library or your institution may have licenses, tutorials, and workshops that you can take advantage of. It is worth investigating those resources as it can ease you into visualization in the classroom by creating opportunities for partnership and guest teaching.

PART III

Forms of Scholarship

Chapter Eight

Digital Archives, Digital Exhibits, and Digital Collections

IN 2012, Kelsey Corlett-Rivera, then the French subject librarian at the University of Maryland, leveraged the Revealing la Révolution project, which catalogued and digitized French pamphlets held in the special collections of the library into a digital history project for use in undergraduate classrooms. Working with Nathan Dize (an undergraduate student proficient in French) and students from classes in the School of Literature, Languages, and Cultures at the University of Maryland (UMD), she created the digital history website A Colony in Crisis, which provides online access to both the French originals and the English translations of key primary sources dealing with the grain shortage faced by the colony of Saint-Domingue in 1789. Students author the translations and contextual materials, as well as introductions to each digitized pamphlet featured on the website.[1] Now publishing its fourth issue focusing on Haitian Creole translations, the project includes dozens of contributors and faculty from across the globe contributing in multiple languages and from specific historical lenses. Part of what motivated Corlett-Rivera to digitize the pamphlets was the need by faculty to have access to primary sources to train students in French translation, history, and public writing. That need, as she found out, was not just local to UMD but was to be found in classrooms across the globe. A Colony in Crisis now has an audience of instructors, librarians and archivists, and students in France as well as in the United States and Haiti. Historian Robert Stephens and his former undergraduate Josh Thumma would note for us that this type of digital history project is likely successful because its core result was the production of a pedagogical work. It's an exemplar of how digital history in the classroom offers us the opportunity to experiment with new forms of historical scholarship including digital archives, digital exhibits, and digital collections.

Asking students to understand digital archives, exhibits, and collections as they relate to historical thinking begins with asking them to understand physical archives. Because many students are exposed to document readers rather than to archives themselves, they are often missing basic knowledge about what an archive is and how it operates. The video series produced by the National Archives UK on archives and archival practice are very useful for K–12 classrooms or for students who might need assistance with basic concepts. In "What Would the World Look Like without Archives?," students learn that archives are as much about imagining the future as preserving the past. In the second video of the series, "What Discoveries Have You Made in Archives?," students are introduced to scholars speaking about the impact of archival research on their knowledge about the past. The brief thirteen-minute sequence closes by asking "What impact have archives had on your life?," where students learn about the personal and communal stakes of archival research for the scholars involved.[2] As your students work through the videos, ask them to identify what assumptions are embedded within how the videos talk about archives. Students will likely note how privileged the archival space of the National Archives is, be it in terms of the resources it can marshal or the types of scholars who engage with it.

You can consider more hands-on activities that center the student within the archival process. For middle school and high school students, I encourage you to take students to a local archive if possible so that they can understand the physical aspects of the archive before you introduce them to digital components. You might work with your local historical society, library, or museum to set up a unit to introduce students to objects and teach them to digitize the documents that align with a topic you will explore that year. Scaffolded assignments can include identification of objects for digitization, the digitization itself, metadata creation, and then contextual research to write an entry about that specific object and its interpretation.

An alternative for those who can't incorporate field trips is to work with your cultural heritage organizations to craft a history-visit-in-a-box. These are reproductions of archival materials that can be brought into the classroom for students to explore. Many teachers have found success with constructing a class-based collection where archives contribute documents that are relevant to topics in their class. You can also embrace personal archiving as part of your approach to digital archives. Personal digital archiving asks individuals to capture their own histories in the form of photographs, films and videos, family documents, personal websites, social media, and email that are created throughout their lives. The US Library of Congress's Personal Digital Archiving site is an excellent resource for this portion of your syllabus.[3] It highlights different forms of media, questions your students will need to ask, and tips on how to handle digitization and access. At the middle school level, you might ask students to work with their families to identify precious family objects as well as born-digital materials that could be incorporated into their own personal digital archive. Students can bring those materials to class, complete digitization activities, merge the digitized surrogates with existing born-digital materials, and create their own digital exhibit about their family history. This activity can be quite exciting for students if coupled with oral history interviews that enable them to understand how they and their families relate to major historical events.

I've seen this same type of sequence deployed where classes of students are trained in personal digital archives and then join with community partners, veterans' groups, and nursing homes to assist in capturing others' histories. Check out the hashtag #historyharvest for examples of this on social media. History Harvest is a program that began at the University of Nebraska–Lincoln to reach out to community members to digitize their personal artifacts.[4] Students in the tenth grade at the International School of the Sacred Heart in Tokyo, Japan, completed their first history harvest in 2014. Working with their teacher, students interviewed classmates and their teachers, then completed independent research on the artifacts brought to the harvest.[5] There are dozens of classroom "harvests" that focus not just on local personal histories but also on major historical events like the COVID-19 pandemic and the 2020 protests against police violence. Personal digital archiving in your course can be a very effective way to develop student interest in history as a craft. It lets students draw on their own experiences and life stories to shape the types of stories that might be told and can lead them to understand how the next generation of archival material is being developed during their lifetime.

Asking students to create materials from a history harvest for teaching purposes can be a very successful strategy. With high school students, you might ask them to approach their project with elementary school students as the audience. With undergraduates, you might ask them to speak to a high school audience. With graduate students, K–12 students or undergraduates might be the audience for lesson plans, digital history content, and analyses. My digital history courses tend to have a high volume of students who are interested in being teachers. Often, I'll group them together and they will work throughout the semester to create materials for use in classrooms. They research the standards used in their history classrooms and create projects that can be inserted into the curriculum. In the most successful case, one group of students used the materials they created in their student teaching. The students in their classrooms provided feedback that they then incorporated into their final digital project.

No matter whether you start with physical archives or ask your students to participate in personal digital archiving activities, the key is that they understand the ways in which archives relate to historical thinking. You might consider beginning this discussion with Terry Cook's essay "The Archive(s) Is a Foreign Country: Historians, Archivists, and the Changing Archival Landscape."[6] Cook argues that historians focus on "issues of power, memory, and identity centered upon the initial inscription of a document (or series of documents). The latter [archivists] concentrates on the subsequent history of documents over time, including the many interventions by archivists (and others) that transform (and change) that original archive into archives."[7] This binary serves as a foil throughout much of the class as students interrogate what happens when historians seek to construct their own archives. I like to pair this reading with Trevor Owens's "What Do You Mean by Archive? Genres of Usage for Digital Preservers" and Kate Theimer's excellent "A Distinction Worth Exploring: 'Archives' and 'Digital Historical Representations.'"[8] Owens highlights a variety of archival definitions and their distinctions: archives as in records management, archives as in "the papers of so and so," archive as in to save, archive as in "tape archive," archive as in "web archive," and archive as in "digital archive." Theimer, meanwhile, sketches the complaints that archivists have when historians are imprecise in their use of the term "archives."[9] Historians use the word "archives" to mean any collection of documents and in doing so frequently get themselves into hot water by assuming a measure of fidelity to archival methods that they just can't meet. Through these readings, students understand this conflict over calling something an "archive" through an introduction to the concept of "digital historical representations."

The primary outputs of digital history courses and even digital history projects themselves are usually titled "archive" but in fact are digital historical representations. That is, they are sources selected through the process of constructing any given project and historical argument. While those sources may follow standards related to metadata creation and provenance sourcing, the product itself does not meet either the Open Archival Information System (OAIS) reference model requirements or the Trusted Repository Archiving Checklist (TRAC), which are the two primary standards that archives must meet to be considered reputable.[10] Rarely do digital history archives created in the classroom maintain multiple copies (preservation, use, and display). Nor do most digital history archives created in the classroom include standards around selection, metadata, digitization, and display; a plan for transforming digital asset formats over time to keep them accessible to the public; and a plan to address long-term access to the technology that supports the archive. With the exceptions of classes that intentionally partner with institutional archives and archivists, most digital history classes are using web-publishing platforms like Omeka and Mukurtu, which are not archival technologies. Instead, they are digital exhibit technologies. Thus, in my classroom I ask students to use terms like "digital historical reproductions," "digital collections," or "digital exhibits" rather than digital archives. This may seem to be a matter of terminology, but in fact it reminds us to respect the work of archival professionals while still achieving our goal of creating historical scholarship that leverages digital collections and datasets.

If I start my course with digital collections rather than archival standards and debate, I like to craft a project-based exploration of how the project identifies, organizes, and publishes individual sources or groups of sources. This approach allows students to track the same project and how it highlights distinctions between archives, collections, and exhibits. The basis for the sequence is Kate Bagnall and Tim Sherratt's Real Face of White Australia.[11] Part of the larger digital project Invisible Australians, which explores how early twentieth-century Australia articulated itself as a "white man's country," the Real Face of White Australia is an experimental project that allows users to navigate the Certificates of Domicile and Certificates of Exemption from Dictation Test series not by the written records of immigrants entering the country but by the photographs that were attached to the certificates (fig. 8.1).

Students begin the sequence by completing a brief reading on the history of immigration into Australia authored by the Migration Heritage Center of New South Wales.[12] They are tasked with locating an immigrant record that meets a subset of criteria (nationality, port of arrival, age, and gender) within the certificates archive provided by the National Archives of Australia and then writing a brief analysis of that person's life as it is reflected by the record. I provide students with the name of the archive and the title of the records series that contains the certificates. They then produce a fifty-word maximum summary of the individual's record. Students turn in both the original record as well as their analysis. I also ask them to write a brief paragraph-long reflection on their experience

Fig. 8.1. The landing page for the Real Face of White Australia project, developed by Kate Bagnall and Tim Sherratt, which demonstrates how images can serve as an interface for users to explore primary source documents. The Real Face of White Australia, accessed November 4, 2018, http://invisibleaustralians.org/faces/.

trying to find the archival material. In almost every instance, students find this assignment incredibly vexing. When using the most common search engine (Google), students are directed not to the individual records that they need but to the landing page for the series created by the archive. This is because in Google's search functionality, the National Archives is a higher-ranked result due to its status as an institution. Because each has been assigned a specific individual and not just any random record, they then will spend long stretches of time clicking around within the archival site trying to navigate to the individual records. It's usually within ten minutes that the first complaint is registered; after twenty, I stop the class and we discuss what their search process looked like. Those who have located the record have much to say about the way the interface to the archive is built. The link to view and save the digital surrogate of the record, for example, is a tiny blue link in the right-hand corner of the metadata records. Most students never find it until I point it out to them.

This initial assignment is built with limited directives intentionally. While I could provide them with the URL to the archives or the even more distinct URL to the series, one of the goals of the assignment is for students to experience what we experience as historians confronting the digital research process and digitized collections. Students are predisposed to assume that information is easy to find and will appear in the form that they want. Yet, as most readers of this volume can attest, locating the sources you need and want can be a long, arduous, and fraught process. You can spend days (and even weeks) making your way through file folder after file folder learning about your topic before you find a single useful piece of information that you will use in your scholarship. Additionally, because digital interfaces facilitate a different type of research process, you can miss relevant documents that may not be indexed or identified similarly. Feminist historian Michelle Moravec has written a useful post about this exact issue that can serve as a supplement for students unfamiliar with in-person archival research.[13] She explores how search functions, keywords, and interfaces can obscure or reveal part of digitized archives. Mar Hicks's recent article on how the Ministry of Pensions computer system was designed to eliminate trans British individuals from view is another excellent article that merges the question of method, interface, and archival view for your considerations of digital archival methods.[14] By encouraging students to problem-solve to find what they need, I am actively developing their digital literacy skills and, just as importantly, sensitizing students to the amount of time and energy that source identification and access can take in a digital space. I am also trying to set them up to think about how they will address the question of navigation when they are creating their own digital projects.

Fig. 8.2. This view of the experimental browser interface for the Real Face of White Australia project, reached when a user selects a face, links a digitized surrogate of the source to the National Archives of Australia files. Users can then back-trace from the face to the individual record and then to the archival series. "Certificate Exempting from Dictation Test, John Baxter," accessed November 4, 2018, http://invisibleaustralians.org/faces/.

In the next stage of the assignment, students are asked to replicate the exercise using the Real Face of White Australia digital collection rather than the National Archives of Australia. As students discover, the project takes them directly to the record using the photographic image of the immigrant associated with the record (fig. 8.2). The red link along the bottom of the digital surrogate returns the students not just to the originating series in the archives but to the appropriate subset (e.g., records 321–30 of the 1906 certificates).

In this sense, the digital interface enables them to avoid what would normally be the intermediate steps of archival negotiation. They don't navigate from collection to series to file to document. Instead, they immediately go from image to document. This mechanism facilitates speedy access, and students can sidestep contextual information about how this specific archive and collection were established. To make this visible, I ask them to compare and contrast their experience with these two different access avenues to the document. On one hand, they often remark that the original archival interface contains much more information that might be relevant to the context of the individual document but that the perceived "hidden" nature of the document itself made it less interesting to them as sleuths. The Real Face interface, on the other hand, offers a more effective way to "see" the immigrants themselves, but students can see that they don't actually have enough information to draw conclusions about immigrants across the archive. If time permits, I like to build in a supplemental track on interpreting photographic images in the historical record, which then allows us to consider how photography, its processes, and its digital interfaces construct racial profiles.

To assist students in considering how the different interfaces of the National Archives and Real Face function, I then have them read Tim Sherratt's "It's All about the Stuff: Collections, Interfaces, Power, and People." He provides a recapitulation of the motivation of Real Face while simultaneously critiquing the ways in which archives function through their adherence to textual information and hierarchies of order. Students are amazed to learn that the Real Face project was built using a facial detection algorithm that sought and extracted all photographs from the digital surrogates made available online by the National Archives. As Sherratt writes, "What we ended up with was a new way of seeing and understanding the records—not as remnants of bureaucratic processes, but as windows onto the lives of people . . . so this is also a finding aid. A finding aid that brings people to the front."[15] I love this example for students because they can begin to draw parallels to larger questions about the archive as a repository that can exist in multiple states at once. It can be liberatory and exclusionary; analog and digital; available and unavailable. And, as Sherratt's project suggests, a digital "archive" can in fact be a subset of an existing archive that looks different than if you approached the source material through traditional archival research and organization.

Michael J. Kramer uses a similar sequence in his advanced undergraduate digital history course, but in reverse. Students first explore Real Face and then listen to an hour-long video podcast of Sherratt speaking about his project.[16] They then are tasked with writing a five-hundred-word nomination of the project for an award. Kramer frames the exercise within a larger unit on "serious history." By asking them to read Carl Smith's "Can You Do Serious History on the Web?," he positions students to question what constitutes serious scholarly engagement.[17] They are also introduced to the ongoing (and never settled) debate of what types of history are considered valid. Some historians trust digital sources less than analog: they are skeptical of preselection processes for digital "archives" and hence of their utility in the classroom.[18] For this reason, they commonly weight their syllabus toward a single-source criticism exercise rather than an exploration of the digital historical representation as a whole archive. What Bagnall and Sherratt show us is that it's possible to teach those very processes of selectivity through a digital interface—arguably in ways that are not so easily done, if at all, via traditional archives, which are in most cases inaccessible in ordinary classroom settings.

Meanwhile, Kramer's framing of "serious history" in relationship to archives raises the question of who history is written for. In digital history classrooms, this question of for whom we write is a significant part of our syllabus. Students often assume that their audience is only their teacher. Digital history projects though can be driven by multiple audiences at once. Whether it is individuals who provide artifacts as part of a harvest, a community group that participates in digitization of their history, or public audiences who are users of your digital projects, there is a need to build into your syllabus the questions of audience. As a reminder from our previous discussion, prioritizing questions about audience requires students to consider what type of history we are exploring, who we are writing that history for, what ethics and methods we utilize, and how our conclusions contribute to the needs of the proposed audience.

Adina Langer's syllabus for her course about special topics in historic preservation is organized around student contributions to an existing digital archive, the Atlanta Rail Corridor Archive project, but it is written explicitly to assist the community in grappling with the history of racial segregation, urbanization, and transportation.[19] The project traces the history of the communities and businesses that lie along Atlanta's historic rail corridor. Students are asked to identify a "neighborhood, a business, a notable individual or group, a church, an environmental feature, or an event that affected more than one location." They research their selected topic and are asked to digitize fifteen to twenty artifacts and craft an online exhibit that incorporates historiographical information with analysis of their selected artifacts. Students are graded on their final exhibit, an annotated bibliography, and their use of best practices and methods in digital public history. For extra credit, they can develop a grant proposal that further expands their exhibit to include other public history outputs. The inclusion of a grant proposal assignment is useful for students because it encourages them to understand funding agencies as one specific type of audience that can directly impact what histories are told and why. It also, though, can assist community partners by providing them access to grant infrastructure and expertise that they may not have.

Let's pause for a moment to recognize that inventing and revising lesson plans and activities can be a significant amount of work. Even those of us with expertise in digital history can be overwhelmed by the cycle of pedagogical creation, deployment, feedback, and revision. For this reason, you may want to think about a longer arc of pedagogical creation than just a single class. Jessica Parr, an Early Americanist, recommends Omeka to her digital history colleagues because they can have students contribute to the same course topic across semesters.[20] She uses it in her upper-division undergraduate digital history course. The benefit to selecting Omeka as the technology is that you can move the technological infrastructure from class to class, keep yourself up to date on any new capabilities, and provide custom training to your students. It also enables you to develop long-term relationships with users and their community that can benefit your students. You might use the same approach as Parr if your class includes individuals with differing levels of expertise in historical thinking. I can imagine, for example, introductory students contributing single documents to a digital collection to develop their historical thinking skills, intermediate students completing digital exhibits using the artifacts contributed by their peers, and advanced students serving as editors, technical specialists, and developers. In my classes, I'll often have this portion of the syllabus organized around five key activities, which are learn, identify, design, draft, and publish, that correlate to tasks that must be completed in Omeka: identify sources, digitize items or create a list of born-digital items, address issues of copyright and permissions, introduce students to metadata including the basics of Dublin Core standards, introduce students to the Omeka dashboard, install and configure any plugins, upload items, complete all metadata for each item, and then begin the digital exhibit process. The digital exhibit tasks include all of the previous in addition to creating a collection, storyboarding or developing an outline of the exhibit including the relationship of items to one another, customizing the theme, drafting page content, and finally creating the associated pages with relevant items. Each of these components can serve as a single assignment throughout the term.

If you are overwhelmed as an instructor, you may be worried that your students will be too. You might find it useful to structure assignments so that they can see progression across tasks as part of how you are keeping them on track. I ask students to work in stages, with each stage including a peer-review exercise as well as an audience-review exercise. In the former, I provide students with a rubric that asks them to confirm that students have completed the task to the standards required. In the latter, I'll bring members of our key audience to class to conduct a feedback session where they can assist students in their work. One note of caution about Omeka and other web-publishing tools: the quality of the work of students in building Omeka projects can vary greatly. When my colleague first started teaching with Omeka in his classes, students ignored how important quality metadata and reliable contextualization were to the success of the digital exhibit. As a result, their final project had items with missing information, poor-quality digitized items, and dozens of problems related to copyright and permission. One way to anticipate this is to develop a controlled vocabulary that accompanies a checklist that students must follow for every item that they include. Another is to assign students to work collaboratively to develop their own schema that they would then utilize as a class. It's important to establish for students what you expect from them not only in terms of the number of items, collections, or pages but also the details associated with each.

These strategies are good in any history classroom, of course. But they pertain especially to the kinds of collaborative work that digital history classrooms are built on. I'm currently working with students via Discover Indiana, a project of the Public History Program at Indiana University–Purdue University Indianapolis (IUPUI), the Indiana Department of Natural Resources Division of Historic Preservation and Archaeology, and the Indiana Historical Society, which uses the Omeka+Curatescape platform to distribute interpretive stories about the history, architecture, culture, and people of the state of Indiana on the web.[21] Omeka provides the repository for digitized artifacts, static and moving images, oral histories, and other sources.[22] Curatescape is a plug-in that allows for the interpretation of these objects through place-based storytelling. The end result is geolocated objects that are wrapped in a narrative framework that is available both online and via mobile application.[23] Now in its eighth year, Discover Indiana offers more than thirty digital tours on topics as diverse as sacred spaces and religious history, sports history, medical history, LGBTQ+ history, art, the experience of African Americans in the state, historic theaters, state parks, recreation, government, the Civil War, railroads, and archaeology. We're actively partnering with cultural heritage organizations throughout the state to develop tours that feature county-based historical content. The content material (via access to primary and secondary sources as well as previous analog walking tours) is provided to students at IUPUI who then consult staff librarians, archivists, and specialists at the originating institutions. Students learn how to create a digital tour as well as how to manage critique and feedback along with skills in historical writing for public audiences. Importantly, each tour includes a curation statement that lists which students authored the tour. We are also able to mentor graduate students to ensure that they learn how to communicate with our partners while developing their mastery of historical short-form writing. Discover Indiana is a riff off community-based archives by extending local resources to a state project. So in this case, the collaborators are multisited, which makes the careful design of work flow and assignment stages all the more critical to student learning.

Community-based archives and digitization initiatives can certainly complicate course planning, but they are critical to questions about audience and can animate the best digital history pedagogy. And they encourage students to engage directly with the desires, needs, and priorities of communities who are seeking both to preserve their past and to make it visible and accessible from whom the materials come and to whom, sometimes literally, they belong. Community-based projects are grounded in collective memory, community control, and a sense that archives should accommodate local contexts and knowledge. They are also some of the fastest-growing segments of digital history classroom work because they are relatively easily tied to local histories of place. My approach to community-based archives is one drawn from the work of noted digital humanist Padmini Ray Murray. "There is a tendency to perceive manifestations of technology as well as of the archive in metaphorical terms," she writes, "which often results in erasure of embodied materiality of the bodies who perform, create, and populate those archives" in "Bringing Up the Bodies."[24] She continues: "As we continue our work here in India, it is crucially important that we constantly remind ourselves that the threats of erasure that endanger corporeal bodies are readily reproduced in the digital archive unless every effort is made to guard against infrastructural violence."[25] Community-based archives have their roots in these concerns of erasure as well as a desire to situate interpretative control in the community. This awareness of erasure and authority is one that deserves attention in digital history classes.

To draw in the work of public and local historians, you might begin your syllabus construction by soliciting partners from your community who either have their own community-based archive or who are interested in creating one. The Documenting Ferguson project, which appears on many digital history syllabi, is one example. The project harnessed a partnership between Washington University, St. Louis and St. Louis–area universities and organizations to launch a digital repository to preserve and make available community content captured and created in the months following the shooting of Michael Brown by Ferguson, Missouri, police.[26] Participants can submit photographs, videos, documents, and creative works. Importantly, the project does not impose any criteria for submission of associated metadata nor does it supply context to the individual artifacts. Members of the community can both determine what information is included with an artifact as well as select the artifact that they believe best represents their interests. The decision to not require adherence to metadata standards was conscious on the part of project creators. They did not want to create any barriers to community participation. Documenting Ferguson has been useful to my students as it allows us to conduct topical conversations around the history of Ferguson, police violence, national media, social media, and Black experiences in America. A colleague uses this same project in a course on the carceral state; a second uses it with other archives related to police and military violence like the digital archive of the Policía Nacional de Guatemala / Guatemalan National Police Historical Archive.[27]

Using a single community-based archive to introduce themes and historical content can be a useful teaching technique. That archive can be reinvoked at key moments in your class where students are asked to reevaluate previous conclusions with new historiographical contexts, add additional interpretations to their work if they are contributing to the archive themselves, or illustrate the impact of a given digital community archive over time. I like to stack the Documenting Ferguson archive with the more recent Documenting the Now (DocNow) project, which lets students create their own data collections from Twitter using hashtags.[28] With contributions from archivists, librarians, computer scientists, historians, software developers, librarians, sociologists, and journalists, DocNow grew out of the Documenting Ferguson project because participants and organizers wanted to include social media content in the archive. The inclusion of this project in the class allows students to consider the technical and ethical issues of social media archiving. They also can craft their own social media collection on a topic of their own interest. I often frame it alongside articles on the US Library of Congress's Twitter Archive. Launched in 2010, this effort to preserve every tweet, beginning with the platform's launch in 2006, provides students with a chance to consider issues of what constitutes public and private speech on the internet, issues of intent and privacy, and the role of the Library of Congress in preserving our shared past.[29] This helps students consider their own social media behaviors and the diverse histories being written on social media, as well as the shifting landscape of access to Twitter. By pivoting to Twitter, I'm also able to ask students to consider social media as a form of historical publication and as a place where future historians will have to conduct research to understand culture, politics, and history being made right now.

By centering community-based archives, I can introduce students to theories, concepts, and practices that come directly out of contemporary social justice and activism. DocNow, for example, uses Alexandra Dolan-Mescal's Social Humans (SH) Labels. SH Labels "empower content creators to indicate if and how they want their data to be used, above and beyond the legal use described in policies of for-profit social media companies."[30] They are designed to be attached to artifacts and signal to future researchers what constitutes ethical research. There are numerous pathways that you can take from here in your syllabus design. You can use SH Labels to explore Local Contexts' Traditional Knowledge Labels, which allow Indigenous communities to add existing local protocols for access and use to artifacts circulating digitally outside the community. This opens an opportunity to explore projects by Indigenous communities that are hosted by Mukurtu, an Indigenous knowledge–based web-publishing tool.[31] Originally developed by the Center for Digital Archeology, Mukurtu is a free tool for publishing cultural heritage content. It allows all users, not just Indigenous community members, to set protocols around cultural and social norms. Culturally sensitive content can be reserved for certain users, those who are identified as being a member with particular roles or sub-groups, or hidden entirely from public view. Part of why I like to incorporate Mukurtu in the classroom is that it can be used to illustrate how cultural knowledge shapes information organization, technology, and practice. Students enjoy comparing Mukurtu with other web-based publishing tools like Omeka and WordPress.

It's important to note that there are lots of available avenues in the digital history classroom to challenge archival methods and historical thinking through the integration of diverse histories. T. L. Cowan, Dayna McLeod, and Jasmine Rault's Cabaret Commons is an online archive and encyclopedia for transfeminist and queer artists, activists, and communities that challenges students to think about how feminist and queer methods can displace archival narratives that privilege white, male, heteronormative status.[32] Avery Dame-Grift recently launched the Queer Digital History Project, which supports an archive of transgender-related UseNet newsgroups that can be used by students to consider how internet technologies created communities for transgender individuals.[33] The Rainbow History Project allows students to explore metropolitan Washington, DC's LGBTQ history through its Omeka-driven online archive.[34] It also pushes students to consider why other DC-based archives haven't focused on collecting LGBTQ histories. Each of these offers plentiful opportunities to explore lesbian, gay, bisexual, transgender, and queer history in the digital history classroom.

No matter what fields you embrace in your digital archival methods, you should consider ending your discussion of digital archival methods with a speculative design exercise. I ask my students to respond to a simple prompt: What does an archive look like fifty years in the future? How do historians engage with it? Which functionalities and approaches last, and which research practices fall to the side as time marches on? Students respond positively to this exercise because they can personalize it. I usually ask them what they would want to retain from their own lives for future digital historians. It is also important as you close this course to discuss with your students not just the ethics of what historians are doing by working in communities but also the unintended consequences of historical research for subjects and their descendant communities. When

I first started teaching digital history, I was less attuned to how digital technologies can extend practices that extract knowledge from communities for the benefit of historians and other researchers. It was only after listening to Native community members talk about what it meant to see their historical artifacts and history digitized, analyzed, and made available outside of their tribal community and without their authorization that I began to trouble my sense of the liberatory possibilities of digital archives, exhibits, and collections.

A digital history colleague likes to ask her students to conduct a harm assessment as part of their concluding work in the class. They're asked three simple questions: What community is tied to this history? How are members of this community incorporated into your work? And what potential harm could come? Importantly, students then present these assessments as part of their possible project to members of the community itself. It seems to me that this type of approach encourages an awareness of scholarly responsibility that students sometimes struggle with. And, by centering this as a community conversation, students are forced to grapple with whose history and for what purpose as part of the organizing ethos of the course. This gives them a sense not only of the power of the digital, but of its politics as well.

Chapter Nine

Storytelling

IN SEASON FOUR OF *Drunk History*, a Comedy Central program that brings together comedians who liberally imbibe alcohol with recognized actors to tell stories from American history, playwright Lin-Manuel Miranda recounts the life and experiences of Alexander Hamilton and his contemporaries.[1] With female leads Alia Shawkat as Hamilton and Aubrey Plaza as Aaron Burr, Miranda spins tales of Hamilton's work with George Washington during the Revolutionary War as well as his duel with then–vice president Burr. Given the now triple-platinum cast album, eleven Tony awards, a Grammy award for Best Musical Theater Album, and the 2016 Pulitzer Prize for Drama, historians of Early America (even those without an interest in Hamilton specifically) cannot avoid being asked what they think of the Broadway show *Hamilton* and Miranda's interpretation of history. The widespread success of *Hamilton* has drawn Early Americanists into conversations with the public about historical accuracy, diversity and representation in historical fiction, and the utility of rap as a means of telling stories. So powerful has the *Hamilton* phenomenon been that an edited collection was recently released exploring the play and its interpretation of historical events.[2] During its release on the

Disney+ platform, Twitterstorians (that is, historians on Twitter: search via #twitterstorians) gathered to live-tweet historical corrections, provide contextual information, and engage with the Broadway cast.

While *Hamilton* may be the most recent example of fictionalized history for public consumption, this is not, of course, the first time that artistic license has been used in telling stories about the past. Many history classrooms utilize plays and film to engage students in exploring the past, even when the history isn't accurate in its depiction. *Gone with the Wind*, *Braveheart*, *Ben-Hur*, *All the President's Men*, *Apocalypse Now*, and *12 Years a Slave* are just a minute sampling of films that can inspire student interest. Asking students to compare and contrast the dramatization of a historical event to the writings it is based on is a tried-and-true classroom exercise. So too is asking students themselves to create digital works like songs, short films, podcasts, and other digital media using historical sources. In light of these possibilities, this chapter turns our attention to forms of nontextual storytelling that the digital history classroom can equip students to think about and produce themselves.

In early 2013, historian Liz Covart began researching podcasts.[3] Frustrated that she couldn't find any history podcasts that spoke to her interests in Early American history, Covart began her own research on the podcast as a form of communication. What made a podcast popular? How were the most effective podcasts structured? How could she reach her target audience of "nonhistorians"? Knowing that her interest was bringing scholarly interviews to the public, Covart developed an "ideal listener" named Janet. Janet was tired of histories that discussed only dates and "dead, white men." Moreover, as a pre-med student, Janet didn't understand why history should matter to her when her interests lay in science. For many of us, these are familiar-enough sentiments. Covart's aim was to appeal to students like Janet and, in the process, bring more nonspecialists into contact with history. The *Ben Franklin's World* podcast that she developed offered listeners interviews with historians, librarians, archivists, and more all talking about history and its relevance in Early America. With over two hundred episodes, Covart now leads the Digital Projects division of the Omohundro Institute of Early American History and Culture. Her podcast is a key publication in that division. Covart's series is undoubtedly successful not just because of the quality of her interviews and the podcast but also because she clearly communicated to her target audience through choices of language, format, length, and style. Along the way, her ideal listener has merged into the average listener: 60 percent of her audience is male; more than 60 percent of her audience is over forty-five years of age; 48 percent has a graduate or professional degree; and only 22 percent are professional historians or K–12 history teachers. Covart's process of identifying a goal as a historian, researching the potential technology that might serve her needs, and crafting a specific strategy to reach her target audience is one that should be replicated in the digital history classroom.

Students in the digital history classroom often welcome podcasting as part of their digital history coursework because they can imagine themselves as the audience for that work. Students might create a singular podcast that the entire class contributes to, or they might craft independent podcasts that speak to their interests. Content can be drawn not just from interviews and secondary sources but from digitized and born-digital primary source materials. From students recording themselves reading written sources to learning how to create audio snippets from the wealth of digitized audio materials available publicly, podcasting offers students an opportunity to craft historical narratives of their own making. While students often turn to the internet as they forage for audio files and music, there are reputable archives and collections that focus on sound that you can gently guide them toward. The National Recording Preservation Board maintains a list of over six hundred significant collections of recorded sound that students can browse through. Musical performances, comedy routines, speeches, radio shows, spoken-word performances, recordings of major events, and oral history recordings from around the world are available for use. By integrating sound into our classroom, I can introduce students to issues around sampling, copyright, and publishing. I can also introduce them to digital musicology, which is an area of research that leverages digital technology to explore music, and sonification studies, which utilize digital tools to explore sound.[4] What's gratifying about this is that they see the wide variety of possibilities that (digital) history opens up for them.

Students might use recordings of famous speeches interspersed with their own commentaries to illustrate specific historical viewpoints. They might also incorporate oral history recordings about a particular moment, event, or topic. The benefit to this integration of archival materials that are sound-based with their podcast is that they learn how to create, edit, and disseminate audio files both as individual assets and as collections in the form of the podcast. Students often eagerly share it with friends and family, particularly when their own oral history interviews are included as part of their podcasts. One student shared with me that three generations of their family gathered at the dinner table during the Christmas holiday to listen to the student interview their grandparent about his military service. The family was thrilled to "capture" these stories, and the student taught other members of the family how to record their own interviews so that they could have a better family history. Many digital historians, aided by the tutorial published by Brandon Walsh in the *Programming Historian*, use the free technology Audacity to record and edit any audio file.[5] It is the perfect tutorial to bring to your classroom as students can download the software and easily work through the steps of the tutorial to consider how sound serves as a source.

Coursework around sound might include a set of evaluation questions. Did students choose the appropriate content? Did they select the best combination of sources for their digital work? Did they demonstrate mastery of both the digital method and the historical content? Did the products of their work meet their intended goals? If you've let students have the freedom to determine their own methods and tools, these questions might be answered preliminarily via a project proposal. Jonathan Loucadellis and Graeme Glebe, undergraduate York University students enrolled in Sean Kheraj's digital history course, developed their project proposal as part of their final project, a public website that explored the history of transportation to York University via bus.[6] They provide an outline of the project and a description, identify necessary skills, provide an itemized workplan, document specific team roles, and highlight key issues they will have to confront. Their "prototype" project includes a map of routes used to get to York University in 1978 as well as a place for oral history interviews to be posted. Here you can use the proposal itself as a point of dialogue between you and the students so that there are frequent check-ins and a genuine exchange of ideas and plans as the project develops. What usually happens is that I am able to identify gaps in a student's historical thinking while asking questions that can nudge the student in many directions they may not have anticipated.

Podcasts aren't the only form of nontextual scholarly communication that is possible in the digital history classroom. Digital documentaries have offered an opportunity for historians to leverage sound, photography, moving image, and digitized documents to produce historical narratives. For analog historians, storytelling generally aligns with the preference for narratives as the primary form of historical thinking. That translates directly to documentary narration. Historians Todd Gernes and Elizabeth Belanger have their undergraduate students complete a written script, an edited film of four to seven minutes, and a contextual essay that reflects on how their source selection related to their historical thinking. Students learn seven key elements to effective digital storytelling (point of view, dramatic question, emotional content, voiceover, soundtrack, economy, and pacing), which are drawn from the Center for Digital Storytelling's training workshop.[7] I like to use Bryan Alexander's chapter, "Story Flow: Practical Lessons on Brainstorming, Planning, and Development," which walks students through those elements and gives them questions they should answer as they craft their historical narrative.[8] Using these elements with students can result in highly personal narratives like those of students at the University of Kragujevac in Serbia, where Eliz Markowitz created a seven-minute-long film about the Kindertransport, which rescued Jewish children during the Holocaust and also saved the lives of her grandmother and her grandmother's twin sister.[9] Images were drawn from her family's personal records as well as historical archives, newspapers, and publicly available footage. A classmate, Chris Stein, developed a ten-minute-long film on his relative Paul Stein, an American who was a prisoner of war during World War II.[10] While these students produced single-author, single-voice narratives for their documentaries, students can also work together to create documentaries that blend a multiplicity of perspectives and viewpoints. These group projects include the seven key elements that Gernes and Belanger utilize. They also include additional assignments built around group collaboration and negotiation. A project charter can outline responsibilities, a project proposal can provide details on the proposed work, and project drafts or mockups can help students move from their topic to the historical question to the development of their narrative strategy. Several colleagues have students present these plans to their peers or to public partners who might be invested in the documentary. A successful version of this that I have used in my classroom is the elevator-pitch exercise, where students must give a two-minute overview that gives us the main points of the project, discusses its primary evidence, and speaks to the significance of the project. Imagine that you are pitching this documentary to investors, I tell students. What compelling vision would convince someone to invest their money in your project? One colleague who does this in his classroom has students pitch their projects at the beginning of the semester. The class then votes for their favorite projects. The biggest vote getters then become project leads whose projects are developed throughout the rest of the semester as group projects. Alternatively, another digital historian has students vote on the class favorite at the close of the semester with that student earning extra credit for being recognized by their peers.

Podcasts and films are not the only genres of digital storytelling available to you as you consider digital narrative methods in your classroom. Most digital historians have embraced some combination of multimodal, multivocal, or nonlinear storytelling as part of their syllabi. Multimodal simply means that the modes of information included are visual, aural, and written. Multivocal utilizes more than one author or set of perspectives, while nonlinear is a narrative technique that portrays information out of chronological or causal order. Historians of Japan David R. Ambaras and Kate McDonald embraced multimodal, multivocal, and nonlinear storytelling in their digital project, Bodies and Structures.[11] The project consists of multiple single-author modules that analyze primary sources to reveal an articulation of space and place as it relates to the spatial history of the

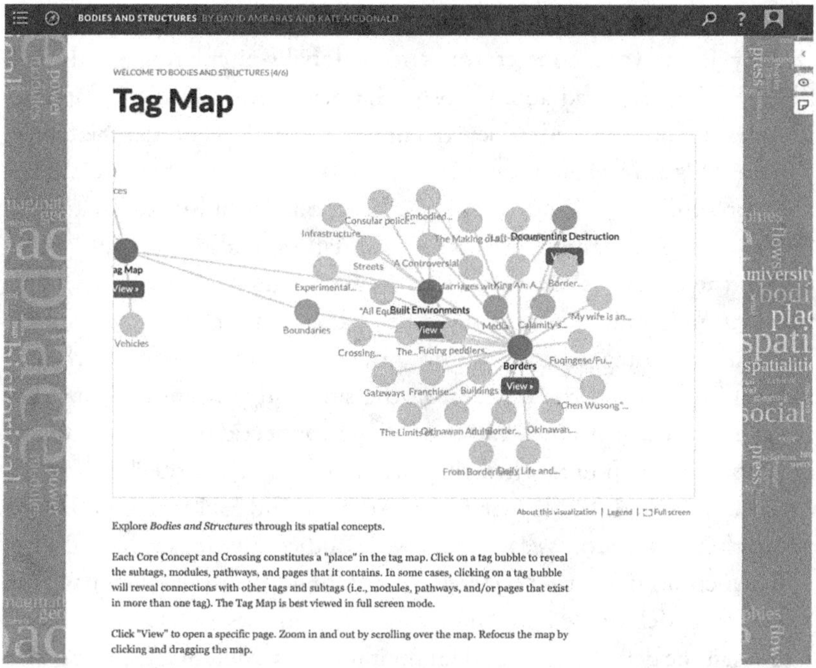

Fig. 9.1. This tag map serves as one way to navigate the Bodies and Structures project created by David Ambaras and Kate McDonald using the Scalar multimodal publishing tool. Here, viewers can see the connections between the concepts, modules, and individual pages. This type of mapping helps students conceptualize the connections between different narrative segments written by a variety of authors. David Ambaras and Kate McDonald, "Tag Map: Bodies and Structures," accessed June 9, 2020, https://scalar.chass.ncsu.edu/bodies-and-structures/tag-map.

Japanese empire. The site organizes the modules thematically through the concepts of space and place as well as "crossings," which are the "boundaries, flows, material culture, vehicles, imaginative geographies, figures, and built environments" that engage with space and place.[12] Users can navigate a module either linearly by following an author-defined pathway or nonlinearly through indexing, hyperlinking, and tags that dynamically call forth content that pertains to one of the crossings (fig. 9.1).

Students working with Bodies and Structures can learn from seven historians about topics that deal with space and place. For example, students can learn from Timothy Yang about how drugstores in early twentieth-century Japan were contact zones for "globally-circulating goods and ideas."[13] They can read about Hoshi Pharmaceuticals, read biographical information on its founder, view documents related to popular medicines and the drugstore, explore visualizations of the networks of wholesale distributors, and more. Yang extends the functionality of his storytelling by incorporating tags and hyperlinks to translations and major concepts, as well as the original source citations. Ambaras and McDonald then link together Yang's module with the other six to create meta-visualizations, including a geotagged map, a grid visualization that illustrates the relationships between the content on the site, and conceptual maps that reveal thematic, historical, and geographic connections. Students appreciate these entry points when they are framed by both the "how to use this site" page and the blog series that Ambaras and McDonald published about the design process associated with Bodies and Structures.[14] Bodies and Structures is what I'd refer to as an umbrella project, which basically means that McDonald and Ambaras serve as editors and assist their colleagues in the development of their digital stories. McDonald equates this type of work to the analog work historians do when creating an edited collection. They select the authors, assist them with revisions, and usher the project to publication. I appreciate this framing with my students for two reasons: one, it suggests that part of what historians do is elevate the work of other scholars by creating multiauthored volumes or states-of-the-field-type work; and, two, it illustrates how digital technologies can build bridges between independently authored digital works to create something more expansive.

This ability to use digital tools to extend the work either through integration of multiple types of primary and secondary sources or through interface layers like visualizations, tags, and cross-hyperlinking is what makes digital storytelling so appropriate for our students. I use Bodies and Structures precisely because it illustrates a layered approach to historical thinking. Students can understand why the editors devote significant time to discussing how space and place both allow and limit certain types of questions, and they can also hear from the other historians independently on their theorization of space and place. "How would we represent the place and movement of people who encountered space differently depending on how spatial structures and physical infrastructures constituted them (e.g., racializing, gendering, disable-izing practices)?" wrote McDonald and Ambaras in their exposition. "How would we incorporate spatial sensibilities that are oriented from the body or the encounter of multiple temporalities in the same locale? And how could we tell spatial stories and make spatial arguments in ways that weren't constrained by the imperatives of linear narrative development, that explicitly reflected on questions of authorial and reader choices?"[15] Bodies and Structures is such a rich pedagogical source because Ambaras and McDonald developed the project explicitly to grapple with limitations in spatial history methods that privilege cartographic mapping. Their "what we learned" section is particularly useful as it highlights how their methodological interventions led to new historical conclusions. Yang, for example, revealed that it was only through his exploration of McDonald's analysis of Cai Peihuo's imaginary of the "inner territory" that he realized the importance of the drugstore clerk as a middleman. While Bodies and Structures was designed with students as users of the project, the model of individually authored essays coupled with a meta-narrative and visualizations is one that could be easily adopted in your classroom.

Scalar, a multimodal digital publishing platform that was developed by the Alliance for Networking Visual Culture, is the storytelling software that was used to develop Bodies and Structures. It lets anyone assemble and annotate digital assets, construct links and pathways between prose and media, and deploy built-in tools to visualize, share, and comment on the work.[16] Scalar can let students import maps, audio, image, text, and video sources; write prose or produce audio and video narrations; and create sequences of content (called "paths") that users can follow. Students can tag anything in their project that then lets them create nonlinear groupings that can be graphed and viewed. It allows you to integrate third-party applications to build out functionalities that you might wish Scalar had for your own narrative work. The benefit of Scalar in the classroom is that it can be used with popular internet media sites like

YouTube and Vimeo as well as archival partners like the Internet Archive, the Shoah Foundation, and major museums and libraries. This makes it easy for students to find and identify content for their projects. Scalar shines with photography, audio, and video materials because students can easily embed them and utilize them in multiple narrative pathways. It also has a built-in editorial workflow that allows you to edit, proof, and comment on student work. Tutorials can easily be integrated into your classroom to assist your students in getting up and running with Scalar.[17] Each portion of the tutorial can be framed as an assignment with students receiving credit for completing each step. By using the Creative Commons standard for importing, Scalar also encourages students to consider fair use, copyright, and source provenance, which can be easily integrated into independent assignments that you scaffold as students work through the construction of their Scalar project.

A brief pause is in order before we close our discussion of Scalar as one possibility for digital storytelling. The Scalar projects that are incorporated into your classroom generally serve as models that students want to emulate. These are often ones with extensive customization that have taken large amounts of time and effort to complete. You and the students should be aware that the out-of-the-box version of Scalar comes with basic aesthetics and functions that don't require programming knowledge or much design ability. This means that students often perceive them as being too simple visually. Either students will need to learn HTML and Cascading Style Sheets to customize the design, or you'll need to bring in a partner who can assist if you are not comfortable assisting students with customization of appearance. Because Scalar utilizes linear and nonlinear structures to organize information, students will need to spend a significant amount of time planning before they ever get to actually building their digital history project. One colleague, for example, has her students complete multiple analog drafts where they first create outlines, then write drafts of content with placeholders for every digital asset, and then literally draw the pathways and linkages between the content they've drafted. That visual rendering becomes a de facto to-do list that orders how they build their project and what visualizations they will have. Another has students organize their content on analog notecards that can be shuffled, reshuffled, and labeled for each pathway. The ability to use source material in many different places is helpful to students, but it can also lead them into repetition if they haven't carefully planned where and when they will discuss certain types of analysis. If you, like me, are someone who thinks very linearly and chronologically, Scalar, with all its possibilities, can feel very overwhelming. Students share that feeling when they confront the blank Scalar install. For this reason, I encourage you to not crowd your syllabus with other tools and methods when working with Scalar. It functions best in the digital history classroom if you unite it with digital source criticism activities and those alone.

There are, of course, alternative approaches to storytelling and narrative methods that you can utilize in digital history classrooms. WordPress, for example, will let students embed digital assets, craft prose narratives, and utilize visualizations including maps.[18] Students can select a given theme that best represents the aesthetics they are interested in, choose plugins that allow them to utilize different functionalities, and publish quickly to the web. It's quite useful to support students building digital narratives around the results of their text analysis work. A colleague of mine asks students to craft Twitter threads where they develop and publish micronarratives on historical topics. Students research a given primary source and then tweet out publicly their analysis and its contextual narrative. Alternatively, if you've planned to integrate cartographic visualization as a primary method in your class, you might wish to select a tool that lets you extend those maps to narration. The ArcGIS StoryMaps tool, which builds on the ArcGIS mapping tools, lets students build stories that combine texts with the maps they've already built in ArcGIS.[19] This enables them to learn spatial history methods and wrap those methods in expositions to guide users to viewpoints and conclusions.

You may find students respond extremely positively to digital storytelling that relies on digital gaming. Historical gaming, which builds on three-dimensional visualization, is one such way to blend historical thinking, narration, and visualization. For those with little familiarity with historical games or their pros and cons, I want to point you to Jeremiah

McCall's 2016 article "Teaching History with Digital Historical Games," which provides a useful overview.[20] Historical games enable you to discuss issues of visual aesthetics and representation, historical accuracy, and authority. Students in Matthew Friedman's undergraduate digital history class at Rutgers University, for example, are asked to write a three-page analysis of a historically themed game and its potential use in teaching history.[21]

When I survey students at the beginning of my introductory courses, many of them point to their experience as players of *Civilization*, *Call of Duty: World at War*, and *Assassin's Creed*. These games have, over time, replaced the classic *Oregon Trail* game that I still use in my classes. Students are provided with sets of secondary and primary source readings related to the Oregon Trail experience, including items from the Library of Congress Oregon Trail collection. Having been sensitized to issues around gender, daily life on the trail, and Native life, we then gather to play both the 1985 Apple II game (via an online simulator) and the fortieth anniversary rerelease (SVG Distribution, 2011) for Wii and Nintendo 3DS.[22] With snacks on hand, students experience the game and its evolution. They research the reception of the various game editions and then are asked to write a new *Oregon Trail* proposal. One student, for example, wrote the game from the point of view of the Native communities whom the trailgoers encountered. Another, using knowledge gained about female mortality due to pregnancy, developed a game sequence where men and women had different outcomes based on age and potential fertility. A third, frustrated with the lack of information about the places that the trailgoers moved through, proposed a game structure that would pull trailgoers off the trail to settlements so that game players could learn about those who established trading outposts. I've found this type of game design exercise is most rewarding in my classes because students' expectations about what it takes to create sophisticated games does not match either their abilities or the amount of time that we have allotted in class. They want professional-level games, and we're more at the stick-figure level in most courses.

James Harry Morris has integrated Twine, which helps students to create interactive text-based games in their browser using HTML, in his undergraduate digital history class.[23] Students can then avoid the technical complexity of building image-based games. He built a Twine based on Commodore Matthew C. Perry's visits to Japan in 1853–54. Students, playing together as a class, are given options that are both historically accurate and alternative realities. Here, the game is driven both by Perry's voyage but also by the students' use of conditions and variables in the game design that place them as a historical actor. Morris's students not only embraced their collective decision making but also wanted to see what alternative game decisions would result.

Austin Mason and Susannah Ottaway have also used Twine in their undergraduate digital history classroom. In their course on the history of poverty and social welfare in England after the Tudor reign, students are asked to create a detailed narrative of the daily life of an individual associated with the Gressenhall House of Industry. They argue that having students use Twine to draft the narrative past increases historical empathy for the "lived experience of the past." Students receive step-by-step instructions on how to use Twine and turn in their final Twine for credit.[24]

No matter which tool you ultimately end up selecting to let students narrate their historical thinking, it is important that you keep in mind that you'll want students to be clear about how their choice of narrative form aligns to their audience. Given not only the density of information on the internet but also the diversity of audiences potentially available, a project that tells a story for the "public" usually ends up amorphous. "Trying to do too much for too many," as one student lamented about a particular history podcast. Another evaluated a Scalar project, with its complex visualizations, as "missing the point" because of its lack of attention to defining terms for the general user. They felt lost from the beginning because it wasn't clear what the historian wanted them to understand about their historical questions, their evidence, or their conclusions. At minimum, the point of the work of any unit on digital storytelling is to make clear that the audience is and should be a major concern of historical thinking and scholarship, regardless of the form it takes. More sophisticated approaches to constructing an audience for a class, though, have significant consequences in terms of course outcomes by encouraging students to understand how issues of audience construction and reception can shape the success or failure of a project and its ability to contribute to historical scholarship. Part of what makes *Ben Franklin's World,* Bodies and Structures, and other projects so effective is that there is a clear understanding of how the digital medium and methods inform and support audiences and their interests. And each explicitly states its historical intervention and why the audience should care, listen, or view.

In our final chapter, we'll consider how your students can contribute to ongoing historical scholarship through the exploration of crowdsourcing. But before we leave digital storytelling, we should stop to remember that the goal of using these tools is to enable your students to be active, critically engaged historians. Digital storytelling can often lead students to use images, sounds, and visualizations as illustrations—things they may not associate with history, and which are exciting and even fun to engage with. But part of a student's work includes how they reveal their historical thinking, and that should be intentional. If they are going to use a person's picture, why that picture? If they are using a song clip, why that song? For what purpose? To what ends? How do these choices impact the story we tell and the history we make? And for whom?

In our last chapter, we'll turn to audience as it relates both to your classroom and to how your students serve as audiences for other digital history projects. There is tremendous opportunity for students to join "the crowd" to contribute to historical collections, projects, and knowledge.

Chapter Ten

Crowdsourcing

WHAT WOULD HAPPEN if hundreds, thousands, or even millions of people around the globe worked on a single digital project? Who would be willing to donate their time and energy to someone else's project? These two questions may seem far-fetched, particularly when so much public rhetoric is about how limited the audiences supposedly are for historians' work. Yet, over the past decade, digital historians have been occupied with exactly these two questions. Crowdsourcing—the reliance on volunteers to work collectively to serve specific project (or organizational) goals—is now so common that people are drawn in without thinking about the fact that they are participating in data gathering for someone else's digital or algorithmic project. Perhaps you use the travel app Waze to get to and from work. Waze uses "the crowd" to provide real-time information on traffic, accidents, police speed traps, and more. But Wikipedia is probably the example of crowdsourcing that your students are most familiar with and that is most frequently discussed in the digital history classroom.

Wikipedia is a freely available encyclopedia that is entirely developed, edited, and promoted by volunteers around the globe.[1] As of March 2020, it has more than fifty-four million articles in more than three hundred languages. It has 1.5 billion unique visitors monthly and is a mainstay for providing historical information on the internet.[2] Historians have long leveraged encyclopedic work in the digital history classroom. Encyclopedias have served as resources for student research, as models for students to emulate in crafting their own entries, and as opportunities to publish our own research. Many historians have learned short-form writing by publishing encyclopedic entries. Digital historians have turned to Wikipedia both as a place to publish historical scholarship but also as a site that can allow us to discuss with students how collective authorship can strain historical argumentation.[3] Adrea Lawrence has her graduate students write a five-hundred-word article that includes scholarly references in their history of education course. Students write a reflection after thirty days that details the reception of their entry, discussions that occurred because of its publications, and revisions that the students made to address any concerns or complaints.[4] Amanda Seligman works through a sequence of Wikipedia-related activities in her undergraduate digital history methods course. Students write a short paper comparing three Wikipedia entries with analog counterparts in specialty print encyclopedias.[5] They are then guided through a discussion of Wikipedia and its editorial practices to understand how historical argumentation is implicit within the entries. And they consider the harmful practices that Wikipedia can encourage due to its restrictive rules around evidence, documentation, and authority. I appreciate Wikipedia's utility in the digital history classroom precisely because it is problematic. It has significant issues with its monitoring system, problems with gender and race, and immense gaps in non-English topics. These problems though are not to be avoided because part of what students can engage with is the rhetorical arguments around public knowledge as positive and a public good. And, when tied to particularly contentious entries, Wikipedia can assist students in considering how objectivity fits within historical thinking and discourse.

In the digital history classroom, crowdsourcing can serve as a powerful tool to generate an audience to engage with students so that students can see the stakes of historical thinking and practice in the digital realm. But participatory digital history isn't limited to Wikipedia. You might consider having students participate as a member of the "crowd" by contributing to existing digital history projects. Examples of these opportunities abound around the globe. One of the most famous projects is Transcribe Bentham, in which people transcribe the unpublished manuscripts of Jeremy Bentham.[6] The Colored Conventions Project documents nineteenth-century African American political life, and it recently launched "Transcribe Minutes" along with two websites focused on providing access to digital records and digital exhibits (fig. 10.1).[7]

Ajapaik is an open-source project developed by the Estonian Photographic Heritage Society that crowdsources geotagging of the historical photos they hold.[8] The University of Iowa's DIYHistory group offers crowdsourcing opportunities in topics as diverse as war diaries and letters, local Iowa and university history, social justice, fanzines, and culinary manuscripts and cookbooks.[9] Ancient Lives asks users to transcribe "papyrus fragments—fragments of texts on a form of paper used in the ancient Mediterranean world."[10] They are currently working on fragments provided by the Egypt Exploration Society. FromthePage, a free software for crowdsourcing transcription, maintains a listing of dozens of historical records and manuscripts that need transcription, indexing, annotation, or other forms of markup.[11] So widespread is crowdsourcing that the Smithsonian Museum system maintains its own Transcription Center for managing crowdsourced projects.[12]

Students as citizen-historians have contributed to several digital history efforts that you can showcase in your classroom. The University of Oxford completed its Great War archive in 2008 using 6,500 digital items contributed by the general public.[13] They then spun that project into a European Union–wide project, Europeana 1914–1918, to tell "untold stories and official histories of World War I in 401,785 items drawn from across Europe."[14] The United States National Archives includes a Citizen Archivist Dashboard, which asks the crowd to create metadata and provide information via tagging and comments.[15] The Tate Museum's AnnoTate effort enables users to transcribe and encode documents from artists' diaries, letters, and sketchbooks.[16] Environmental history courses might have students engage with Old Weather, a project that helps "scientists recover

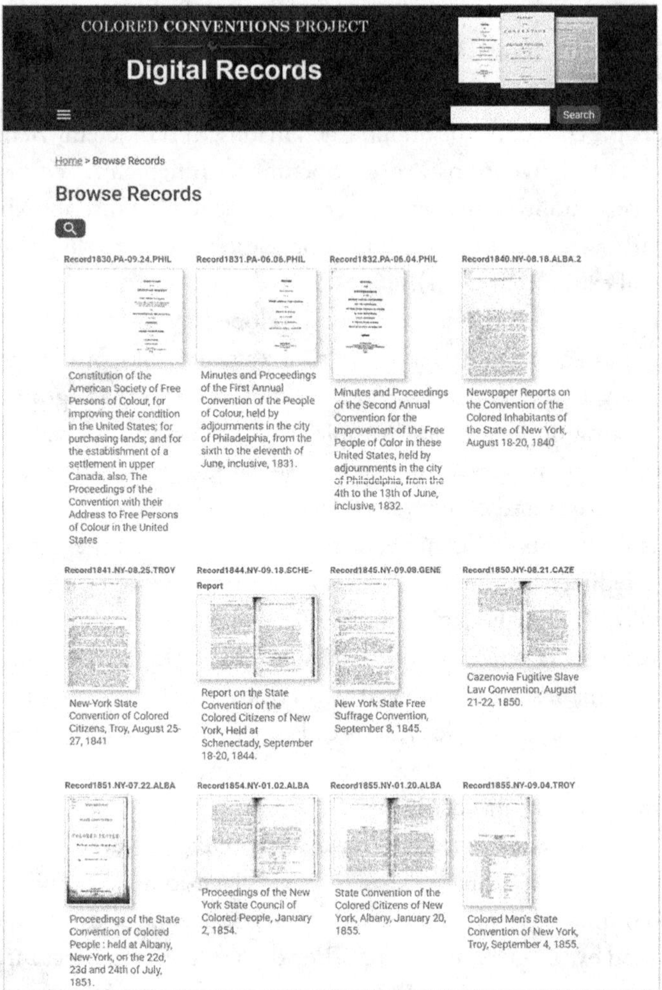

Fig. 10.1. The landing page for the Digital Records section of the Colored Conventions Project offers students the opportunity to see individual digital surrogates organized by title. This type of digital collection work not only gives students access to primary sources but also serves as a model of how instructors might have distinct digital projects developed around the same topical area. This site is a parallel to the digital exhibits and teaching materials offered at the coloredconvention.org site. P. Gabrielle Foreman, Jim Casey, and the Colored Conventions Project Team, "Digital Records," accessed November 1, 2020, https://omeka.coloredconventions.org/browse-records.

Arctic and worldwide weather observations recorded in ship's logs since the mid-19th century."[17]

For each of these crowdsourced endeavors, you can ask students not only to complete the requested task but also to use the project as a jumping-off point for their own research and learning. For example, the Colored Conventions Project includes assignments, research guides, contextual resources, and teachers' guides that you could build an entire class around. A course in Civil War history might utilize one of the dozens of available crowdsourcing projects around diaries to research soldiers' experiences and other pertinent issues. I can easily imagine dividing the class up to transcribe and research an experience from the North and one from the South to ultimately compare and contrast the language of war. One reason you might consider crowdsourcing as the structure of your course is that it encourages students to join existing historical research and, in some cases, historiographical debates. Students can readily see their contributions and can see how those contributions enter public knowledge almost immediately. For students who often view historical research as a long, slow process without a payoff, participation in one or more crowdsourced projects can shift their perspective.

You might also complement students' contributions to an existing crowdsourcing project by developing your entire course around a local crowdsourcing project. Scripto is freely available software that you can use to create crowdsourced transcriptions of any item you've uploaded to the Omeka digital exhibit software if you host the Omeka installation on your own server. Students can register as users, view your digital assets, transcribe them, and then, after they've completed the transcriptions, create digital exhibits using their work. You'll need to either have developed or develop with students transcription guides to address things like spelling, punctuation, formatting, marginalia, and other editorial practices. The Papers of the War Department project, for example, provides its users with these guidelines as well as step-by-step directions with screenshots of how to use the tool and contribute to the project.[18] For introductory courses, you may want to determine the mechanics of the project before the class starts so that students spend most of their time transcribing and researching context for their exhibit. For more advanced courses though there is tremendous opportunity to use the development and launch of Scripto+Omeka as applied learning. Students could create a list of steps that would need to be taken to get the technology set up, make methodological and editorial decisions about the workflow and its content, and then complete their research tasks. This type of procedural work mimics the full cycle of a digital history crowdsourcing project, particularly if part of what they have to do is build their own crowd of contributors.

It is key as you think about building a crowd and having students contribute to crowdsourcing projects to discuss the ethics of working freely as a historian, even if students are novices. As one crowdsourcing team at the Getty Museum noted, there is a need to be "mindful of the link between crowdsourcing and outsourcing, and that this practice could be viewed as a way of externalizing labor traditionally done by hired staff, despite the fact that this type of labor isn't typically paid by institutions."[19] Digital history classrooms should also be careful not to use students as "free labor" for the instructors' own research.[20] As one graduate student noted when we discussed this issue, the devaluing of the humanities and history is rampant both inside and outside higher education. Thinking that anyone can be a historian through crowdsourcing is both an oversimplification and reductionist in its framing. People I spoke to about this question were eager to encourage students' interest in working on a historical project. In addition to the labor issue, they were also keen to emphasize that, as a profession, history has standards that students should be mindful of if they aspire to be citizen-scholars.

If you are concerned about the ethics of using students in these types of projects, you might consider building an entire network of interconnected digital projects that ask students to consider the ethics of crowdsourcing the past. I've developed a unit where students explore the ethics of crowdsourcing via the National Archives and Records Administration (NARA) and Ancestry.com. Students contribute to the transcription efforts around the US Census, then learn about the agreements between NARA and Ancestry.com that effectively embargoes the work they've completed. They also read about how prisoners in the United States serve as unpaid corporate labor for transcribing cultural heritage through FamilySearch, a project of the Church of Jesus Christ of Latter-day Saints.[21] What does it mean that our cultural record is being privatized? Are there ethical considerations around using prison labor? What does the practice of embargoing do for historians or the NARA?

There are plenty of options for your digital history classroom to contribute to or create crowdsourcing projects. Be sure to keep in mind your own balancing act as a teacher, however, because this work can be labor-intensive. If the scope of the work is limited (say a few dozen documents) or you only intend to have crowdsourcing as a small portion of your syllabus, it may not be worth your time to develop and deploy your own technology for crowdsourcing. When you use the term "crowd," you might wish to substitute the words "community-based" or "openly public" to signal the limits of the reach of the "crowd." Most digital history projects in the classroom are not crowdsourcing projects in the commercial sense of the term. One digital history colleague will post digital assets to a folder in their campus learning management system. Students are assigned one asset and asked to transcribe the handwritten text by using a word-processing program like Microsoft Word. Students then submit their plain-text files for a grade. It is only after the instructor combines all of the plain-text files received that the students have a full transcript to go with the digital asset. The benefit to this approach is that it requires less technical infrastructure, almost no consideration of issues of audience participation and monitoring/moderating, and little time to get students up and running with their coursework. I also like this approach because I can quickly vary the digital assets and approaches to respond to student interests. This contrasts with a full-scale classroom crowdsourcing project where the wealth of data might overwhelm the interpretive work. Students are our "crowd" and generally number in the dozens. We don't normally build a massive user base in our classes. As a result, some digital historians avoid using the term "crowd" and instead refer to this segment on their syllabus as "participatory" history.

Yet, as a concept, crowdsourcing in the digital history classroom serves our quest to broaden students' appreciation for how the past is made by encouraging students to consider who is writing history publicly, how "the public" might be collectively imagined, and how they can actively participate in those processes. They can see how technological systems and their practices (like Wikipedia) can construct different historical representations and user groups. This kind of collaborative, outward-facing work reminds us that part of our responsibility as historians and teachers is to develop historical knowledge that is useful to our peers, communities, and the general public. When students understand crowdsourcing in this context, they glimpse the wide variety of individuals who participate in historical scholarship under a broad set of titles: citizen-archivist, citizen-historian, genealogist, librarian, or even hobbyist.

Remember that you are part of a broad and diverse community of teachers and researchers that can assist you in your course pedagogy. Asking students to join an existing project is just one way to illustrate those connections to community.

Conclusion

EMBRACING DIGITAL HISTORY

IT USED TO BE THAT only a few historians were charged with creating a robust digital history curriculum. I used to be able to count on two hands the number of institutions of higher education that had a course titled Digital History. Now, thankfully, that's changed as more schools are embracing curricula that rely on digital history methods and approaches. You see that change playing out in the pages of this text. Many of the included examples are drawn from courses that aren't titled Digital History Methods or Introduction to Digital History. Instead, they are topical courses organized geographically, thematically, or conceptually. They are courses that aren't singular occurrences in their departments; instead, they represent a variety of historical subfields that bring their own questions and concerns to digital history methods. And they are drawn from historians actively teaching across the globe at a variety of types of institutions with quite different audiences.

As we close our principles for teaching digital history, it's important that we discuss at least briefly how to embrace digital history beyond a single class and instead as an integrated strategy in your curriculum. I spend a lot of time thinking about this question as I codirect a US-based digital humanities training institute, the Humanities Intensive Learning and Teaching Institute (HILT).[1] Every year, we select around a dozen courses taught by the best instructors we can find. For four consecutive days, we let those instructors shine as they work with undergraduate students, graduate students, faculty, cultural heritage professionals, and members of the public to learn methods, tools, and professional skills. I've been truly lucky to learn from these instructors because they are both passionate about their teaching and incredibly articulate in how pedagogy aligns to the digital. Every year, at the end of our institute, we gather to discuss what worked, what didn't, and what we might do in the future. Sometimes that conversation results in new courses with different methods; at other times, it includes bringing in new instructors with capabilities that we hadn't considered before. But every year, what that discussion reveals is a deep desire by those instructors to continually improve their teaching by challenging themselves and their students. Much of that improvement is tied to a sense that there is now space for curricular arcs that students can follow. This book represents one curricular arc for digital history. We move from datasets to learning outcomes, from learning outcomes to new types of assignments, from those assignments to concerns over methodological approaches. And, once we've chosen our methods, we consider what types of historical thinking digital history can represent. The list is truly overwhelming: models, graphs, maps, archives, exhibits, collections, digital editions, podcasts, short digital documentaries, multimodal linear narratives, multimodal nonlinear narratives, Wikipedia articles, websites, and crowdsourced digital projects. Digital history in the classroom can offer a place for all of these. But digital history can also offer an arc for your entire curriculum. As students move thorough a degree program or curriculum sequence, you want them to develop progressively more complex abilities. If your curriculum doesn't build on itself, you may find that students lose interest as they make their way from course to course.

So how do you approach designing an entire sequence of courses without becoming overwhelmed? One way is to begin by asking colleagues to identify digital methods they've encountered in existing historical scholarship or that they use themselves. Digital history methods that are being utilized in existing scholarship are generally methods that are well developed, have tutorials and extensive documentation, and are used in most digital history classrooms. These methods are represented in conference programs and are readily identified in existing digital history syllabi. Digital archives, digital collections, digital exhibits, mobile applications, spatial analysis, text analysis, and even 3D and augmented reality all fit easily into this category. So too does digital source criticism, as even the most analog historians are using digital sources and can be gently prodded into incorporating a digital component and set of evaluation questions into their existing courses. Perhaps every course in your curriculum could incorporate a single digital source criticism exercise.

From there, you might consider identifying for each of your courses a dataset that could underlie the course syllabus. At the college level, all the instructors who teach a given course might join together to prepare a dataset that every section of the class could use. Once that dataset is established, that same group may elect a method or two that could be incorporated into every section of the class. The benefit to this is that you can divide the work of crafting any tutorials, lesson plans, or assignment prompts that you might need. Alternatively, every teacher could select a different method to use and then come back together at the end of the course to evaluate how students responded to the method. Were the learning outcomes associated with crafting a dynamic map in OpenGIS, for example, more successful than those that asked students to do textual analysis with Voyant? The benefit to this is that you can work collaboratively to identify the types of methods that align best to the course outcomes. You also can then share the materials you've created for the following year, providing everyone with more methodological options for the course. This is particularly attractive, I imagine, for history teachers in the high school environment where prescriptive content may limit their ability to broaden a student's historical thinking with supplemental materials. I can easily see high school history teachers working together to share this type of pedagogical work.

A different approach to a curricular arc could be developed for history majors only. You might consider using beginning, intermediate, and advanced as the organizing frame for your curricular development exercise. Beginning courses introduce students to digital history concepts and methods and are taught by less digitally confident colleagues. Usually, these courses are tightly controlled in both their learning outcomes and their course assignments. They tend to be titled "introduction to" courses and fulfill general core and survey requirements. Intermediate courses are usually topical courses that are tied to methodological approaches and should be taught by those confident in their knowledge of the method and its assumptions. For example, at the intermediate level students generally dig deeply into a small handful of methods that allow them to ask specific historical questions. Advanced courses give students the latitude to self-select their digital method and generally serve as capstones to their degree. These usually are independent research–driven courses that ask students to challenge their abilities. In this approach, you'd take our sequential list of courses that students must take and align them to methodological complexity. You may select a set of tutorials from the *Programming Historian* that can be assigned to different courses. For example, you may have students in your lower-level course develop visualizations with Tableau Public and learn HTML, Cascading Style Sheets, and JavaScript. Students in upper-division courses would then use those skills to compare and contrast cartographic mapping approaches between Tableau and Leaflet. Similarly, lower-level history courses might encourage easy-to-use text analysis methods like frequency, collocation, and named entity recognition, while upper-division courses could build a text analysis project from scratch that requires coding and programming skills. The benefit to this type of technical complexity approach is that you are building proficiency over long periods of time. This reduces the burden on instructors because you can work collaboratively to staff office hours or consultations. It lets materials be shared across multiple classes to support each other. And, by using tutorials already designed and peer reviewed, you are assured that the technical aspects of the course are appropriate to the types of historical knowledge you wish students to develop.

Independent learning might fit into a third approach to your curriculum integration. Because I currently teach a variety of courses across both undergraduate and graduate curricula, I rarely get more than one class with any student. While my colleagues are moving toward more digital history in their classrooms, I most frequently am brought in to work with students on honors projects, senior thesis projects, or graduate-level dissertations and theses. The student is interested in digital history, but generally they haven't had a complete digital history curriculum. How I deal with this is through independent study. I will often gauge a student's base abilities for historical thinking and technical proficiency with a questionnaire. Then, once I know where the student is at, I will select tutorials and scaffold them sequentially to get them to the level they need to be at to successfully complete their research project. Individual curricular arcs are a form of ad hoc training that can be quite valuable because they ask the students to take agency in their own learning. I can also partner with colleagues from other departments and institutions to deliver the training. Many of the attendees at HILT are crafting their own curricular arcs, either through self-interest or because their employer wishes to move into a given method or approach. This independent study plus ad hoc training institute approach, by the way, is how many digital historians develop their own expertise in programming and methods. They assign, iterate, and master tutorials, moving slowly from least complex to most complex, either independently or through a community-training experience.

Don't think though that you need to be an expert in a method before incorporating it in a curricular arc. In digital history courses, you'll need to update your course to match innovations in method and historical scholarship. Sometimes the most exciting lessons in historical thinking are the ones where you are learning alongside the students. A colleague, for example, throws one new method or tool into their course every year to keep their own thinking and approaches fresh. Ten years ago, only the most adventurous digital historian worked with three-dimensional representation in their courses. Now, thanks to its growth both as a set of methods and as part of digital pedagogy, I can "play" alongside my students. I want to encourage you to embrace the scholarship of teaching and learning about digital history. When discussing this book with peers who teach digital history, one thing we all agreed upon was a desire to have more example assignments, syllabi, rubrics, tutorials, and the like that we can use to diversify our courses. These are important contributions that you can make as you improve your digital history proficiency.

I'd like us to return briefly to a thread that has run throughout this book: the relationship between history, digital history, audience, and the ethics of our classrooms. Theorist and artist micha cárdenas draws on the work of Donna Haraway, Jasbir Puar, Audre Lorde, Gloria Anzaldúa, and others to argue that digital tools can serve as a site of resistance against knowledges and practices that have defined Black people, women, trans individuals, Indigenous peoples, and others as less than human.[2] In our classrooms, that "less than" tendency has played out in learning and writing the histories of these individuals and their communities without their consultation, consideration, or inclusion. It has shaped US laws that support the rights of corporations and the public over descendant communities who would like the images and records of their families repatriated and removed from the public domain. And it has played out in digital history through the separation between the communities we study and descendants who might feel strongly about being treated as an object of study rather than as the primary historian of their past. Digital history as method and practice compels us to understand our data not as separate from their conditions and contexts of production—this is nothing different than our analog practice. It also pushes us to consider how the systems of access, analysis, and delivery that we must utilize perpetuate systems of oppression and inequality. Computers, data, software, and the internet are not value-neutral. Digital history, though, can also offer us the possibility of creating full partnerships among the various audiences our work might have. This is, after all, the strength of the social web. You should consider partnership not as an albatross but as a way to illustrate for students the diverse voices that might shape our history. The more participants they encounter, the more they will see exactly how immersive history truly is in the surrounding world.

Finally, as we close this work, it would be remiss of me not to bring us back to the beginning. Digital history is currently being practiced, written, revised, and negotiated around the world. Each of these sites and the individuals who inhabit them bring their own local, regional, national, or personal concerns to their work as teachers. I am ever more convinced that, as teachers and historians, our responsibility is to embrace those local contexts and questions. They help us to tell more nuanced stories, craft more complex histories, and experience the broad array of pedagogical practices. Don't be afraid to reach out and learn more from other historians working digitally. Don't be afraid to struggle. Don't be shy about iterating. And, most importantly, don't forget that what makes you a great teacher is your desire to continually improve your own pedagogy.

Glossary and Resources

ABBYY FineReader An optical character recognition program that enables users to convert images to machine-readable text. Limited free trial. https://pdf.abbyy.com/.

aggregator A website or computer program that brings together information, usually in the form of hyperlinks or data, from disparate digital sources.

Ajapaik A software program that allows you to geotag historical imagery, particularly maps. Free to use. Created by the Estonian Photographic Heritage Society. https://ajapaik.ee/.

algorithm A sequence of step-by-step instructions for a program or computer behavior. Generally used in this text in refer to search algorithms that guide the results shown from a website or search box.

Ancient Lives A project in which members of the public can transcribe papyrus fragments from the Ancient World. Free to contribute. Created by Zooniverse for the University of Minnesota, University of Oxford, Middle Tennessee State University, and University of Waterloo. https://www.ancientlives.org/.

AnnoTate A project in which members of the public can transcribe diaries, letters, sketchbooks, and other materials from the Tate Galleries UK. Free to contribute. Created by Zooniverse for the Tate Museum. https://anno.tate.org.uk/.

ArcGIS Software to create, manage, and share geographical information via maps, layers, and other geographical renderings. Paid. https://www.arcgis.com/index.html.

ArcGIS StoryMaps An extension of the ArcGIS mapping software that enables users to embed their maps within narrative frameworks. Paid. https://storymaps.arcgis.com; https://storymaps.arcgis.com/en/.

Atlanta Rail Corridor Archive An Omeka-based project developed by students in the Heritage Preservation Program at Georgia State University about the historic rail corridor that is being redeveloped as part of the Atlanta BeltLine. Free to use. http://atlrailcorridorarchive.org/.

Audacity Digital software that allows users to create, edit, and share audio files. Free to use. Created by Dominic Mazzoni, Roger Dannenberg, and the Audacity Team and Community Developers. https://www.audacityteam.org/

audio analysis Using computers to extract acoustic features of sound files for the purposes of classification, clustering, and visualization.

augmented reality A method of superimposing computer-generated content over a user's view of the physical world to create a compositive view that blends artificial content and what the user can see.

Ben Franklin's World A podcast created by Liz Covart about topics in Early American history that is currently hosted by the Omohundro Institute. Free to listen. https://benfranklinsworld.com/.

beta-tester A phase of project or software testing where the intended audience reviews and provides feedback on their experience for the purpose of improving the final output.

big data Any data that is too large or complex to analyze using traditional data-processing software or personal computers. For historians, big data is generally in the eye of the beholder.

Black Ships & Samurai: Commodore Perry and the Opening of Japan (1853–1854) A website built using hypertext markup language to publish primary source documents, pedagogical materials, and scholarly interpretations. This site is hosted by Asia for Educators at Columbia University. Free to use. Created by MIT Visualizing Cultures. https://ocw.mit.edu/ans7870/21f/21f.027/black_ships_and_samurai/index.html.

Bloom's Revised Taxonomy for Learning, Teaching, and Assessing The 2001 updating of a framework of knowledge and cognitive processes, originally created in 1956. It is used to develop learning outcomes and standardized curriculums. Created by Iowa State University Center for Excellence in Learning and Teaching. http://www.celt.iastate.edu/teaching/effective-teaching-practices/revised-blooms-taxonomy/.

Bodies and Structures A Scalar-based project that focuses on space and place as it relates to the Japanese empire. Free to use. Created by David R. Ambaras and Kate McDonald. https://scalar.chass.ncsu.edu/bodies-and-structures/index.

born-digital Materials that originate in digital form only.

Cabaret Commons An online archive and encyclopedia for Trans-Feminist and Queer Artists, Activists, and Audiences that is hosted by the Canadian Writing Research Collaboratory repository. Free to use. Created by T. L. Cowan, Dayna McLeod, and Jasmine Rault. https://cwrc.ca/projects/infrastructure-projects/pilot-projects/cabaret-commons.

Cascading Style Sheets (CSS) A style-sheet language that describes how elements should be rendered visually digitally or in analog form.

Century America A website built in WordPress that explores World War I and the Spanish influenza epidemic from local and community histories. Free to use. Created by Ellen Pearson and Jeffrey McClurken. http://course.centuryamerica.org/.

Citizen Archivist Dashboard A program hosted by the National Archives and Records Administration that allows the public to transcribe, tag, and comment on primary sources held by the institution. Free to contribute. https://www.archives.gov/citizen-archivist.

Clio A website and mobile application that allows users to document historical and cultural sites throughout the United States. Free to use. Created by David Trowbridge and Strictly Business Computer Systems. https://theclio.com.

close listening A method of analyzing sound at the level of an individual sound.

close reading A method of analyzing text at the level of a single document and its component parts.

close viewing A method of analyzing visual material to focus on the elements that compose an image.

CMS *See* **content management system.**

code A system of rules that converts information, be it visual, textual, or auditory, into binary code that can be read by a computer.

code repository A centralized file storage of computer code.

A Colony in Crisis: The Saint-Domingue Grain Shortage of 1789 A digital publishing project from the University of Maryland libraries that provides access to digital manuscripts, translations, and historical introductions to documents about the colony of Saint-Domingue. Free to use. Created by Kelsey Corlett-Rivera, Nathan H. Dize, and Abby Broughton. https://colonyincrisis.lib.umd.edu.

Colored Conventions Project A project that uses the Omeka content management system to provide primary sources about state and national political meetings held by Black Americans from 1830 to the 1890s. The project now includes opportunities for transcription, teaching materials, and bibliographies. Free to use and free to contribute. Created by P. Gabrielle Foreman, Jim Casey, and Sarah Lynn Patterson. http://coloredconventions.org/.

comma-separated value file A text file that uses a comma to separate and store tabular data in plain-text form. An alternative to the proprietary format of Microsoft Excel or Apple's Numbers software.

command line A text interface to your computer and its programming that enables you to navigate and run programs directly from the operating system.

community-based archive An archive developed by a community that collects, preserves, and makes accessible information documenting and recognizing their own authority and knowledge about a given event, topic, and so forth.

computational analysis The use of mathematical models and principles to organize and analyze digital assets.

Computational Historical Thinking A textbook developed by Dr. Lincoln A. Mullen that teaches readers to conduct historical research through computational methods, including data analysis, mapping, text analysis, and network analysis. Free to use. http://dh-r.lincolnmullen.com/.

Connected Histories A website that utilizes a search engine to provide access to digital content already available publicly from other websites about early modern and nineteenth-century British history. Free to use. Directed by Tim Hitchcock, Robert Shoemaker, and Jane Winters. http://www.connectedhistories.org/.

content management system A software that allows you to create, modify, and publish digital content. Most systems allow for individual and collaborative authoring of material. Common systems used by historians include WordPress, Joomla, Drupal, Mukurtu, and Omeka.

corpora A set or group of materials, generally made available in a homogenous form of text, visual, or audio format.

corpus analysis Defined by the *Programming Historian* website as a form of text analysis that lets you make comparisons between textual objects at a large scale. Often synonymous with distant reading and corpus linguistics, which explores the study of language as corpora.

counterdata A term used by Lauren Klein and Catherine D'Ignazio that refers to the opportunity to quantify and visualize structural oppression.

Creative Commons An American nonprofit organization that has made available copyright licenses that are free of charge to the public. Free to use. https://creativecommons.org/.

crowdsourcing The practice of soliciting communities of users to contribute either paid or unpaid work to complete a given task or project.

CSS *See* **Cascading Style Sheets (CSS).**

Curatescape A theme and associated tools for use with WordPress that allows you to publish location-based content for mobile application tours. Paid. https://curatescape.org/.

data A general concept of information that is represented or coded to communicate knowledge. It is often used in both singular and plural form and can be used interchangeably with sources in digital history practice.

data aggregation Data that is identified and summarized collectively.

database A structured set of data that allows for searching, analyzing, publishing, and so on.

data curation The management of data through its life cycle to ensure that it can be retrieved for future use or reuse.

Data Curation Guide A digital publication of a compilation of articles that directs readers to trusted information about data management. Free to use. https://guide.dhcuration.org/.

data literacy The ability to understand, manipulate, analyze, and argue with data as a form of scholarship.

data mining The practice of computationally analyzing datasets to generate new information.

dataset A collection of data.

data standardization The process of amending data to create a common format that is usable with a given tool or methodology.

DH Box A grouping of digital humanities tools, including Omeka, IPython, RStudio, and the Natural Language Toolkit, that enables users to deploy the tools in a browser window without installing the tools on their computer. Free to use. Created by Stephen Zweibel, Patrick Smyth, and Jojo Karlin. http://dhbox.org/.

digital archive A term that refers to a collection of materials that might be born-digital or were analog materials that have been digitized. Used appropriately, it should adhere to the technical standards of archives as established by archival specialists.

digital asset Any digital file that incorporates the right to use it.

digital collection A grouping of materials that is available in digital form.

digital documentary edition A set of digital materials that is compiled and annotated with historically and contextually important information.

digital ethnography The study of kinship, relational analysis, and cultural and linguistic custom analysis, as well as techniques of observation and interview, associated with the digital sphere.

digital exhibit Selected materials that are used to craft narratives and layouts for online display.

digital historical representation A term authored by Kate Theimer to refer to digital materials that are collected, combined, or recombined outside of institutional archives for the purposes of access. Note: These do not necessarily meet archival standards for preservation and provenance.

digital history A spectrum of digital methods used by historians to take advantage of the affordances of digital technologies including software, tools, and infrastructure.

digital humanities Any form of humanities scholarship that uses computers to present, analyze, or publish scholarship digitally.

Digital Humanities Manifesto 2.0 An opinion piece authored by Jeffrey Schnapp, Todd Presner, Peter Lunenfeld, and Johanna Drucker in 2008 about what the humanities can and should be doing related to twenty-first-century research. http://manifesto.humanities.ucla.edu/.

Digital Karnak A three-dimensional reconstruction project of the Egyptian site of Karnak built using the VSim software. Created by Diane Favro, Willeke Wendrich, and Elaine Sullivan in 2017. https://vsim.library.ucla.edu/xmlui/handle/20.500.11991/1012.

digital literacy The ability to use digital technologies to find, analyze, and create information.

Digital Mappa A browser-based tool that lets you mark up, annotate, link, and share digital images and texts. Free to use. Requires setting up your own Digital Mappa server or partnership with an existing Digital Mappa user. https://www.digitalmappa.org.

digital musicology An area of research that leverages digital technologies to understand music.

digital object identifier (DOI) A persistent identifier used to uniquely identify an object.

Digital Panopticon The digital project "The Digital Panopticon: Tracing London Convicts in Britain and Australia, 1780–1925" uses MediaWiki, d3.js, and bootstrap to present and visualize datasets related to London convicts in Britain and Australia, 1780–1925. Free to use. Created by Barry Godfrey. https://www.digitalpanopticon.org/.

Digital Public Library of America (DPLA) A search engine that aggregates metadata that is used to describe an item from libraries, museums, and institutions around the United States. The site includes primary resource sets for teaching. Free to use. https://dp.la/.

digital repository A collection of resources usually hosted by an institution, organization, or group of individuals.

digital reproduction The use of computing technology to re-create an object, environment, or experience.

digital source criticism An extension of source criticism that takes into account the digital aspects of historical sources, be they sources converted from analog to digital or sources that exist only digitally. Digital source criticism can also involve the exploration and analysis of digital environments, platforms, and the internet.

digital storytelling Using digital technologies to tell narrative interactive stories.

digital surrogate A digital reproduction, either through photography or scanning, of an analog object.

digitization The process of converting information into a digital format.

directory structure The organization of information as files into an organized hierarchy.

Discover Indiana A statewide public history project created with Omeka with the Curatescape theme to provide cultural and historical information to the public. Free to use. Created by Rebecca Shrum. https://publichistory.iupui.edu/.

distant listening The process of using sound analysis to analyze and visualize an auditory collection at the level of a corpora.

distant reading The process of using text analysis to analyze, mine, visualize, and understand textual corpora.

distant viewing The process of using image analysis to understand still or moving images at the level of a corpus.

Distant Viewing Toolkit A package of Python code that can be used to conduct computational analysis of visual culture. Free to use. Created by Taylor Arnold and Lauren Tilton. https://distant-viewing.github.io/dvt/index.html.

DIYHistory A crowdsourced project in which users can transcribe historical materials held by the University of Iowa's libraries. https://diyhistory.lib.uiowa.edu/.

Documenting Ferguson An Omeka-based community project that makes available digital media related to the shooting death of Michael Brown in Ferguson, Missouri, in 2014. Free to use. Created by Rudolph Clay, Shannon Davis, Chris Freeland, Nadia Ghasedi, Sonya Rooney, Andrew Rouner, Rebecca Wanzo, and Micah Zeller. http://digital.wustl.edu/ferguson/.

Documenting the American South A digital project that publishes texts, images, and audio sources related to Southern history, literature, and culture. Sponsored by the Wilson Library at the University of North Carolina. https://www.docsouth.unc.edu/.

Documenting the Now A project that provides tools to help those interested in working with social media data. Free to use. Created by Meredith Clark, Bergis Jules, Trevor Muñoz, and the Documenting the Now Project Team. https://www.docnow.io/.

Dublin Core Metadata A set of controlled vocabulary terms used to describe assets. https://dublincore.org/.

DuckDuckGo An American company that provides a search engine where all users receive the same search results regardless of an individual's profile. Free to use. https://duckduckgo.com/.

dynamic visualization Preset visualizations that are made available to the viewer based on queries that are predetermined by the visualization author.

Europeana A digital platform that aggregates metadata information from cultural heritage organizations in the European Union. Free to use. Created by the Europeana Foundation. https://pro.europeana.eu/.

Europeana 1914–1918 A digital project that provides access to metadata and hyperlinks of objects about World War I held by institutions that are part of Europeana. Free to use. https://www.europeana.eu/portal/en/collections/world-war-I.

Facebook A social media platform that allows users to share, communicate, and promote information about themselves and others. Free to use. https://www.facebook.com/.

Flickr A PHP-based image and video hosting service. Paid. https://www.flickr.com/.

frequency analysis A study of the frequency of letters or words as they appear in a given textual document or corpus.

FromthePage Open-source software that allows users to correct, transcribe, index, annotate, and share digital assets. Paid. Created by Benjamin Brumfield and Sara Brumfield. https://fromthepage.com/.

game design A discipline at the intersection of computer programming, arts and graphic design, media, and narration that results in a playable product.

geographic information systems A system for gathering, managing, analyzing, visualizing, and sharing data related to geography.

Gephi An open-source software package that allows users to create, analyze, and visualize networks. Free to use. https://gephi.org/.

Git A version-control system for programming code.

GitHub A cloud-based service that lets you share code. Free or paid, depending on capabilities. https://github.com.

GitHub Pages An HTML, CSS, and JavaScript tool from GitHub that lets you host and publish websites and projects directly from your code repository. https://pages.github.com/.

Google A US company that provides a search engine, cloud-based hosting, software, and hardware to users. Free to use. https://www.google.com/.

Google Earth A software package that enables users to create three-dimensional representations based on satellite images, aerial photography, and geographic data. Free to use. https://www.google.com/earth/.

Google Lit Trips An educational project that lets users build and share three-dimensional field trips based on literary works. Free to use. http://www.googlelittrips.org/.

Google Maps An online software for mapping locations to contemporary maps. It offers satellite imagery, aerial photography, street maps, and panoramic views of streets, as well as the ability to create custom map tours. Free to use. https://www.google.com/maps.

Great War Archive A digital project containing more than 6,500 items related to World War I (1914–18) contributed by the general public between March and June 2018. Created by Stuart Lee and hosted by the University of Oxford. http://www.oucs.ox.ac.uk/ww1lit/gwa.

hashtag A form of information tagging used on social media, particularly Twitter.

high-performance computing The ability to process data beyond the capabilities of a user's desktop computer.

Historian's Macroscope The online textbook *Exploring Big Historical Data: The Historian's Macroscope* focuses on how historians can use big data in their research. Free to use. Created by Shawn Graham, Ian Milligan, and Scott Weingart. http://www.themacroscope.org/2.0/.

History Harvest An initiative that brings together the general public with historians to share and digitize letters, photographs, objects, and other physical ephemera. Founded by William G. Thomas III and sponsored by the University of Nebraska, Lincoln. https://historyharvest.net/.

Historypin A platform that allows users to "pin" historical photographs, videos, and other content to Google Maps, build a collection of pins, and compare them to contemporary location images. Free to use. https://www.historypin.org/en/.

Hollerith Machine A physical machine built by Herman Hollerith that used electrical and mechanical signals to count data provided on paper punch cards.

Homicide in Chicago 1870–1930 A website and database that focuses on the Chicago Police Department Homicide Record Index between 1870 and 1930. The site is hosted by Northwestern University School of Law. Free to use and free to download the complete database. Created by Leigh Bienan. http://homicide.northwestern.edu/.

Hypertext Markup Language (HTML) The first standard markup language for all digital assets that are designed to be displayed on the internet.

Hypertext Markup Language (HTML) 5 The current version of markup language for digital assets that defines both properties and behaviors of the material on the internet.

Hypothes.is A browser-based tool that allows users to annotate any content available on the internet, regardless of format. Free to use. Created by Lyza Danger Gardner, Jon Betts, Sean Hammond, Kyle Keating, and Robert Knight. https://web.hypothes.is/.

Humanities Intensive Learning and Teaching Institute (HILT) A digital humanities training institute offering courses in methods, approaches, and disciplinary studies including history and area studies. Founded by Jennifer Guiliano and Trevor Muñoz. http://dhtraining.org/hilt/.

image analysis The process of extracting information from images.

immersive experiences Technology that enables a user to experience a virtual environment in the form of historical reproductions, artificial environments, or simulations. Immersive experiences can contain visual, aural, tactile, and scent-based content.

influence mapping A visualization model that reveals the influence of factors on one another; it usually displays information about personal relationships.

information literacy The ability to understand how information is created, valued, analyzed, and shared.

Instagram A photo and video-based sharing service owned by Facebook. Free to use. https://instagram.com/.

interactive visualization A visualization that allows users to select variables that will delimit the visualization and adjust it accordingly.

interface A space where two computers or the computer and user interact. Usually used as a shorthand for the portion of a program, project, archive, or website that is available to the user.

Internet Archive A nonprofit digital library that offers free access to books, movies, music, and archived webpages. It includes the Wayback Machine, a service for archiving webpages. Often, Internet Archive and Wayback Machine are used synonymously. Free to use. https://archive.org/.

Invisible Australians A series of digital projects that explore Australian governmental records about Indigenous Australians as well as Chinese, Japanese, Indian, Afghan, Syrian, and Malay individuals. It includes the Real Face of White Australia project, which explores image-based browsing of the collection. Free to use. http://invisibleaustralians.org/.

IPython A toolkit that enables you to use the Python programming language interactively. Free to use. https://ipython.org/.

JavaScript A scripted programming language for HTML and the web.

JavaScript Object Notation (JSON) data format A standard file format that uses human-readable text to transmit data.

Jekyll A tool written in the Ruby programming language to generate a static site for websites and project sites. Free to use. https://jekyllrb.com/.

Jupyter notebook A web-based computer program for creating, executing, and visualizing code. Free to use. https://www.jupyter.org.

Leaflet A JavaScript library for mapping that helps users build a mobile-friendly map. Free to use. Created by Vladimir Agafonkin and the Leaflet Programming Community. https://leafletjs.com/.

LGBTQ+ The abbreviation for lesbian, gay, bisexual, transgender, queer, and gender-nonconforming individuals.

Liberated Africans A digital project that uses the KORA platform developed by Michigan State University to provide access to primary source materials about the more than 250,000 people emancipated as part of the abolition of slavery. Free to use. Created by Henry P. Lovejoy and the Liberated Africans Project Team. https://liberatedafricans.org/.

link rot The process by which hyperlinks that point to other information on the internet become unavailable. When hyperlinks are unresolvable, they are also known as broken links.

Liverpool as a Trading Port An HTML- and PHP-based website that provides access to a database of information related to Liverpool residents between 1704 and 1860 as well as voyages from and to Liverpool between 1759 and 1809. Free to use. Created by Stephen D. Behrendt. http://www.liverpoolmaritime.org/.

Locating London's Past A digital project that provides users access to datasets and demographic data about London in the eighteenth century that is georeferenced to historical maps. Free to use. Directed by Matthew Davies, Tim Hitchcock, and Robert Shoemaker. https://www.locatinglondon.org/.

London Lives, 1690–1800 A digital project of 240,000 manuscript and printed pages from London archives as well as fifteen supporting datasets to research the role of plebeians in London. Free to use. Directed by Tim Hitchcock, Robert Shoemaker, Sharon Howard, and Jamie McLaughlin. https://www.londonlives.org/.

macro-history A historical method that explores long-term trends and patterns at the level of entire cultures or groups of people, usually globally.

Madison Historical A digital project built in Omeka and WordPress that provides a digital collection and encyclopedia of information about Madison County, Illinois. Free to use. Created by Steve Hansen, Jeff Manuel, Robert Paulett, and Jason Stacy. https://madison-historical.siue.edu/encyclopedia/.

MALLET A Java programming language–based package for analyzing, classifying, and visualizing language. Free to use. Created by Andrew Kachites McCallum. http://mallet.cs.umass.edu/.

Mapping Ararat—An Imaginary Jewish Homelands A digital project that uses augmented reality to illustrate Major Mordechai Noah's plans to transform Grant Island, New York, into a city for Jewish people. Free to use. Created by Melissa Shiff and Louis Kaplan. http://www.mappingararat.com/.

Mappingthenation.com A digital companion project to Susan Schulten's "Capturing the Past through Maps." Free to use. http://mappingthenation.com/index.php/viewer/index/2/2.

Mapping the Republic of Letters A complex network visualization project that graphs correspondence networks of Enlightenment thinkers. The project utilizes Palladio, Timechart, and Gephi software as its technical platform. Free to use. Created by Paula Findlen, Dan Edelstein, Nicole Coleman, and Humanities+ Design at CESTA, Stanford University. http://republicofletters.stanford.edu/.

markup Standardized notations used to annotate a plain-text document. Also used to refer to the annotation of digital assets generally.

metadata Information that is created to describe other data and that is associated with that data.

micro-history A method of historical research that focuses on discrete categories at the level of an individual, event, community, and so forth.

Mining the Dispatch A topic-modeling project hosted by the University of Richmond that analyzed the *Daily Dispatch* newspaper from November 1860 to April 1865. Free to use. https://dsl.richmond.edu/dispatch/.

mobile application Software designed to run on a mobile device, such as a phone, tablet, or watch.

Mukurtu A content management system that uses traditional knowledge labels and Indigenous ways of knowing to manage digitized or born-digital cultural heritage. Free to use on your own server. Created by Kimberly Christen and Craig Dietrich. https://mukurtu.org/.

multimodal The use of multiple forms of textual, visual, aural, or other modes of information to convey meaning.

named entity recognition A form of information extraction that seeks to identify and classify named entities mentioned in texts. This includes names of persons, places, organizations, and others.

Natural Language Toolkit Tools that include libraries and programs for processing written language texts that are created in the Python programming language. Free to use. https://stanfordnlp.github.io/CoreNLP/.

network A way of visually presenting and analyzing information as connected entities.

network analysis A method of analyzing and visualizing interconnected components using individual items and their relationships to one another. Often used to explore social media, correspondence flows, and other social relationships.

1911 Triangle Factory Fire project A web exhibit and archive that presents primary and secondary sources, including oral histories, photographs, and testimonies about the Triangle Waist Factory fire. Free to use. Created by Curtis Lyons, Patrizia Sione, Barbara Morley, and John Peters. http://trianglefire.ilr.cornell.edu/.

OCRopus A command-line interface tool that allows users to complete tasks associated with optical character recognition to transform images into machine-readable text. Free to use. https://github.com/tmbarchive/ocropy.

Old Bailey Proceedings Online A digital project focused on the digitization, transcription, markup and display of all surviving editions of the Proceedings of the Old Bailey from 1674 to 1913 and associated documents via a database. Free to use. Created by Tim Hitchcock, Robert Shoemaker, Clive Emsley, Sharon Howard, and Jamie McLaughlin. https://www.oldbaileyonline.org/.

Old Weather A project created by Zooniverse to have members of the public transcribe Arctic and other weather observations from United States log books from the mid-nineteenth century onward. Free to contribute. https://www.oldweather.org/.

Omeka An open-source content management system for publishing digital collections of cultural heritage materials on the web. Free to use. https://omeka.org/.

Open Archival Information System (OAIS) reference model A requirements model for an archive or repository to ensure the long-term preservation of digital information. http://www.oais.info/.

open educational resource A free, publicly available digital asset for the purposes of teaching. Usually used in the context of textbooks, document readers, or other pedagogical materials.

OpenRefine A Java-based program that enables users to clean and transform data into other formats. Free to use. https://openrefine.org/.

optical character recognition The process of converting images of handwritten or typed text into machine-readable text.

oral history A methodology for studying historical information gathered through sound recordings with individuals.

Oral History in the Digital Age A digital project at Michigan State University that provides information on oral history and digital oral history methods. Free to use. Created by Doug Boyd, Steve Cohen, Kurt Dewhurst, Brad Rakerd, and Dean Rehberger. http://ohda.matrix.msu.edu/.

ORBIS: The Stanford Geospatial Network Model of the Roman World A geospatial database and project that maps communication costs in the Roman empire in terms of both time and expense. The project includes interactive models and simulations of the Roman world. Free to use. Created by Elijah Meeks, Karl Grossner, Noemi Alvarez, and Ashley Ngu. http://orbis.stanford.edu/.

Palladio A tool for visualization. Free to use. https://hdlab.stanford.edu/palladio/.

Papers of the War Department Project A digital project that incorporates over 42,000 primary source documents of the US War Department between 1784 and 1800. The project includes contextual, pedagogical, and other relevant information about historical documentary editing. Free to use. Created by Ted Crackel; Roy Rosenzweig Center for History and New Media, George Mason University; Christopher Hamner; Jim Safley; Kim Nguyen; Megan Brett; and Jessica Dauterive. https://wardepartmentpapers.org/s/home/page/home.

Pelagios Network A network of researchers and organizations interested in working with geographic data in humanities contexts. The network provides tools for annotation, collaboration, pedagogy, and visualization. Free to join and contribute. https://pelagios.org/.

personal digital archiving A process of digitizing or gathering born-digital assets about one's own history.

Personal Histories A digital exhibit of the United States Holocaust Memorial Museum that provides access to oral histories, including video recordings of Holocaust survivors. Free to view and listen. https://www.ushmm.org/exhibition/personal-history/.

Photogrammar A visualization project that depicts all photographs taken between 1935 and 1945 by the United States Farm Security Administration and Office of War Information. Free to use. Created by Laura Wexler, Lauren Tilton, and Taylor Arnold. http://photogrammar.yale.edu/.

photogrammetry A computational process that records, measures, and interprets photographic images. Photogrammetry is commonly used to transform static photographs into two- and three-dimensional digital models.

platform A term used to refer to the operating system of the computer.

platform studies A field of study that explores the relationship between the hardware of a computer system and the software that operates the computer.

Play the Past A collaboratively authored and edited website that focuses on discussions of cultural heritage, games, and meaningful play. https://www.playthepast.org/.

podcast A series of audio or video files that are offered as episodes for download or streaming. Can be used both in the singular to refer to one episode and in the plural to refer to all episodes.

Policía Nacional de Guatemala / Guatemalan National Police Historical Archive A digital archive hosted by the University of Texas at Austin that replicates and extends the physical archive held at the Historic Archive of the National Police of Guatemala. Free to use. Created by the Archivo Histórico de la Policía Nacional and University of Texas at Austin. https://ahpn.lib.utexas.edu/.

Portal to Texas History A digital collection of over 1.5 million items hosted by the University of North Texas libraries that includes content from cultural heritage partners across the state of Texas. Free to use. Created by the University of North Texas Library. https://texashistory.unt.edu/.

probability analysis A branch of mathematics that analyzes how likely it is that an event or variable is going to occur. It is also used to consider the reliability of a variable.

Programming Historian The site provides open-source, peer-reviewed tutorials written for use by historians that are available in English, Spanish, and French. Free to use. Founded by William J. Turkel and Alan MacEachern. https://programminghistorian.org/.

Prospect A WordPress-based plug-in that enables you to curate and visualize data that was developed by the University of North Carolina at Chapel Hill. Free to use. https://wordpress.org/plugins/prospect/.

Python An open-source computer programming language that is commonly used to build digital tools. Free to use. https://www.python.org/.

QGIS A desktop-based geographic information system to view, edit, and analyze geospatial data. Free to use. https://qgis.org/en/site/.

qualitative data Information that can be observed or collected but not measured.

qualitative history A method of research that utilizes biography, case study, discourse, ethnography, and the like to explore history.

Quality Matters A framework for evaluating the design of educational, particularly online, course design. https://www.qualitymatters.org/.

Quantifying Kissinger A text analysis project that explores the National Security Archive's Kissinger Collection Memcons and Telcons. The complete title of this project is "'Everything on Paper Will Be Used against Me': Quantifying Kissinger | Text Analysis, Visualization and Historical Interpretation of the National Security Archive's Kissinger Correspondence." Free to use. Created by Micki Kaufman. https://blog.quantifyingkissinger.com/.

quantitative data Statistical, survey, or numerical information that can be recorded or measured.

quantitative history A method of history that uses statistical, survey, and numerical data to analyze history.

Queer Digital History Project A digital project to document pre-2010 LGBTQ digital spaces online. Free to use. Created by Avery Dame-Griff. http://queerdigital.com/.

R A computer programming language used for statistical programming that is commonly used for data analysis. Free to use. https://www.r-project.org/about.html.

Rainbow History Project A community-based project that collects, preserves, and promotes the history and culture of Washington, DC's LGBTQ+ community. Free to use. Created by the Rainbow History Project Foundation. https://archives.rainbowhistory.org/.

Ranke.2 A digital platform for teaching students digital source criticism; content is written in English, French, and German. Free to use. Created by the Luxembourg Centre for Contemporary and Digital History. https://ranke2.uni.lu/.

Real Face of White Australia A digital project, part of the Invisible Australians portfolio of scholarship, that uses a face-detection algorithm to construct a visual interface that then navigates the records of the National Archive of Australia Series ST84/1. Free to use. Created by Kate Bagnall and Tim Sherratt. http://invisibleaustralians.org/faces/.

Reclaim Hosting A commercial web-hosting service that has common digital history software available for installation. Paid. https://reclaimhosting.com/.

Recogito An annotation tool that allows users to identify and mark up texts and images. Free to use. Created by Pelagios Commons. https://recogito.pelagios.org/.

Recogito2 An annotation tool that allows users to identify and mark up texts and images. As of August 2021, the current version of the software is 3.3. Free to use. Created by Pelagios Commons. https://github.com/pelagios/recogito2.

regression analysis A statistical method for analyzing the relationship between two or more variables where at least one variable is dependent.

regular expression Strings of text that describe a pattern used to search within any given set of characters. Think "find and replace."

repository A centralized location for storing data. Usually used to refer to a digital collection or archive.

research data Data identified, created, analyzed, or published as part of the process of historical research.

research life cycle The stages of work completed as part of research processes. Historians generally focus on identifying, gathering, analyzing, visualizing/writing, and publishing.

RStudio A tools package that uses the programming language R for statistical analysis. Free to use. Developed by RStudio, PBC. https://rstudio.com/.

Scalar A digital publishing platform that allows users to create networked, nonlinear, multimedia-based narratives. Free to use. Developed by the Alliance for Networking Visual Culture. Founded by Tara McPherson, Wendy Chun, Brian Goldfarb, Nicholas Mirzoeff, and Joan Saab. https://scalar.usc.edu/.

Sci2 tool A modular set of digital tools that helps users to clean, analyze, and visualize temporal, geospatial, topical, and network-based data. Free to use. Developed by the Sci2 Team at the School of Science at Indiana University. https://sci2.cns.iu.edu/user/index.php.

Scripto An extension to the Omeka CMS that enables you to create crowdsourced transcription and other crowdsourcing activities. Free to use. Created by Christopher Hamner and Jim Safley. https://scripto.org/.

Segrada An open-source tool for graphing networks. Free to use. Created by Max Kalus. https://opensource.com/life/15/11/segrada-open-source-semantic-graph-database.

sentiment mapping A process of analysis that allows users to interpret and classify emotions within textual data that can then be visualized.

SketchUp A program that lets you develop three-dimensional models. Free or paid, depending on the level of use. Developed by Trimble Inc. https://www.sketchup.com/.

Slave Revolt in Jamaica, 1760–1761 A digital project that explores insurrection through an animated thematic map. Free to use. Created by Vincent Brown. http://revolt.axismaps.com/.

Snapchat A multimedia messaging application. Free to use. Developed by Snap Inc. https://www.snapchat.com.

Social Humans Labels A set of labels for social media creators to indicate how and if they wish their social media content to be used. Free to use. Created by Alexandra Dolan-Mescal. https://www.docnow.io/social-humans/.

software A set of instructions and data that tells the computer how to work.

sonification studies The use of digital tools and methods to analyze sound computationally.

SoundCloud A web-based audio distribution platform and sharing site. Free to use. Developed by SoundCloud. https://soundcloud.com/.

source criticism A process of analyzing a source to identify pertinent information.

SourceLab An initiative of the Department of History at the University of Illinois that trains students in source criticism and digital documentary edition work.

Available for partnership opportunities through a Call for Proposals. Created by John Randolph. https://sourcelab.history.illinois.edu/.

spatial history A method of historical analysis that emphasizes visualization and the movement of landscape to understand how and what space means as a historical process.

Stanford Named Entity Recognizer Java-based software that enables users to computationally label sequences of words in a text. Free to use. Created by the Stanford Natural Language Processing Group. https://nlp.stanford.edu/software/CRF-NER.html.

static visualization A visualization that is one-dimensional and includes no dynamic or interactive elements.

StoryMapJS A tool that lets users tell narrative stories about locations related to a series of events. Free to use. Created by Knight Lab, Joe Germuska, Rebecca Poulson, and Scott Bradley. https://storymap.knightlab.com.

structured data Data that is organized according to a data model that results in consistent structure.

"A Student Collaborators' Bill of Rights" A document that explicitly details issues of credit, citation, payment, working conditions, and so on to guide collaborations. Free to cite. Created by Haley Di Pressi, Stephanie Gorman, Miriam Posner, Raphael Sasayama, and Tori Schmitt for the Center for Digital Humanities—UCLA. https://humtech.ucla.edu/news/a-student-collaborators-bill-of-rights/.

Tableau Public A visualization tool that allows users to develop one hundred different visualizations via a drag-and-drop interface. Students and current instructors receive a free one-year use license. Free and paid, depending on capabilities. https://public.tableau.com/en-us/s/.

tabular data Data that follows a data model of rows and columns that result in a table.

TAPoR3 A digital collection of both text analysis tools and curated lists of tools for use in research. Free to use. Created by R. Geoffrey Rockwell, Stéfan Sinclair, and Milena Radzikowska. http://tapor.ca/home.

Tesseract An optical character recognition software in the C++ language that lets users transform images into machine-readable text via the command line. Free to use. Created by Hewlett-Packard Laboratories Bristol; Google, Inc.; and the Tesseract Open Source Community. https://github.com/tesseract-ocr/tesseract.

text analysis A process of extracting, classifying, and visualizing information from textual data through statistical analysis. Often also called "text mining."

text encoding The process of adding structural and descriptive elements of a text to a digital asset.

three-dimensional digitization The process of imaging an artifact to capture geometry, texture, and scale to form a three-dimensional model that can be used digitally or as the source file to create duplicates of physical objects.

three-dimensional visualization The process of rendering graphics and designs in three dimensions using software.

Tiki-Toki A web-based software for creating interactive timelines. Free to use. Created by Webalon LTD. https://www.tiki-toki.com/.

TimelineJS A tool for creating interactive timelines with a Google spreadsheet as its base. Free to use. Created by Knight Lab, Joe Germuska, Rebecca Poulson, and Scott Bradley. https://timeline.knightlab.com/.

tool A software program that lets a user accomplish a specific task or tasks.

topic modeling A form of textual analysis that allows users to computationally detect and organize words and phrase patterns within documents using statistical algorithms and natural language processing.

Traditional Knowledge Labels Information added to a digital asset to communicate access and use protocols for Indigenous cultural heritage. Free to use; registration required. https://localcontexts.org/.

Transcribe Bentham A digital project to transcribe previously unpublished manuscripts of Jeremy Bentham. Free to contribute. Created by University College London. Contributions by Philip Schofield, Melissa Terras, Tom Couch, and the Bentham Project. http://blogs.ucl.ac.uk/transcribe-bentham/.

transcription The process of recording information that appears within a digital asset as an associated text file.

Tropy A digital platform that allows you to organize and describe photographs taken of analog materials. Free to use. Created by Sylvester Keil and Roberto Martínez. https://tropy.org.

Trove A digital archive of Australian cultural heritage provided by the National Library of Australia. Free to use. Created by the National Library of Australia. https://trove.nla.gov.au/.

Trusted Repository Archiving Checklist (TRAC) A checklist used to verify and certify that digital repositories can preserve digital content for future use. https://www.crl.edu/archiving-preservation/digital-archives/metrics-assessing-and-certifying/trac.

Tumblr A microblogging and social network website. Free to use. Created by Tumblr. https://www.tumblr.com/.

Twine A tool for creating interactive text-based games in HTML. Free to use. Created by Chris Klimas. https://twinery.org/.

Twitter A microblogging and social network website. Free to use. Created by Jack Dorsey, Noah Glass, Biz Stone, and Evan Williams. https://twitter.com/.

uniform resource locator (URL) A string of characters that specifies a location on a computer network. Also referred to as a web address.

unstructured data Data that does not conform to a predetermined data model or structure.

The Valley of the Shadow A digital project that provides access to letters, diaries, newspapers, and other records of the US Civil War in Augusta County, Virginia, and in Franklin County, Pennsylvania. Free to use. Created by Edward L. Ayers, Anne Rubin, William G. Thomas III, and Andrew J. Torget. https://valley.lib.virginia.edu/.

Virtual Angkor A digital reconstruction of the Cambodian city of Angkor and its surroundings around 1300 built using the Unity software. Created by Tom Chandler, Adam Clulow, Bernard Keo, Mike Yeates, and Martin Polkinghorne. https://www.virtualangkor.com.

Virtual Paul's Cross A digital project that incorporates three-dimensional modeling of St. Paul's Cathedral and Churchyard in seventeenth-century London alongside audio files of John Donne's historic sermon. Free to use. Created by John N. Wall. https://vpcp.chass.ncsu.edu/.

virtual reality A simulation model of an experience that does not exist currently.

visualization A process of communicating information through visual imagery and display.

Voyant Tools A web-based application for text analysis. Free to use. Developed by Stéfan Sinclair and R. Geoffrey Rockwell. https://voyant-tools.org/.

VSim A tool for developing virtual reality simulations. Free to use. Developed by Lisa M. Snyder, Scott Friedman, David Stephan, and the VSim project team. https://idre.ucla.edu/research/active-research/vsim/.

Wakelet An online website that allows students to bookmark, save, and share any content from the internet. Free to use. Developed by Wakelet Limited. https://wakelet.com/.

Wayback Machine *See* **Internet Archive**.

website A set of content published on the internet with a specified domain name and server.

Who Built America? A textbook with accompanying CD-ROM that was published by Bedford/St. Martin's and the American Social History Project in 2000. Volume 1 was authored by Christopher Clark and Nancy Hewitt. Volume 2 was authored by Roy Rosenzweig and Nelson Lichtenstein. All print versions are currently out of print; the digital version is being updated as of August 2021. https://ashp.cuny.edu/who-built-america-textbook.

Wikipedia A free, online, collaboratively written encyclopedia. Free to use and contribute. Created by the Wikimedia Foundation. https://www.wikipedia.org/.

WordPress A content management system that uses a database to publish content to the web. Free to use. Developed by Matt Mullenweg and Mike Little. https://wordpress.com/.

YouTube A video-sharing website. Free to use. Developed by Steve Chen, Chad Hurley, and Jawed Karim. https://www.youtube.com/.

Zotero A reference management software for creating, managing, and sharing bibliographic information in standardized bibliographic formats. Free to use. Created by the Roy Rosenzweig Center for History and New Media, George Mason University. https://www.zotero.org/.

Notes

Introduction

1 Bernard Marr, "How Much Data Do We Create Every Day? The Mind-Blowing Stats Everyone Should Read," *Forbes*, accessed October 10, 2018, https://www.forbes.com/sites/bernardmarr/2018/05/21/how-much-data-do-we-create-every-day-the-mind-blowing-stats-everyone-should-read/.

2 Born-digital materials originate in digital form in contrast to digitized materials, which are reformatted from analog to digital form. Common born-digital materials include digital photographs, electronic records, and content created on the internet and via software platforms.

3 LIBER: Association of European Research Libraries, "European Commission's Recommendation on Digitisation and Digital Preservation," *LIBER* (blog), accessed October 14, 2018, https://libereurope.eu/european-commission-s-recommendation-on-digitisation-and-digital-preservation/; National Archives and Records Administration, "Digitization at the National Archives," June 26, 2017, https://www.archives.gov/digitization; Commonwealth of Australia, "Digital Transformation Agenda," accessed October 14, 2018, https://www.dta.gov.au/what-we-do/transformation-agenda/.

4 Adam Crymble, *Technology and the Historian: Transformations in the Digital Age*, Topics in the Digital Humanities (Urbana: University of Illinois Press, 2021); Jennifer Hart, "Introduction: Digital History in African Studies," *History in Africa* 47 (2020): 269–74; Hannu Salmi, *What Is Digital History?* (Cambridge: Polity Books, 2020).

5 Play the Past, accessed June 12, 2020, https://www.playthepast.org/.

6 Petri Paju, Mila Oiva, and Mats Fridlund, "Digital and Distant Histories: Emergent Approaches within the New Digital History," in *Digital Histories: Emergent Approaches within the New Digital History*, ed. Mats Fridlund, Mila

Oiva, and Petri Paju (Helsinki: Helsinki University Press, 2020), 3–4, https://doi.org/10.2307/j.ctv1c9hpt8.6.

7 Salmi, *What Is Digital History?*, 7.

8 Jo Guldi, "The Common Landscape of Digital History: Universal Methods, Global Borderlands, Longue-Durée History, and Critical Thinking about Approaches and Institutions," in *Digital Histories: Emergent Approaches within the New Digital History*, ed. Mats Fridlund, Mila Oiva, and Petri Paju (Helsinki: Helsinki University Press, 2020), 328, https://doi.org/10.2307/j.ctv1c9hpt8.23.

9 Guldi, "Common Landscape of Digital History," 331.

10 Sheila A. Brennan, "Digital History," *The Inclusive Historian's Handbook*, June 4, 2019, https://inclusivehistorian.com/digital-history/. For an alternative framing of digital history, see Crymble, *Technology and the Historian*.

11 Margo Anderson, "Quantitative History," in *The Sage Handbook of Social Science Methodology*, ed. William Outhwaite and Stephen P. Turner (London: SAGE, 2007), 248–64, doi: 10.4135/9781848607958.n14.

12 Robert W. Fogel and Stanley L. Engerman, *Time on the Cross: The Economics of American Negro Slavery* (Boston: Little, Brown, 1974).

13 Fogel and Engerman, *Time on the Cross*.

14 Sharon Leon, "Returning Women to the History of Digital History," accessed June 1, 2016, http://www.6floors.org/bracket/2016/03/07/returning-women-to-the-history-of-digital-history/.

15 Lisa Nakamura and Peter Chow-White, *Race after the Internet* (New York: Routledge, 2013); Radhika Gajjala, *Cyberculture and the Subaltern: Weavings of the Virtual and Real* (Lanham, MD: Rowman and Littlefield, 2013); Ruha Benjamin, "Assessing Risk, Automating Racism," *Science* 366, no. 6464 (2019): 421–22.

16 Wendy Hui Kyong Chun, "Race and/as Technology, or How to Do Things to Race," in Nakamura and Chow-White, *Race after the Internet*, 38–60; Natalia Rybas and Radhika Gajjala, "Developing Cyberethnographic Research Methods for Understanding Digitally Mediated Identities," *Forum Qualitative Sozialforschung / Forum: Qualitative Social Research* 8, no. 3 (2007), https://www.qualitative-research.net/index.php/fqs/article/view/282; Marisa Elena Duarte, *Network Sovereignty: Building the Internet across Indian Country* (Seattle: University of Washington Press, 2017); Miriyam Aouragh and Paula Chakravartty, "Infrastructures of Empire: Towards a Critical Geopolitics of Media and Information Studies," *Media, Culture and Society* 38, no. 4 (2016): 559–75.

17 Hart, "Introduction," 269.

18 Hart, "Introduction," 271.

19 Safiya Umoja Noble, *Algorithms of Oppression: How Search Engines Reinforce Racism* (New York: New York University Press, 2018).

20 Jill E. Kelly and Omar Badsha, "Teaching South African History in the Digital Age: Collaboration, Pedagogy, and Popularizing History," *History in Africa* 47 (June 2020): 297–325, https://doi.org/10.1017/hia.2020.6.

21 Linda Tuhiwai Smith, *Decolonizing Methodologies: Research and Indigenous Peoples* (London: Zed, 2013).

One. Sources as Data

1 Jennifer Guiliano and Carolyn Heitman, "Difficult Heritage and the Complexities of Indigenous Data," *Journal of Cultural Analytics* 4, no. 1 (August 13, 2019), https://doi.org/10.22148/16.044. Portions of this paragraph are drawn from this article.

2 Miriam Posner, "Humanities Data: A Necessary Contradiction," accessed June 7, 2020, http://miriamposner.com/blog/humanities-data-a-necessary-contradiction/.

3 Jill Walker Rettberg, "Situated Data Analysis: A New Method for Analysing Encoded Power Relationships in Social Media Platforms and Apps," *Humanities and Social Sciences Communications* 7, no. 1 (June 17, 2020): 1–13, https://doi.org/10.1057/s41599-020-0495-3; Roopika Risam, "'It's Data, Not Reality': On Situated Data with Jill Walker Rettberg," *Medium* (blog), June 29, 2020, https://medium.com/nightingale/its-data-not-reality-on-situated-data-with-jill-walker-rettberg-d27c71b0b451.

4 Risam, "'It's Data, Not Reality.'"

5 Jay Burns, "Beyond 'Founded by Abolitionists': Students and Faculty Undertake a More Inclusive Examination of Bates' Founding Story," Bates, February 6, 2020, https://www.bates.edu/news/2020/02/26/going-beyond-founded-by-abolitionists-students-and-faculty-undertake-a-more-inclusive-examination-of-bates-founding-story/.

6 Katherine McKittrick, "Mathematics Black Life," *Black Scholar* 44, no. 2 (2014): 16–28.

7 Lindsey Passenger Wieck, "Tutorial—Gathering and Curating Data," 2016, http://lindseywieck.com/fall_2016_sf/gatheringdatatutorial.html.

8 Seth van Hooland, Ruben Verborgh, and Max De Wilde, "Cleaning Data with OpenRefine," *Programming Historian*, August 5, 2013, http://programminghistorian.org/lessons/cleaning-data-with-openrefine.html; Thomas Padilla, "Getting Started with OpenRefine," accessed June 30, 2015, http://thomaspadilla.org/dataprep/.

9 Julia Flanders and Trevor Muñoz, "An Introduction to Humanities Data Curation," in *Digital Humanities Data Curation*, accessed February 15, 2015, http://guide.dhcuration.org/intro/.

10 Daniel van Strien, "An Introduction to Version Control Using GitHub Desktop," *Programming Historian*, June 17, 2016, https://programminghistorian.org/en/lessons/getting-started-with-github-desktop.

11 Benjamin Schmidt, "Sapping Attention: Reading Digital Sources: A Case Study in Ship's Logs," *Sapping Attention* (blog), November 15, 2012, http://sappingattention.blogspot.com/2012/11/reading-digital-sources-case-study-in.html.

12 Catherine D'Ignazio and Lauren F. Klein, *Data Feminism* (Cambridge, MA: MIT Press, 2020).

13 D'Ignazio and Klein, *Data Feminism*, 8.

14 Katie Rawson and Trevor Muñoz, "Against Cleaning," *Curating Menus* (blog), July 6, 2016, http://www.curatingmenus.org/articles/against-cleaning/.

15 Ellen Gruber Garvey, "'facts and FACTS': Abolitionists' Database Innovations," in *"Raw Data" Is an Oxymoron*, ed. Lisa Gitelman (Cambridge, MA: MIT Press, 2013), 89–102.

16 Documenting the American South, "North American Slave Narratives," accessed November 23, 2020, https://docsouth.unc.edu/neh/.

17 Mimi Onuoha, "On Missing Data Sets," 2019, https://github.com/MimiOnuoha/missing-datasets.

18 Mimi Onuoha, "On Missing Data Sets."

19 D'Ignazio and Klein, *Data Feminism*, 72.

Two. Learning Outcomes

1 David R. Krathwohl and Lorin W. Anderson, eds., *A Taxonomy for Learning, Teaching, and Assessing: A Revision of Bloom's Taxonomy of Educational Objectives* (London: Longman, 2009); Iowa State University, "Revised Bloom's Taxonomy," Iowa State University Center for Excellence in Learning and Teaching, accessed October 14, 2018, http://www.celt.iastate.edu/teaching/effective-teaching-practices/revised-blooms-taxonomy/.

2 Seyyed Mohammad Ali Soozandehfar and Mohammad Reza Adeli, "A Critical Appraisal of Bloom's Taxonomy," *American Research Journal of English and Literature* 2 (2016), https://www.arjonline.org/papers/arjel/v2-i1/14.pdf.

3 Anelise H. Shrout, "Data Cultures," accessed June 23, 2020, https://docs.google.com/document/d/1DSB20K-GTPMcQkqoPG5d8JZYyOMU51vrbiUmxqI15PA/edit.

4 Danielle Picard and Derek Bruff, "Digital Timelines," Vanderbilt University Center for Teaching and Learning, April 20, 2016, https://wpo.vanderbilt.edu/cft/guides-sub-pages/digital-timelines/.

5 Picard and Bruff, "Digital Timelines."

6 Brandon T. Locke, "Digital Humanities Pedagogy as Essential Liberal Education: A Framework for Curriculum Development," *Digital Humanities Quarterly* 11, no. 3 (October 2, 2017), http://www.digitalhumanities.org/dhq/vol/11/3/000303/000303.html.

7 Leah Potter, "Creating Digital History," Fall 2017, https://s18798.pcdn.co/archivesandpublichistory/wp-content/uploads/sites/5465/2018/06/Fall-17-Creating-DH-Potter.pdf.

8 Jeffrey McClurken, "Digital History Reviews," accessed July 12, 2019, http://jah.oah.org/submit/digital-history-reviews/.

9 Robert Stephens and Josh Thumma, "Faculty-Undergraduate Collaboration in Digital History at a Public Research University," *History Teacher* 38, no. 4 (2005): 525–42, https://doi.org/10.2307/30036719.

10 Stephens and Thumma, "Faculty-Undergraduate Collaboration in Digital History at a Public Research University," 529–30.

11 Tom Scheinfeldt, "Stuff Digital Humanists Like: Defining Digital Humanities by Its Values," *Found History* (blog), December 2, 2010, http://foundhistory.org/2010/12/stuff-digital-humanists-like/; *Digital Humanities Manifesto 2.0*, http://manifesto.humanities.ucla.edu/; Marin Dacos, "Manifesto for the Digital Humanities," *THATCamp Paris* (blog), accessed September 5, 2018, https://tcp.hypotheses.org/411; Lisa Spiro, "'This Is Why We Fight': Defining the Values of the Digital Humanities," in *Debates in the Digital Humanities*, ed. Matthew K. Gold (Minneapolis: University of Minnesota Press, 2012), 16–36, http://dhdebates.gc.cuny.edu/debates/text/13.

12 Lincoln A. Mullen, *Computational Historical Thinking*, accessed April 4, 2018, http://dh-r.lincolnmullen.com/.

13 Simon Appleford, personal email to author, August 2018.

14 Columbia University, "The Open Syllabus Project," July 8, 2019, https://blog.opensyllabus.org/about-the-open-syllabus-project/; Lisa Spiro and Members of the Digital Humanities Education Group, "Digital Humanities Education," accessed June 15, 2020, https://www.zotero.org/groups/25016/digital_humanities_education?; City University of New York Academic Commons, "DH Syllabi—CUNY Academic Commons Wiki Archive," accessed June 15, 2020, https://wiki.commons.gc.cuny.edu/dh_syllabi/.

Three. New Forms of Assignments

1 Emily Suzanne Clark, "The Unessay," August 1, 2016, https://emilysuzanneclark.wordpress.com/2016/08/01/the-unessay/.

2 Ryan Cordell, "How Not to Teach Digital Humanities," accessed June 13, 2020, https://ryancordell.org/teaching/how-not-to-teach-digital-humanities/.

3 Daniel O'Donnell, "The Unessay," accessed October 16, 2014, http://people.uleth.ca/~daniel.odonnell/Teaching/the-unessay.

4 Cate Denial, "The Unessay," accessed June 13, 2020, https://catherinedenial.org/blog/uncategorized/the-unessay/.

5 Denial, "The Unessay."

6 Lucinda Matthews-Jones, "Assessing Creatively, or Why I've Embraced the #unessay," September 11, 2019, https://lucindamatthewsjones.com/2019/09/11/assessing-creatively-or-why-ive-embraced-the-unessay/.

7 TimelineJS, accessed June 25, 2020, https://timeline.knightlab.com/; SIMILE Widgets, accessed June 9, 2011, http://www.simile-widgets.org/.

8 Google Maps, accessed May 10, 2020, http://www.google.com/maps/; ArcGIS, accessed May 7, 2020, http://www.esri.com/software/arcgis.

9 R Foundation, "R: What Is R?," accessed July 6, 2020, https://www.r-project.org/.

10 Mukurtu CMS, accessed June 1, 2019, https://mukurtu.org/; Clio, accessed July 6, 2020, https://theclio.com.

11 Trevor Owens, "2019 (Spring) Digital History Methods AMU—Digital History Methods," accessed May 16, 2019, http://www.dighist.org/syllabi/syllabus-2019-amu-digital-history/.

12 Erin Bush, "Schedule," *Spring 2018—The Digital Past* (blog), accessed June 12, 2019, http://teaching.erinbush.org/s18h390/schedule/.

13 The Triangle Factory Fire, accessed January 25, 2011, http://trianglefire.ilr.cornell.edu/; Homicide in Chicago 1870–1930, accessed June 12, 2019, http://homicide.northwestern.edu/.

14 StoryMapJS, accessed June 25, 2020, https://storymap.knightlab.com.

15 Wakelet, accessed July 6, 2020, https://wakelet.com/.

16 Rebecca Wingo, "Cincinnati's West End," accessed September 16, 2019, https://rebeccawingo.com/courses/hist2098/.

17 Century America, accessed January 12, 2019, http://course.centuryamerica.org/.

18 Haley Di Pressi et al., "A Student Collaborators' Bill of Rights," Center for Digital Humanities, University of California, Los Angeles, June 8, 2015, https://humtech.ucla.edu/news/a-student-collaborators-bill-of-rights/.

19 Here is an example of the note included in my syllabus: "It is important to recognize that you have your own technical skills, abilities, and experiences with platforms. As your first assignment in this course, write the instructor a brief email outlining what technical skills and abilities you may have. Be clear about which skills you are fully proficient in versus things you may just be familiar with. This may include, but is not limited to, the following: HTML, CSS, PHP, Java, SQL/MySQL, Twitter, Facebook, Instagram, SnapChat, WordPress, Drupal, Adobe Suite (Photoshop, Illustrator, Indesign, etc.), Sketchup or other 3D rendering software, Audio Editing Software, Video Editing Software, Graphic Design, Multimedia Design, OpenRefine, Gephi, NodeXL, R, MALLET, etc."

Four. The Basics of Digital Methods

1 Oral History in the Digital Age, accessed June 20, 2020, http://ohda.matrix.msu.edu/.

2 ProgHist Limited, *Programming Historian*, accessed February 2, 2020, https://programminghistorian.org/.

3 Adam Crymble, "Introduction to Gravity Models of Migration and Trade," *Programming Historian*, March 18, 2019, https://programminghistorian.org/en/lessons/gravity-model.

4 Crymble, "Introduction to Gravity Models of Migration and Trade."

5 IPython Project and Jupyter Community, *Project Jupyter*, accessed July 6, 2020, https://www.jupyter.org.

6 Shawn Graham, "Crafting Digital History," accessed August 11, 2019, http://workbook.craftingdigitalhistory.ca/. This site was updated in June 2020 to https://craftingdh.netlify.app.

7 DH Box, accessed October 12, 2019, http://dhbox.org/.

8 Shawn Graham, "Capstone Exercise," in "Course Manual for Crafting Digital History HIST38140|DIGH38140 @ Carleton U Summer 2019," accessed October 12, 2019, https://site.craftingdigitalhistory.ca/capstone-exercise-1.html.

9 Taylor Arnold, "Statsmaths/Hilt2019-Image-Analysis," Jupyter notebook, 2019, https://github.com/statsmaths/hilt2019-image-analysis.

10 Taylor Arnold and Lauren Tilton, Distant Viewing Toolkit (DVT), version 0.3.1, Python, accessed August 12, 2019, https://distant-viewing.github.io/dvt/index.html.

11 Digital Mappa, version 2.0, accessed October 12, 2019, https://www.digitalmappa.org.

12 Arguing with Digital History Working Group, "Digital History and Argument," white paper (Roy Rosenzweig Center for History and New Media, November 13, 2017), https://rrchnm.org/argument-white-paper/.

Five. Digital Source Criticism

1 Roopika Risam, "Decolonizing the Digital Humanities in Theory and Practice," May 2018, https://digitalcommons.salemstate.edu/cgi/viewcontent.cgi?article=1006&context=english_facpub.

2 Risam, "Decolonizing the Digital Humanities."

3 British Library, accessed January 15, 2015, https://www.bl.uk/; Bibliothèque Nationale de France, accessed September 4, 2016, http://www.bnf.fr/en/tools/a.welcome_to_the_bnf.html; National Library of Australia, Trove, accessed September 4, 2017, https://trove.nla.gov.au/; National Archives of India, accessed March 4, 2018, http://nationalarchives.nic.in/.

4 Digital Public Library of America (DPLA), accessed September 4, 2014, https://dp.la/.

5 Smithsonian Institution Learning Lab, accessed July 6, 2020, https://learninglab.si.edu/.

6 Tropy, accessed June 6, 2019, https://tropy.org.

7 Luxembourg Centre for Contemporary and Digital History, "A Series of Lessons on Digital Source Criticism," accessed October 1, 2019, https://ranke2.uni.lu/.

8 Luxembourg Centre for Contemporary and Digital History, "Why Digital Source Criticism? About the Platform," accessed October 1, 2019, https://ranke2.uni.lu/about-platform/.

9 Trevor Owens, "Digital Sources and Digital Archives: The Evidentiary Basis of Digital History (Draft)," December 5, 2015, http://www.trevorowens.org/2015/12/digital-sources-digital-archives-the-evidentiary-basis-of-digital-history-draft/.

10 Internet Archive, accessed September 6, 2010, https://archive.org/web/. The "Wayback Machine" is another name for the Internet Archive site.

11 Hypothes.is, accessed October 1, 2019, https://web.hypothes.is/.

12 SourceLab, accessed June 3, 2019, https://sourcelab.history.illinois.edu/. John Randolph and the SourceLab team are in the process of publishing their workflows and guides.

13 Antonis Hadjikyriacou, "Using Recogito in the (Ottoman History) Classroom," *Europeana Pro*, no. 12 (March 2019), https://pro.europeana.eu/page/issue-12-pelagios. For Recogito, see Pelagios Commons, Recogito2, Scala (2016; repr., Pelagios Project, 2019), https://github.com/pelagios/recogito2.

Six. Text and Network Analysis

1 See Kirsten Bussière, "Chapter 4—Text Analysis," in *Digital Humanities—A Primer*, 2018, https://carletonu.pressbooks.pub/digh5000/chapter/chapter-4-text-analysis/, for an excellent overview of text analysis that would be appropriate for students to use in the classroom.

2 Voyant Tools, accessed November 4, 2019, http://voyant-tools.org.

3 Digital Scholarship Commons, Robert W. Woodruff Library, Emory Libraries, "Text Mining with Voyant," *Lincoln Logarithms: Finding Meaning in Sermons* (blog), February 21, 2013, http://lincolnlogs.digitalscholarship.emory.edu/voyant/.

4 Micki Kaufman, "Everything on Paper Will Be Used against Me": Quantifying Kissinger | Text Analysis, Visualization and Historical Interpretation of the National Security Archive's Kissinger Correspondence, accessed January 12, 2019, https://blog.quantifyingkissinger.com/.

5 Tesseract-OCR/Tesseract, C++ (2014; repr., tesseract-ocr, 2020), https://github.com/tesseract-ocr/tesseract; Tmbarchive/OCRopy, Jupyter notebook, 2020, https://github.com/tmbarchive/ocropy; ABBYY FineReader Online, accessed June 25, 2020, https://finereaderonline.com/en-us.

6 Robert Nelson, Mining the *Dispatch*, accessed September 7, 2011, http://dsl.richmond.edu/dispatch/pages/intro.

7 Nelson, Mining the *Dispatch*.

8 Nelson, Mining the *Dispatch*.

9 Portions of this paragraph are drawn from my previous work.

10 Rebecca Sutton Koeser, "Trusting Others to 'Do the Math,'" *Interdisciplinary Science Reviews* 40, no. 4 (October 2, 2015): 376–92, https://doi.org/10.1080/03080188.2016.1165454.

11 Koeser, "Trusting Others to 'Do the Math,'" 377.

12 Benjamin M. Schmidt, "Words Alone: Dismantling Topic Models in the Humanities," *Journal of Digital Humanities* 2, no. 1 (Winter 2012), http://journalofdigitalhumanities.org/2-1/words-alone-by-benjamin-m-schmidt/.

13 University of Massachusetts Amherst, "MALLET Homepage," Machine Learning for Language Toolkit, accessed September 7, 2011, http://mallet.cs.umass.edu/; Shawn Graham, Scott Weingart, and Ian Milligan, "Getting Started with Topic Modeling and MALLET," *Programming Historian 2*, September 2, 2012; updated September 3, 2021, http://programminghistorian.org/lessons/topic-modeling-and-mallet.

14 Sharon Leon, "The Digital Past Syllabus," Fall 2016, http://www.6floors.org/teaching/.

15 The Stanford Natural Language Processing Group, accessed June 25, 2020, https://nlp.stanford.edu/software/CRF-NER.html.

16 Caleb McDaniel et al., "Digital History Methods," syllabus, accessed August 20, 2018, http://ricedh.github.io/#our-data.

17 Ian Milligan, "Network Analysis Fundamentals" and "Networks Analysis," in Shawn Graham, Ian Milligan, and Scott Weingart, *Exploring Big Historical Data: The Historian's Macroscope*, 2016, http://web.archive.org/web/20200618171130/http://www.themacroscope.org/?page_id=584.

18 Center for History and Economics at Harvard University, "Visualizing Historical Networks," accessed October 16, 2019, https://histecon.fas.harvard.edu/visualizing/index.html.

19 Scott Weingart, "Demystifying Networks," *Scottbot Irregular* (blog), December 14, 2011, http://www.scottbot.net/HIAL/?p=6279; Sci2 tool, https://sci2.cns.iu.edu/user/index.php..

20 Segrada, accessed July 16, 2019, https://opensource.com/life/15/11/segrada-open-source-semantic-graph-database; Palladio, accessed March 16, 2015, http://palladio.designhumanities.org/.

21 Shin-Kap Han, "The Other Ride of Paul Revere: The Brokerage Role in the Making of the American Revolution," *Mobilization: An International Quarterly* 14, no. 2 (2009): 143–62, http://www.sscnet.ucla.edu/polisci/faculty/chwe/ps269/han.pdf; Mapping the Republic of Letters, 2013, http://republicofletters.stanford.edu/index.html; Caroline Winterer, "Where Is America in the Republic of Letters?," *Modern Intellectual History* 9, no. 3 (November 2012): 597–623, https://doi.org/10.1017/S1479244312000212.

22 Jason A. Heppler, "Directed Readings in Digital History (Spring 2018)," accessed August 17, 2021, https://jasonheppler.org/courses/unodh.2018/.

23 "MEAD: The Magazine of Early American Datasets," PennLibraries, University of Pennsylvania," accessed January 29, 2022, https://repository.upenn.edu/mead/.

24 Jean-Paul Rehr, "Re-mapping the 'Great Inquisition' of 1245–46: The Case of Mas-Saintes-Puelles and Saint-Martin-Lalande," *Open Library of Humanities* 5, no. 1 (April 16, 2019): 28, https://doi.org/10.16995/olh.414.

25 Rehr, "Re-mapping the 'Great Inquisition' of 1245–46," 22.

Seven. Visualization

1 Photogrammar, 2011, http://photogrammar.yale.edu/.

2 Jeffrey Heer, Michael Bostock, and Vadim Ogievetsky, "A Tour through the Visualization Zoo," accessed June 27, 2020, https://homes.cs.washington.edu/~jheer//files/zoo/.

3 Shawn Graham, Ian Milligan, and Scott Weingart, *Exploring Big Historical Data: The Historian's Macroscope*, accessed July 6, 2020, http://www.themacroscope.org/2.0/.

4 Michael Sandberg, "DataViz as History: When Napoleon Ventured East—Revisiting Minard's Map," *Michael Sandberg's Data Visualization Blog*, December 27, 2017, https://datavizblog.com/2017/12/27/dataviz-as-history-when-napoleon-ventured-east/.

5 Betsy Mason, "The Underappreciated Man behind the 'Best Graphic Ever Produced,'" *National Geographic*, March 16, 2017, https://www.nationalgeographic.com/culture/article/charles-minard-cartography-infographics-history.

6 Edward R. Tufte, *The Visual Display of Quantitative Information* (Cheshire, CT: Graphics Press, 1983).

7 John Theibault, "Visualizations and Historical Arguments," in *Writing History in the Digital Age*, ed. Kristen Nawrotzki and Jack Dougherty, Digital Humanities (University of Michigan Press, 2013), 173–85, https://quod.lib.umich.edu/d/dh/12230987.0001.001/1:8/—writing-history-in-the-digital-age?g=dculture;rgn=div1;view=fulltext;xc=1.

8 Jack Fleisher, Jae Ha, and Joey Hammel, "Guest Post: Tuberculosis in California: A Statistical Analysis from 1880–1910," *Medical Heritage Library* (blog), accessed October 4, 2019, http://www.medicalheritage.org/2017/03/24/guest-post-tuberculosis-in-california-a-statistical-analysis-from-1880–1910/.

9 Fleisher, Ha, and Hammel, "Guest Post."

10 TAPoR3, accessed October 14, 2019, http://tapor.ca/home.

11 Sarah J. Purcell, "Visualizing Data (Excel PivotTables and Tableau)—Fall 2019: Digital History at Grinnell College," accessed June 28, 2020, https://his100.sarahjpurcell.sites.grinnell.edu/fall-2019/tutorials/data-analysis-and-visualization/visualizing-data/.

12 Arguing with Digital History Working Group, "Digital History and Argument," white paper (Roy Rosenzweig Center for History and New Media, November 13, 2017), https://rrchnm.org/argument-white-paper/.

13 Edward Ayers, "Turning toward Place, Space, and Time," in *The Spatial Humanities: GIS and the Future of the Humanities Scholarship*, ed. David J. Bodenhamer, John Corrigan, and Trevor M. Harris (Bloomington: Indiana University Press, 2010), 1–13, https://scholarship.richmond.edu/history-faculty-publications/98.

14 Nick Bartel, "The Travels of Ibn Battuta," accessed October 7, 2019, https://orias.berkeley.edu/resources-teachers/travels-ibn-battuta.

15 Susan Schulten, "Capturing the Past through Maps," in *Mapping the Nation: History and Cartography in Nineteenth-Century America* (Chicago: University of Chicago Press, 2012), 41–76.

16 Mapping the Nation, accessed June 28, 2020, http://mappingthenation.com/index.php/viewer/index/2/2.

17 Slave Revolt in Jamaica, 1760–1761, accessed June 28, 2020, http://revolt.axismaps.com/.

18 Leaflet, accessed June 28, 2020, https://leafletjs.com/.

19 An excellent tutorial on Leaflet is available from Shawn Graham: "Getting Started with Leaflet," accessed August 20, 2021, https://workbook.craftingdigitalhistory.ca/supporting%20materials/leaflet.txt/.

20 Lara Putnam, "The Transnational and the Text-Searchable: Digitized Sources and the Shadows They Cast," *American Historical Review* 121, no. 2 (April 1, 2016): 377–402, https://doi.org/10.1093/ahr/121.2.377.

21 Jessica Marie Johnson, "Diaspora," in *Digital Pedagogy in the Humanities: Concepts, Models, and Experiments* (MLA Commons, 2016), https://digitalpedagogy.mla.hcommons.org/keywords/diaspora/.

22 Vincent Brown, "Project," Slave Revolt in Jamaica, 1760–1761, accessed June 28, 2020, http://revolt.axismaps.com/project.html.

23 Hadjikyriacou, "Using Recogito."

24 Europeana Network Association, Europeana Pro, accessed June 28, 2020, https://pro.europeana.eu/network-association/sign-up.

25 Tyechia Lynn Thompson, "Baldwin's Paris," accessed October 14, 2018, https://www.google.com/maps/d/viewer?mid=1RZRF9kyQy9woabmAeQIYECnLuaI.

26 GLT Global ED, "Google Lit Trips," accessed June 4, 2019, http://www.googlelittrips.org/.

27 Victoria Szabo, "Knowledge in 3D: How 3D Data Visualization Is Reshaping Our World," *Items* (blog), accessed June 28, 2020, https://items.ssrc.org/parameters/knowledge-in-3d-how-3d-data-visualization-is-reshaping-our-world/.

28 Digital Karnak, 2008, http://vsim.library.ucla.edu/xmlui/handle/20.500.11991/1012.

29 Virtual Angkor, accessed November 18, 2018, https://www.virtualangkor.com.

30 Colin Rose, "HIST2P26: Intro to Digital History," accessed September 17, 2019, https://colinrose.ca/teaching/hist2p26/.

31 John Bonnett, "Following in Rabelais' Footsteps: Immersive History and the *3D Virtual Buildings Project*," *History and Computing* 13, no. 2 (June 2001): 107–50, https://doi.org/10.3366/hac.2001.13.2.107; Caterina Balletti and Francesco Guerra, "Historical Maps for 3D Digital City's History," *Cartographica: The International Journal for Geographic Information and Geovisualization* 51, no. 3 (September 15, 2016): 115–26, https://doi.org/10.3138/cart.51.3.3140.

32 W3C Web Accessibility Initiative (WAI), "Home," accessed July 6, 2020, https://www.w3.org/WAI/; WebAIM at Utah State University, WAVE Web Accessibility Evaluation Tool, accessed July 6, 2020, https://wave.webaim.org/.

Eight. Digital Archives, Digital Exhibits, and Digital Collections

1 Sarah Benharrech, Valerie K. Orlando, and Kelsey Corlett-Rivera, "Revealing la Révolution," accessed September 5, 2018, https://www.lib.umd.edu/special/guides/frenchpamphlets; Kelsey Corlett-Rivera, Nathan H. Dize, and Abby Broughton, "A Colony in Crisis: The Saint-Domingue Grain Shortage of 1789," accessed September 5, 2018, https://colonyincrisis.lib.umd.edu/.

2 National Archives UK, "What Would the World Look Like without Archives?," YouTube, November 14, 2013, https://www.youtube.com/watch?v=Rbs5UnzDQdY; National Archives UK, "What Discoveries Have You Made in the Archives?," YouTube, November 14, 2013, https://www.youtube.com/watch?v=h92aWHUsVrk.

3 Library of Congress, "Personal Digital Archiving," accessed October 3, 2019, http://digitalpreservation.gov/personalarchiving/index.html.

4 University of Nebraska–Lincoln, "The History Harvest Community | Community and Pedagogy," accessed June 27, 2020, http://historyharvest.net/.

5 Saya, "First History Harvest: Teachers Share Their Prized Artifacts," *The International*, The International School of Sacred Heart, January 2014.

6 Terry Cook, "The Archive(s) Is a Foreign Country: Historians, Archivists, and the Changing Archival Landscape," *American Archivist* 74, no. 2 (2011): 600–632.

7 Cook, "The Archive(s) Is a Foreign Country," 600.

8 Trevor Owens, "What Do You Mean by Archive? Genres of Usage for Digital Preservers," February 27, 2014, //blogs.loc.gov/thesignal/2014/02/what-do-you-mean-by-archive-genres-of-usage-for-digital-preservers/; Kate Theimer, "A Distinction Worth Exploring: 'Archives' and 'Digital Historical Representations,'" *Journal of Digital Humanities* 3, no. 2 (August 4, 2014), http://journalofdigitalhumanities.org/3-2/a-distinction-worth-exploring-archives-and-digital-historical-representations/.

9 Kate Theimer, "Archives in Context and as Context," *Journal of Digital Humanities* 1, no. 2 (June 26, 2012), http://journalofdigitalhumanities.org/1-2/archives-in-context-and-as-context-by-kate-theimer/.

10 Brian Lavoie, "Meeting the Challenges of Digital Preservation: The OAIS Reference Model," *OCLC Newsletter*, January/February 2000, https://www.oclc.org/research/publications/2000/lavoie-oais.html; Center for Research

Library, "TRAC Metrics," accessed October 10, 2019, https://www.crl.edu/archiving-preservation/digital-archives/metrics-assessing-and-certifying/trac.

11 The Real Face of White Australia, 2011, http://discontents.com.au/the-real-face-of-white-australia/.

12 Migration Heritage Center at the Powerhouse Museum, "Australia's Migration History," accessed July 12, 2019, http://www.migrationheritage.nsw.gov.au/belongings-home/about-belongings/australias-migration-history/index.html.

13 Michelle Moravec, "How Digitized* Changed Historical Research," *Medium* (blog), January 24, 2017, https://medium.com/on-archivy/how-digitized-changed-historical-research-d77c78540878.

14 Mar Hicks, "Hacking the Cis-Tem," *IEEE Annals of the History of Computing* 41, no. 1 (January 2019): 20–33, https://doi.org/10.1109/MAHC.2019.2897667.

15 Tim Sherratt, "It's All about the Stuff: Collections, Interfaces, Power, and People," *Journal of Digital Humanities*, March 9, 2012, http://journalofdigitalhumanities.org/1-1/its-all-about-the-stuff-by-tim-sherratt/.

16 Michael J. Kramer, "Syllabus: Approaching Digital History 2.0, Fall 2015—Michael J. Kramer," 2015, http://www.michaeljkramer.net/approaching-digital-history-2-0/; Tim Sherratt, "Exposing the Archives of White Australia," accessed July 12, 2019, https://vimeo.com/60639104.

17 Carl Smith, "Can You Do Serious History on the Web?," *Perspectives on History: The Newsmagazine of the American Historical Association*, February 1998, https://www.historians.org/publications-and-directories/perspectives-on-history/february-1998/can-you-do-serious-history-on-the-web.

18 John Rosinblum, "Teaching with Digital Archives," *Perspectives on History: The Newsmagazine of the American Historical Association*, November 2017, https://www.historians.org/publications-and-directories/perspectives-on-history/november-2017/teaching-with-digital-archives.

19 Adina Langer, "HIST 8885 Syllabus" (Digital History class blog), accessed July 3, 2019, http://sites.gsu.edu/mhp-digital-history/syllabus/; Atlanta Rail Corridor Archive, accessed January 31, 2022, https://atlrailcorridorarchive.org/.

20 Jessica Parr, "Reflecting on Digital History," *Junto* (blog), January 26, 2017, https://earlyamericanists.com/2017/01/26/reflecting-on-digital-history/.

21 Discover Indiana, accessed August 10, 2019, https://indyhist.iupui.edu/.

22 Omeka, 2015, http://omeka.org/; Jeffrey W. McClurken, "Teaching with Omeka," *Chronicle of Higher Education* (ProfHacker blog), August 9, 2010, http://chronicle.com/blogs/profhacker/teaching-with-omeka/26078; Allison C. Marsh, "Omeka in the Classroom: The Challenges of Teaching Material Culture in a Digital World," *Literary and Linguistic Computing* 28, no. 2 (June 1, 2013): 279–82, https://doi.org/10.1093/llc/fqs068.

23 Curatescape, 2015, http://curatescape.org/.

24 Padmini Ray Murray, "Bringing Up the Bodies," in *Bodies of Information: Intersectional Feminism and the Digital Humanities*, ed. Elizabeth Losh and Jacqueline Wernimont (Minneapolis: University of Minnesota Press, 2018), 188.

25 Murray, "Bringing Up the Bodies," 188.

26 Documenting Ferguson, accessed October 3, 2019, http://digital.wustl.edu/ferguson/purpose.html.

27 Archivo Histórico de la Policía Nacional (AHPN) and University of Texas at Austin, Digital Archive of the Guatemalan National Police Historical Archive (AHPN), accessed January 15, 2019, https://ahpn.lib.utexas.edu/.

28 DocNow, accessed October 3, 2019, https://www.docnow.io/.

29 Gayle Osterberg, "Update on the Twitter Archive at the Library of Congress," *Library of Congress Blog*, December 26, 2017, https://blogs.loc.gov/loc/2017/12/update-on-the-twitter-archive-at-the-library-of-congress-2/.

30 Social Humans Labels, accessed October 3, 2019, https://www.docnow.io/social-humans/.

31 Mukurtu CMS, accessed June 1, 2019, https://mukurtu.org/.

32 Cabaret Commons, accessed October 3, 2019, https://cwrc.ca/projects/infrastructure-projects/pilot-projects/cabaret-commons; T. L. Cowan, Dayna McLeod, and Jasmine Rault, "Speculative Praxis towards a Queer Feminist Digital Archive: A Collaborative Research-Creation Project," *Ada: A Journal of Gender, New Media, and Technology*, no. 5 (2014), https://doi.org/10.7264/N3PZ573Z.

33 Queer Digital History Project, accessed October 3, 2018, http://queerdigital.com/.

34 Rainbow History Project, accessed October 3, 2019, https://archives.rainbowhistory.org/.

Nine. Storytelling

1 Derek Waters and Jeremy Konner, "Hamilton" episode of *Drunk History* (Comedy Central, November 22, 2016), http://www.cc.com/episodes/y51rso/drunk-history-hamilton-season-4-ep-410.

2 Renee C. Romano and Claire Bond Potter, eds., *Historians on "Hamilton": How a Blockbuster Musical Is Restaging America's Past* (New Brunswick, NJ: Rutgers University Press, 2018).

3 Sadie Bergen, "Inside Ben Franklin's World: An Interview with Podcaster Liz Covart," *AHA Today* (blog), April 18, 2016, https://www.historians.org/publications-and-directories/perspectives-on-history/april-2016/inside-ben-franklins-world-an-interview-with-podcaster-liz-covart.

4 Johanna Devaney, ed., "Digital Musicology," accessed June 29, 2020, https://www.frontiersin.org/journal/digital-humanities/section/digital-musicology; "Archives," National Recording Preservation Plan, accessed January 31, 2022, https://www.loc.gov/programs/national-recording-preservation-plan/tools-and-resources/online-resources/archives/.

5 Brandon Walsh, "Editing Audio with Audacity," *Programming Historian*, August 5, 2016, https://programminghistorian.org/en/lessons/editing-audio-with-audacity; Audacity, accessed June 28, 2020, https://www.audacityteam.org/.

6 Jonathan Loucadellis and Graeme Glebe, "About—Digital History Project Proposal," accessed August 27, 2018, https://dhprojectproposal.wordpress.com/about/.

7 Todd Gernes and Elizabeth Belanger, "Digital Storytelling in Teaching History," H-Digital-History, accessed June 29, 2020, https://networks.h-net.org/node/3276/pages/3699541/digital-storytelling-teaching-history.

8 Bryan Alexander, "Story Flow: Practical Lessons on Brainstorming, Planning, and Development," in *The New Digital Storytelling: Creating Narratives with New Media* (Santa Barbara, CA: Praeger, 2011), 177–200.

9 Eliz Markowitz, *Kindertransport: The Unknown Children of the Holocaust*, accessed June 29, 2020, https://digitalstorytelling.coe.uh.edu/view_story.cfm?vid=409&categoryid=16&d_title=History.

10 Chris Stein, *Missing in Action*, accessed June 29, 2020, https://digitalstorytelling.coe.uh.edu/view_story.cfm?vid=328&categoryid=16&d_title=History.

11 Bodies and Structures, accessed June 29, 2020, https://scalar.chass.ncsu.edu/bodies-and-structures/what-were-doing.

12 Bodies and Structures, "How to Use This Site," accessed June 29, 2020, https://scalar.chass.ncsu.edu/bodies-and-structures/how-to-use-this-site.

13 Timothy Yang, "Bodies and Structures: The Drugstore as Contact Zone," Bodies and Structures, accessed June 29, 2020, https://scalar.chass.ncsu.edu/bodies-and-structures/drugstore-landing-page.

14 David R. Ambaras et al., "Building a Multivocal Spatial History: Scalar and the Bodies and Structures Project," *PLATFORM* (blog), accessed June 29, 2020, https://www.platformspace.net/home/building-a-multivocal-spatial-history-scalar-and-the-bodies-and-structures-project-part-1.

15 Ambaras et al., "Building a Multivocal Spatial History."

16 Scalar, 2015, http://scalar.usc.edu/.

17 Alliance for Networking Visual Culture at the University of Southern California, "Scalar 2 User's Guide: Getting Started," accessed June 29, 2020, https://scalar.usc.edu/works/guide2/getting-started; Dan Tracy, "LibGuides: Scalar:

An Introduction: Home," accessed June 29, 2020, //guides.library.illinois .edu/c.php?g=348220&p=2348685.

18 WordPress, 2015, https://wordpress.com.

19 ArcGIS StoryMaps, accessed June 29, 2020, https://storymaps.arcgis.com.

20 Jeremiah McCall, "Teaching History with Digital Historical Games: An Introduction to the Field and Best Practices," *Simulation and Gaming* 47, no. 4 (August 1, 2016): 517–42, https://doi.org/10.1177/1046878116646693.

21 Matthew Friedman, "New Viewpoints in American History: Digital History in Theory and Practice Syllabus," 2016, https://sasn.rutgers.edu/sites/default/files/sites/default/files/inline-files/Friedman%20Digital%20History%20Syllabus%202016.pdf.

22 *Oregon Trail*, Classic Reload, accessed January 31, 2022, https://classicreload.com/oregon-trail.html.

23 James Harry Morris, "Historical Storytelling with Twine," *Digital Orientalist* (blog), May 27, 2019, https://digitalorientalist.com/2019/05/27/historical-storytelling-with-twine/.

24 Austin Mason and Susannah Ottaway, "Twine Storyboards," *Bringing the Past to Virtual Life* (course website), accessed January 17, 2016, https://blogs.carleton.edu/hist235/twine-storyboards/.

Ten. Crowdsourcing

1 Wikipedia, 2015, http://www.wikipedia.org/.

2 "Wikipedia: About," June 6, 2020, https://en.wikipedia.org/w/index.php?title=Wikipedia:About&oldid=961166598.

3 Margaret Conrad, "2007 Presidential Address of the CHA: Public History and Its Discontents or History in the Age of Wikipedia," *Journal of the Canadian Historical Association / Revue de La Société Historique du Canada* 18, no. 1 (2007): 1–26; Adam Jatowt, Daisuke Kawai, and Katsumi Tanaka, "Digital History Meets Wikipedia: Analyzing Historical Persons in Wikipedia," in *2016 IEEE/ACM Joint Conference on Digital Libraries (JCDL)* (Piscataway, NJ: Institute of Electrical and Electronics Engineers, 2016), 17–26; Murray G. Phillips, "Wikipedia and History: A Worthwhile Partnership in the Digital Era?," *Rethinking History* 20, no. 4 (2016): 523–43; Mia Ridge, "New Challenges in Digital History: Sharing Women's History on Wikipedia," 2013, http://repository.brynmawr.edu/greenfield_conference/papers/saturday/37?utm_source=repository.brynmawr.edu%2Fgreenfield_conference%2Fpapers%2Fsaturday%2F37&utm_medium=PDF&utm_campaign=PDFCoverPages; Roy Rosenzweig, "Can History Be Open Source? Wikipedia and the Future of the Past," *Journal of American History* 93, no. 1 (2006): 117–46; Robert Wolff, "The

Historian's Craft, Popular Memory, and Wikipedia," in *Writing History in the Digital Age*, ed. Kristen Nawrotzki and Jack Dougherty (Ann Arbor: University of Michigan Press, 2013), 64–74.

4 Adrea Lawrence, "Learning How to Write Analog and Digital History," in *Writing History in the Digital Age*, ed. Kristen Nawrotzki and Jack Dougherty (Ann Arbor: University of Michigan Press, 2013), https://quod.lib.umich.edu/d/dh/12230987.0001.001/1:6/--writing-history-in-the-digital-age?g=dculture;rgn=div1;view=fulltext;xc=1.

5 Amanda Seligman, "Teaching Wikipedia without Apologies," in *Writing History in the Digital Age*, ed. Kristen Nawrotzki and Jack Dougherty (Ann Arbor: University of Michigan Press, 2013), https://quod.lib.umich.edu/d/dh/12230987.0001.001/1:6/--writing-history-in-the-digital-age?g=dculture;rgn=div1;view=fulltext;xc=1.

6 Transcribe Bentham, accessed September 5, 2018, http://blogs.ucl.ac.uk/transcribe-bentham/.

7 The Colored Conventions Project, 2015, http://coloredconventions.org/.

8 Ajapaik, accessed September 5, 2018, https://ajapaik.ee/.

9 DIYHistory, "Iowa Women's Lives: Letters and Diaries," accessed February 11, 2015, http://diyhistory.lib.uiowa.edu/collections/show/9.

10 Zooniverse et al., "Ancient Lives," accessed September 5, 2018, https://www.ancientlives.org/.

11 FromThePage, 2015, http://beta.fromthepage.com/.

12 Smithsonian Digital Volunteers, accessed September 8, 2018, https://transcription.si.edu/.

13 The Great War Archive, accessed October 7, 2021, http://www.oucs.ox.ac.uk/ww1lit/gwa.

14 Europeana, "1914–1918," Europeana Collections, accessed October 10, 2018, https://www.europeana.eu/portal/en/collections/world-war-I.

15 National Archives and Records Administration, Citizen Archivist Dashboard, October 6, 2015, https://www.archives.gov/citizen-archivist.

16 Tate Museum, "AnnoTate," accessed September 5, 2018, https://anno.tate.org.uk/#/.

17 Old Weather—Our Weather's Past, the Climate's Future, 2013, http://www.oldweather.org/.

18 Scripto, accessed July 1, 2020, https://scripto.org/; Ted Crackel et al., "Papers of the War Department Project," accessed July 1, 2020, https://wardepartmentpapers.org/s/home/page/transcribing-guide.

19 Nathaniel Deines, Melissa Gill, Matthew Lincoln, and Marissa Clifford, "Six Lessons Learned from Our First Crowdsourcing Project in the Digital Human-

ities," *Getty Iris* (blog), February 7, 2018, http://blogs.getty.edu/iris/six-lessons-learned-from-our-first-crowdsourcing-project-in-the-digital-humanities/.

20 Spencer D. C. Keralis, "Milking the Deficit Internship," *Disrupting the Digital Humanities* (blog), January 6, 2016, http://www.disruptingdh.com/milking-the-deficit-internship/; Spencer D. C. Keralis, "Disrupting Student Labor in the Digital Humanities Classroom; or, The Classroom Is Not Your Crowd," in *Disrupting the Digital Humanities*, ed. Dorothy Kim and Jesse Stommel (Punctum, 2018), 273–94, https://hcommons.org/deposits/item/hc:22295/; Katrina Anderson et al., "Student Labour and Training in Digital Humanities," *Digital Humanities Quarterly* 10, no. 1 (2016), http://www.digitalhumanities.org/dhq/vol/10/1/000233/000233.html; Aaron Mauro et al., "Towards a Seamful Design of Networked Knowledge: Practical Pedagogies in Collaborative Teams," *Digital Humanities Quarterly* 11, no. 3 (October 2, 2017), http://www.digitalhumanities.org/dhq/vol/11/3/000322/000322.html.

21 Church of Jesus Christ of Latter-day Saints, "Inmates Serve in FamilySearch Indexing Program," *Newsroom*, February 5, 2015, https://web.archive.org/web/20150205150137/http://www.mormonnewsroom.org/article/service-helps-inmates-look-beyond-themselves; Glen N. Greener, "Pioneers Are Now Found in Local Jails," *FamilySearch* (blog), August 26, 2015, https://www.familysearch.org/blog/en/pioneers-local-jails/; Shane Bauer, "Did an Inmate Digitize Your Genealogical Records?," *Mother Jones*, accessed July 1, 2020, https://www.motherjones.com/politics/2015/08/mormon-church-prison-geneology-family-search/.

Conclusion

1 Humanities Intensive Learning and Teaching, accessed July 2, 2020, http://dhtraining.org/hilt/.

2 micha cárdenas, "The Android Goddess Declaration: After Man(ifestos)," in *Bodies of Information: Intersectional Feminism and the Digital Humanities*, ed. Elizabeth Losh and Jacqueline Wernimont (Minneapolis: University of Minnesota Press, 2018), 25–38.

Bibliography

Note: Software and digital projects that are included in the notes and glossary are not included in this bibliography. I encourage you, if you are looking for specific software or projects, to consult the glossary first.

Abebe, Rediet, Solon Barocas, Jon Kleinberg, Karen Levy, Manish Raghavan, and David G. Robinson. "Roles for Computing in Social Change." In *Proceedings of the 2020 Conference on Fairness, Accountability, and Transparency*, 252–60. New York: Association for Computing Machinery, 2020.

ADA National Network. "Understanding Disability Statistics." Accessed September 6, 2018. https://adata.org/factsheet/understanding-disability-statistics.

Adelusi-Adeluyi, Ademide. "New Maps of Old Lagos." Accessed July 9, 2019. http://newmapsoldlagos.com/index.html.

Alegi, Peter. "Podcasting the Past: Africa Past and Present and (South) African History in the Digital Age." *South African Historical Journal* 64, no. 2 (2012): 206–20. https://www.tandfonline.com/doi/abs/10.1080/02582473.2011.640344.

Alexander, Bryan. "Story Flow: Practical Lessons on Brainstorming, Planning, and Development." In *The New Digital Storytelling: Creating Narratives with New Media*, 177–200. Santa Barbara, CA: Praeger, 2011.

Alliance for Networking Visual Culture at the University of Southern California. "Scalar 2 User's Guide: Getting Started." Accessed June 29, 2020. https://scalar.usc.edu/works/guide2/getting-started.

Ambaras, David R., Curtis Fletcher, Erik Loyer, and Kate McDonald. "Building a Multivocal Spatial History: Scalar and the Bodies and Structures Project." *PLATFORM* (blog). Accessed June 29, 2020. https://www.platformspace.net/home/building-a-multivocal-spatial-history-scalar-and-the-bodies-and-structures-project-part-1.

American Historical Association. "AHA History Tuning Project: 2016 History Discipline Core." 2016. https://www.historians.org/teaching-and-learning/tuning-the-history-discipline/2016-history-discipline-core.

American Historical Association. "Historical Thinking Skills." Accessed July 8, 2019. https://www.historians.org/teaching-and-learning/teaching-resources-for-historians/teaching-and-learning-in-the-digital-age/the-history-of-the-americas/the-conquest-of-mexico/for-teachers/setting-up-the-project/historical-thinking-skills.

American Historical Association. "Session 6913: 126th Annual Meeting (January 5–8, 2012)—The Future Is Here: Pioneers Discuss the Future of Digital Humanities." Accessed June 15, 2020. https://aha.confex.com/aha/2012/webprogram/Session6913.html.

Anderson, Katrina, Lindsey Bannister, Janey Dodd, Deanna Fong, Michelle Levy, and Lindsey Seatter. "Student Labour and Training in Digital Humanities." *Digital Humanities Quarterly* 10, no. 1 (2016). http://www.digitalhumanities.org/dhq/vol/10/1/000233/000233.html.

Anderson, Margo. "Quantitative History." In *The Sage Handbook of Social Science Methodology*, edited by William Outhwaite and Stephen P. Turner, 248–64. London: SAGE, 2007. doi: 10.4135/9781848607958.n14.

Aouragh, Miriyam, and Paula Chakravartty. "Infrastructures of Empire: Towards a Critical Geopolitics of Media and Information Studies." *Media, Culture and Society* 38, no. 4 (2016): 559–75.

Arguing with Digital History Working Group. "Digital History and Argument." White paper. Roy Rosenzweig Center for History and New Media, November 13, 2017. https://rrchnm.org/argument-white-paper/.

Armitage, David, and Jo Guldi. "Longing for the Longue Durée." *Isis* 107, no. 2 (June 1, 2016): 353–57. https://doi.org/10.1086/687179.

Arnold, Taylor. "Statsmaths/Hilt2019-Image-Analysis." Jupyter notebook. 2019. https://github.com/statsmaths/hilt2019-image-analysis.

ASCD Guest Blogger. "Bringing Digital Learning into the History Classroom." *ASCD Inservice*. Accessed July 12, 2019. http://inservice.ascd.org/bringing-digital-learning-into-the-history-classroom/.

Ayers, Edward L. "Turning toward Place, Space, and Time." In *The Spatial Humanities: GIS and the Future of the Humanities Scholarship*, edited by David J. Bodenhamer, John Corrigan, and Trevor M. Harris, 1–13. Bloomington: Indiana University Press, 2010. https://scholarship.richmond.edu/history-faculty-publications/98.

Ballantyne, Tony. "On Place, Space and Mobility in Nineteenth-Century New Zealand." *New Zealand Journal of History* 45, no. 1 (April 2011): 50–70.

Balletti, Caterina, and Francesco Guerra. "Historical Maps for 3D Digital City's History." *Cartographica: The International Journal for Geographic Information and Geovisualization* 51, no. 3 (September 15, 2016): 115–26. https://doi.org/10.3138/cart.51.3.3140.

Barnette, Adena. "Commodore Perry's Expedition to Japan." Digital collection. DPLA Primary Source Sets, n.d. https://dp.la/primary-source-sets/commodore-perry-s-expedition-to-japan/teaching-guide#tabs.

Bartel, Nick. "The Travels of Ibn Battuta." Accessed October 7, 2019. https://orias.berkeley.edu/resources-teachers/travels-ibn-battuta.

Bauer, Shane. "Did an Inmate Digitize Your Genealogical Records?" *Mother Jones*. Accessed July 1, 2020. https://www.motherjones.com/politics/2015/08/mormon-church-prison-geneology-family-search/.

Benharrech, Sarah, Valerie K. Orlando, and Kelsey Corlett-Rivera. "Revealing la Révolution." Accessed September 5, 2018. https://www.lib.umd.edu/special/guides/frenchpamphlets.

Benjamin, Ruha. "Assessing Risk, Automating Racism." *Science* 366, no. 6464 (2019): 421–22.

Bergen, Sadie. "Inside Ben Franklin's World: An Interview with Podcaster Liz Covart." *AHA Today* (blog). April 18, 2016. https://www.historians.org/publications-and-directories/perspectives-on-history/april-2016/inside-ben-franklins-world-an-interview-with-podcaster-liz-covart.

Bialik, Kristen. "7 Facts about Americans with Disabilities." *Pew Research Center* (blog). July 27, 2017. http://www.pewresearch.org/fact-tank/2017/07/27/7-facts-about-americans-with-disabilities/.

Birnbaum, David J., Sheila Bonde, and Mike Kestemont. "The Digital Middle Ages: An Introduction." *Speculum* 92, no. S1 (October 2017): S1–S38. https://doi.org/10.1086/694236.

Black, Edwin. *IBM and the Holocaust: The Strategic Alliance between Nazi Germany and America's Most Powerful Corporation*. New York: Random House, 2001.

Bonnett, John. "Following in Rabelais' Footsteps: Immersive History and the *3D Virtual Buildings Project*." *History and Computing* 13, no. 2 (June 2001). https://doi.org/10.3366/hac.2001.13.2.107.

Bonnett, John. "History 4F30: Topics in History and Computing." Syllabus, 2010. http://spartan.ac.brocku.ca/~jbonnett/Syllabus.html.

Brennan, Sheila A. "Digital History." *The Inclusive Historian's Handbook*, June 4, 2019. https://inclusivehistorian.com/digital-history/.

Broussard, Meredith. *Artificial Unintelligence: How Computers Misunderstand the World*. Cambridge, MA: MIT Press, 2018.

Brown, Vincent. "Project." Slave Revolt in Jamaica, 1760–1761. Accessed June 28, 2020. http://revolt.axismaps.com/project.html.

Bullen, Mark, Tannis Morgan, Karen Belfer, and Adnan Qayyam. "The Digital Learner at BCIT and Implications for an E-Strategy." Accessed August 24, 2018. https://app.box.com/s/fxqyutottt.

Burns, Jay. "Beyond 'Founded by Abolitionists': Students and Faculty Undertake a More Inclusive Examination of Bates' Founding Story." Bates, February 6, 2020. https://www.bates.edu/news/2020/02/26/going-beyond-founded-by-abolitionists-students-and-faculty-undertake-a-more-inclusive-examination-of-bates-founding-story/.

Burton, Antoinette M. *Dwelling in the Archive: Women Writing House, Home, and History in Late Colonial India*. Oxford: Oxford University Press, 2010.

Burton, Orville Vernon. "American Digital History." *Social Science Computer Review* 23, no. 2 (2005): 206–20.

Bush, Erin. "Schedule." *Spring 2018—The Digital Past* (blog). Accessed June 12, 2019. http://teaching.erinbush.org/s18h390/schedule/.

Bussière, Kirsten. "Chapter 4—Text Analysis." In *Digital Humanities—A Primer*. 2018. https://carletonu.pressbooks.pub/digh5000/chapter/chapter-4-text-analysis/.

Butler, Kim D. "Defining Diaspora, Refining a Discourse." *Diaspora: A Journal of Transnational Studies* 10, no. 2 (2001): 189–219. https://doi.org/10.1353/dsp.2011.0014.

cárdenas, micha. "The Android Goddess Declaration: After Man(ifestos)." In *Bodies of Information: Intersectional Feminism and the Digital Humanities*, edited by Elizabeth Losh and Jacqueline Wernimont, 25–38. Minneapolis: University of Minnesota Press, 2018.

Caswell, Michelle. "Seeing Yourself in History: Community Archives and the Fight against Symbolic Annihilation." *Public Historian* 36, no. 4 (November 2014): 26–37. https://doi.org/10.1525/tph.2014.36.4.26.

Caswell, Michelle, Joyce Gabiola, Jimmy Zavala, Gracen Brilmyer, and Marika Cifor. "Imagining Transformative Spaces: The Personal–Political Sites of Community Archives." *Archival Science* 18, no. 1 (2018): 73–93. https://doi.org/10.1007/s10502-018-9286-7.

Caswell, Michelle, Christopher Harter, and Bergis Jules. "Diversifying the Digital Historical Record: Integrating Community Archives in National Strategies for Access to Digital Cultural Heritage." *D-Lib Magazine* 23, no. 5/6 (May 2017). https://doi.org/10.1045/may2017-caswell.

Caswell, Michelle, Alda Allina Migoni, Noah Geraci, and Marika Cifor. "'To Be Able to Imagine Otherwise': Community Archives and the Importance of Representation." *Archives and Records* 38, no. 1 (January 2, 2017): 5–26. https://doi.org/10.1080/23257962.2016.1260445.

Cefalo, Raffaela, Janusz B. Zieliński, and Maurizio Barbarella. *New Advanced GNSS and 3D Spatial Techniques: Applications to Civil and Environmental Engineering, Geophysics, Architecture, Archeology and Cultural Heritage*. New York: Springer, 2017.

Center for History and Economics at Harvard University. "Visualizing Historical Networks." Accessed October 16, 2019. https://histecon.fas.harvard.edu/visualizing/index.html.

Center for Research Library. "TRAC Metrics." Accessed October 10, 2019. https://www.crl.edu/archiving-preservation/digital-archives/metrics-assessing-and-certifying/trac.

Christen, Kimberly. "Tribal Archives, Traditional Knowledge, and Local Contexts: Why the 's' Matters." *Journal of Western Archives* 6, no. 1 (January 7, 2015). https://digitalcommons.usu.edu/westernarchives/vol6/iss1/3.

Christian-Lamb, Caitlin, and Anelise Hanson Shrout. "Starting from Scratch? Workshopping New Directions in Undergraduate Digital Humanities." *Digital Humanities Quarterly* 11, no. 3 (October 2, 2017). http://digitalhumanities.org:8081/dhq/vol/11/3/000311/000311.html.

Chun, Wendy Hui Kyong. "Race and/as Technology, or How to Do Things to Race." In *Race after the Internet*, ed. Lisa Nakamura and Peter Chow-White, 38–60. New York: Routledge, 2013.

Church of Jesus Christ of Latter-day Saints. "Inmates Serve in FamilySearch Indexing Program." *Newsroom*, February 5, 2015. https://web.archive.org/web/20150205150137/http://www.mormonnewsroom.org/article/service-helps-inmates-look-beyond-themselves.

City University of New York Academic Commons. "DH Syllabi—CUNY Academic Commons Wiki Archive." Accessed June 15, 2020. https://wiki.commons.gc.cuny.edu/dh_syllabi/.

Clark, Emily Suzanne. "The Unessay." August 1, 2016. https://emilysuzanneclark.wordpress.com/2016/08/01/the-unessay/.

Coates, Colin, Jim Clifford, Ewan Klein, Claire Grover, Beatrice Alex, Clare Llewellyn, Aaron Quigley, et al. *Trading Consequences* (blog). Accessed October 7, 2019. http://tradingconsequences.blogs.edina.ac.uk/.

Columbia University. "The Open Syllabus Project." July 8, 2019. https://blog.opensyllabus.org/about-the-open-syllabus-project/.

Commonwealth of Australia. "Digital Transformation Agenda." 2019. https://www.dta.gov.au/digital-transformation-strategy-2019.

Conrad, Margaret. "2007 Presidential Address of the CHA: Public History and Its Discontents or History in the Age of Wikipedia." *Journal of the Canadian Historical Association / Revue de La Société Historique du Canada* 18, no. 1 (2007): 1–26.

Conway, Paul, and Ricardo Punzalan. "Fields of Vision: Toward a New Theory of Visual Literacy for Digitized Archival Photographs." *Archivaria* 71 (May 2011): 63–97.

Cook, Terry. "The Archive(s) Is a Foreign Country: Historians, Archivists, and the Changing Archival Landscape." *American Archivist* 74, no. 2 (2011): 600–632.

Cook, Terry. "Evidence, Memory, Identity, and Community: Four Shifting Archival Paradigms." *Archival Science* 13, no. 2–3 (June 2013): 95–120. https://doi.org/10.1007/s10502-012-9180-7.

Cordell, Ryan. "How Not to Teach Digital Humanities." Accessed June 13, 2020. https://ryancordell.org/teaching/how-not-to-teach-digital-humanities/.

Cowan, T. L., Dayna McLeod, and Jasmine Rault. "Speculative Praxis towards a Queer Feminist Digital Archive: A Collaborative Research-Creation Project." *Ada: A Journal of Gender, New Media, and Technology*, no. 5 (2014). https://doi.org/10.7264/N3PZ573Z.

Craig, Kalani. "History and the Digital World." Accessed October 16, 2019. http://www.kalanicraig.com/courses/history-and-the-digital-world/.

Crymble, Adam. "Introduction to Gravity Models of Migration and Trade." *Programming Historian*, March 18, 2019. https://programminghistorian.org/en/lessons/gravity-model.

Crymble, Adam. *Technology and the Historian: Transformations in the Digital Age*. Topics in the Digital Humanities. Urbana: University of Illinois Press, 2021.

Cultural Heritage Imaging. "Digital Lab Notebook." Accessed August 12, 2019. http://culturalheritageimaging.org/Technologies/Digital_Lab_Notebook/.

Dacos, Marin. "Manifesto for the Digital Humanities." *THATCamp Paris* (blog). Accessed September 5, 2018. https://tcp.hypotheses.org/411.

Davis, Ann Marie, Jessica McCullough, Ben Panciera, and Rebecca Parmer. "Faculty–Library Collaborations in Digital History: A Case Study of the Travel Journal of Cornelius B. Gold." *College and Undergraduate Libraries* 24, no. 2–4 (April 2017): 482–500. https://doi.org/10.1080/10691316.2017.1325347.

Deines, Nathaniel, Melissa Gill, Matthew Lincoln, and Marissa Clifford. "Six Lessons Learned from Our First Crowdsourcing Project in the Digital Humanities." *Getty Iris* (blog), February 7, 2018. http://blogs.getty.edu/iris/six-lessons-learned-from-our-first-crowdsourcing-project-in-the-digital-humanities/.

Denial, Cate. "The Unessay." Accessed June 13, 2020. https://catherinedenial.org/blog/uncategorized/the-unessay/.

Devaney, Johanna, ed. "Digital Musicology." Accessed June 29, 2020. https://www.frontiersin.org/journal/digital-humanities/section/digital-musicology.

Digital Humanities Lab: Russian and East European Studies. "Topic Modeling the Slavic Review." *DHREES* (blog). Accessed August 8, 2018. http://dhrees.yale.edu/dhrees-project/avante-gardes-and-emigres/age-project-two/.

Digital Scholarship Commons, Robert W. Woodruff Library, and Emory Libraries. "Text Mining with Voyant." *Lincoln Logarithms: Finding Meaning in Sermons* (blog). February 21, 2013. http://lincolnlogs.digitalscholarship.emory.edu/voyant/.

D'Ignazio, Catherine, and Lauren F. Klein. *Data Feminism*. Cambridge, MA: MIT Press, 2020.

Di Pressi, Haley, Stephanie Gorman, Miriam Posner, Raphael Sasayama, and Tori Schmitt, with Roderic Crooks, Megan Driscoll, Amy Earhart, Spencer Keralis, Tiffany Naiman, and Todd Pressner. "A Student Collaborators' Bill of Rights." Center for Digital Humanities, University of California, Los Angeles, June 8, 2015. https://humtech.ucla.edu/news/a-student-collaborators-bill-of-rights/.

Duarte, Marisa Elena. *Network Sovereignty: Building the Internet across Indian Country*. Seattle: University of Washington Press, 2017.

Eltis, David, Allen Tullos, and the Trans-Atlantic Slave Trade Database Development Team. "SlaveVoyages." Digital project. 2013. http://www.slavevoyages.org/.

Erickson, Ansley T. "Historical Research and the Problem of Categories: Reflections on 10,000 Digital Note Cards." In *Writing History in the Digital Age*, edited by Kristen Nawrotzki and Jack Dougherty, 133–45. Ann Arbor: University of Michigan Press, 2013. https://quod.lib.umich.edu/d/dh/12230987.0001.001/1:7/—writing-history-in-the-digital-age?g=dculture;rgn=div1;view=fulltext;xc=1.

Etcheson, Nicole. "Microhistory and Movement: African American Mobility in the Nineteenth Century." *Journal of the Civil War Era* 3, no. 3 (August 1, 2013): 392–404. https://doi.org/10.1353/cwe.2013.0065.

Everett, Anna. "The Revolution Will Be Digitized: Afrocentricity and the Digital Public Sphere." *Social Text* 20, no. 2 (2002): 125–46.

Ewing, E. Thomas. "Will It Come Here? Using Digital Humanities Tools to Explore Medical Understanding during the Russian Flu Epidemic, 1889–90." *Medical History* 61, no. 3 (July 2017): 474–77. https://doi.org/10.1017/mdh.2017.53.

Flanders, Julia, and Trevor Muñoz. "An Introduction to Humanities Data Curation." In *Digital Humanities Data Curation*. Accessed February 15, 2015. https://guide.dhcuration.org/contents/intro/.

Fleisher, Jack, Jae Ha, and Joey Hammel. "Guest Post: Tuberculosis in California: A Statistical Analysis from 1880–1910." *Medical Heritage Library* (blog). Accessed October 4, 2019. http://www.medicalheritage.org/2017/03/24/guest-post-tuberculosis-in-california-a-statistical-analysis-from-1880-1910/.

Flinn, Andrew, Mary Stevens, and Elizabeth Shepherd. "Whose Memories, Whose Archives? Independent Community Archives, Autonomy and the Mainstream." *Archival Science* 9, no. 1–2 (June 2009): 71–86. https://doi.org/10.1007/s10502-009-9105-2.

Fogel, Robert W., and Stanley L. Engerman. *Time on the Cross: The Economics of American Negro Slavery*. Boston: Little, Brown, 1974.

Friedman, Matthew. "New Viewpoints in American History: Digital History Theory and Practice Syllabus." 2016. https://sasn.rutgers.edu/sites/default/files/sites/default/files/inline-files/Friedman%20Digital%20History%20Syllabus%202016.pdf.

Fuentes, Marisa J. *Dispossessed Lives: Enslaved Women, Violence, and the Archive*. Philadelphia: University of Pennsylvania Press, 2016.

Gajjala, Radhika. *Cyberculture and the Subaltern: Weavings of the Virtual and Real*. Lanham, MD: Rowman and Littlefield, 2013.

Gajjala, Radhika. *Cyber Selves: Feminist Ethnographies of South Asian Women*. New York: AltaMira, 2004.

Gajjala, Radhika. "An Interrupted Postcolonial/Feminist Cyberethnography: Complicity and Resistance in the 'Cyberfield.'" *Feminist Media Studies* 2, no. 2 (2002): 177–93.

Garvey, Ellen Gruber. "'facts and FACTS': Abolitionists' Database Innovations." In *"Raw Data" Is an Oxymoron*, edited by Lisa Gitelman, 89–102. Cambridge, MA: MIT Press, 2013.

Gernes, Todd, and Elizabeth Belanger. "Digital Storytelling in Teaching History." H-Digital-History. Accessed June 29, 2020. https://networks.h-net.org/node/3276/pages/3699541/digital-storytelling-teaching-history.

Graham, Shawn. "Capstone Exercise." In "Course Manual for Crafting Digital History HIST38140|DIGH38140 @ Carleton U Summer 2019." Accessed October 12, 2019. https://site.craftingdigitalhistory.ca/capstone-exercise-1.html.

Graham, Shawn. "Cities & Countryside in the Ancient World." Accessed August 10, 2018. http://www.scottbot.net/HIAL/wp-content/uploads/2012/09/hist3902a-Graham-fall-2012-sept-10-version.pdf.

Graham, Shawn. "Crafting Digital History." Accessed June 2020. https://craftingdh.netlify.app/.

Graham, Shawn. "Crafting Digital History." Accessed August 11, 2019. http://workbook.craftingdigitalhistory.ca/.

Graham, Shawn. "Getting Started with Leaflet." Accessed August 20, 2021. https://workbook.craftingdigitalhistory.ca/supporting%20materials/leaflet.txt/.

Graham, Shawn, Scott Weingart, and Ian Milligan. "Getting Started with Topic Modeling and MALLET." *Programming Historian 2* (September 2, 2012; updated September 3, 2021). http://programminghistorian.org/lessons/topic-modeling-and-mallet.

Graham, Shawn, Ian Milligan, Scott Weingart, and Kim Martin. *Exploring Big Historical Data: The Historian's Macroscope*. 2nd edition. London: Imperial College Press, forthcoming.

Green, James N., Patricia Figueroa, and Staff of the Center for Digital Scholarship at Brown University. "Latin American Travelogues." Accessed October 7, 2019. https://library.brown.edu/cds/travelogues/index.html.

Greener, Glen N. "Pioneers Are Now Found in Local Jails." *FamilySearch* (blog), August 26, 2015. https://www.familysearch.org/blog/en/pioneers-local-jails/.

Gregory, Ian. "Challenges and Opportunities for Digital History." *Frontiers in Digital Humanities* 1, no. 1 (2014). https://doi.org/10.3389/fdigh.2014.00001.

Guiliano, Jennifer, and Carolyn Heitman. "Difficult Heritage and the Complexities of Indigenous Data." *Journal of Cultural Analytics* 4, no. 1 (August 13, 2019). https://doi.org/10.22148/16.044.

Guldi, Jo. "The Common Landscape of Digital History: Universal Methods, Global Borderlands, Longue-Durée History, and Critical Thinking about Approaches and Institutions." In *Digital Histories: Emergent Approaches within the New Digital History*, edited by Mats Fridlund, Mila Oiva, and Petri Paju, 327–46. Helsinki: Helsinki University Press, 2020. https://doi.org/10.2307/j.ctv1c9hpt8.23.

Guldi, Joanna. "The History of Walking and the Digital Turn: Stride and Lounge in London, 1808–1851." *Journal of Modern History* 84, no. 1 (March 1, 2012): 116–44. https://doi.org/10.1086/663350.

Hadjikyriacou, Antonis. "Using Recogito in the (Ottoman History) Classroom." *Europeana Pro*, no. 12 (March 2019). https://pro.europeana.eu/page/issue-12-pelagios.

Han, Shin-Kap. "The Other Ride of Paul Revere: The Brokerage Role in the Making of the American Revolution." *Mobilization: An International Quarterly* 14, no. 2 (2009): 143–62. http://www.sscnet.ucla.edu/polisci/faculty/chwe/ps269/han.pdf.

Hangen, Tona. "Historical Digital Literacy, One Classroom at a Time." *Journal of American History* 101, no. 4 (March 1, 2015): 1192–203. https://doi.org/10.1093/jahist/jav062.

Harbison, Thomas, and Luke Waltzer. "Toward Teaching the Introductory History Course, Digitally." In *Writing History in the Digital Age*, edited by Kristen Nawrotzki and Jack Dougherty, 97–109. Ann Arbor: University of Michigan Press, 2013. https://quod.lib.umich.edu/d/dh/12230987.0001.001/1:6/—writing-history-in-the-digital-age?g=dculture;rgn=div1;view=fulltext;xc=1#6.1.

Hart, Jennifer. "Introduction: Digital History in African Studies." *History in Africa* 47 (2020): 269–74.

Hathorn, Michael. "Creating a 3-D History." Accessed September 5, 2018. https://sites.google.com/a/gradschool.marlboro.edu/creating-a-3-d-history/home.

Heer, Jeffrey, Michael Bostock, and Vadim Ogievetsky. "A Tour through the Visualization Zoo." Accessed June 27, 2020. https://homes.cs.washington.edu/~jheer//files/zoo/.

Heppler, Jason. "Directed Readings in Digital History (Spring 2018)." Accessed August 17, 2021. https://jasonheppler.org/courses/unodh.2018/.

Heppler, Jason, and Gabriel K. Wolfenstein. "Crowdsourcing Digital Public History." *American Historian*. Accessed July 1, 2020. https://tah.oah.org/content/crowdsourcing-digital-public-history/.

Hicks, Mar. "Hacking the Cis-Tem." *IEEE Annals of the History of Computing* 41, no. 1 (January 2019): 20–33. https://doi.org/10.1109/MAHC.2019.2897667.

Hill, Mark J., and Simon Hengchen. "Quantifying the Impact of Dirty OCR on Historical Text Analysis: Eighteenth Century Collections Online as a Case Study." *Digital Scholarship in the Humanities* 34, no. 4 (December 1, 2019): 825–43. https://doi.org/10.1093/llc/fqz024.

History and Public Policy Program, Woodrow Wilson International Center for Scholars. "Digital Archive: International History Declassified." Accessed January 2, 2019. https://digitalarchive.wilsoncenter.org/.

History Relevance Initiative. "History Relevance." Accessed August 6, 2019. https://www.historyrelevance.com.

Jatowt, Adam, Daisuke Kawai, and Katsumi Tanaka. "Digital History Meets Wikipedia: Analyzing Historical Persons in Wikipedia." In *2016 IEEE/ACM Joint Conference on Digital Libraries (JCDL)*, 17–26. Piscataway, NJ: Institute of Electrical and Electronics Engineers, 2016.

Johnson, Jessica Marie. "Diaspora." In *Digital Pedagogy in the Humanities: Concepts, Models, and Experiments*. MLA Commons, 2016. https://digitalpedagogy.mla.hcommons.org/keywords/diaspora/.

Kaplan, Elisabeth. "We Are What We Collect, We Collect What We Are: Archives and the Construction of Identity." *American Archivist* 63, no. 1 (January 2000): 126–51. https://doi.org/10.17723/aarc.63.1.h554377531233l05.

Kaplan, Louis, and Melissa Shiff. "Mapping Ararat: An Augmented Reality Walking Tour for an Imaginary Jewish Homeland." *Anthrovision*, December 31, 2016. https://doi.org/10.4000/anthrovision.2339.

Kelly, Jill E., and Omar Badsha. "Teaching South African History in the Digital Age: Collaboration, Pedagogy, and Popularizing History." *History in Africa* 47 (June 2020): 297–325. https://doi.org/10.1017/hia.2020.6.

Keralis, Spencer D. C. "Disrupting Student Labor in the Digital Humanities Classroom; or, The Classroom Is Not Your Crowd." In *Disrupting the Digital Humanities*, edited by Dorothy Kim and Jesse Stommel, 273–94. Punctum, 2018. https://hcommons.org/deposits/item/hc:22295/.

Keralis, Spencer D. C. "Milking the Deficit Internship." *Disrupting the Digital Humanities* (blog). January 6, 2016. http://www.disruptingdh.com/milking-the-deficit-internship/.

Koeser, Rebecca Sutton. "Trusting Others to 'Do the Math.'" *Interdisciplinary Science Reviews* 40, no. 4 (October 2, 2015): 376–92. https://doi.org/10.1080/03080188.2016.1165454.

Kolko, Beth, Lisa Nakamura, and Gilbert Rodman. *Race in Cyberspace*. New York: Routledge, 2013.

Kramer, Michael J. "Syllabus: Approaching Digital History 2.0, Fall 2015—Michael J. Kramer." 2015. http://www.michaeljkramer.net/approaching-digital-history-2-0/.

Krathwohl, David R., and Lorin W. Anderson, eds. *A Taxonomy for Learning, Teaching, and Assessing: A Revision of Bloom's Taxonomy of Educational Objectives*. London: Longman, 2009.

Langer, Adina. "HIST 8885 Syllabus." Digital History class blog. Accessed July 3, 2019. http://sites.gsu.edu/mhp-digital-history/syllabus/.

Lavoie, Brian. "Meeting the Challenges of Digital Preservation: The OAIS Reference Model." *OCLC Newsletter*, January/February 2000. https://www.oclc.org/research/publications/2000/lavoie-oais.html.

Lawrence, Adrea. "Learning How to Write Analog and Digital History." In *Writing History in the Digital Age*, edited by Kristen Nawrotzki and Jack Dougherty, 110–20. Ann Arbor: University of Michigan Press, 2013. https://quod.lib.umich.edu/d/dh/12230987.0001.001/1:6/—writing-history-in-the-digital-age?g=dculture;rgn=div1;view=fulltext;xc=1.

Leon, Sharon. "The Digital Past Syllabus." Fall 2016. http://www.6floors.org/teaching.

Leon, Sharon. *Doing Digital History* (blog). Fall 2019. https://www.6floors.org/teaching/H251/f2019/.

Leon, Sharon. "Returning Women to the History of Digital History." Accessed June 1, 2016. http://www.6floors.org/bracket/2016/03/07/returning-women-to-the-history-of-digital-history/.

Lester, Peter. "Of Mind and Matter: The Archive as Object." *Archives and Records* 39, no. 1 (January 2, 2018): 73–87. https://doi.org/10.1080/23257962.2017.1407748.

LIBER: Association of European Research Libraries. "European Commission's Recommendation on Digitisation and Digital Preservation." *LIBER* (blog). Accessed October 14, 2018. https://libereurope.eu/european-commission-s-recommendation-on-digitisation-and-digital-preservation/.

Library of Congress. "National Recording Preservation Board." Accessed July 7, 2021. https://www.loc.gov/programs/national-recording-preservation-board/about-this-program.

Library of Congress. "Personal Digital Archiving." Accessed October 3, 2019. http://digitalpreservation.gov/personalarchiving/index.html.

Library of Congress. "Traveling on the Overland Trails, 1843–1860." Accessed May 17, 2019. //www.loc.gov/teachers/classroommaterials/presentationsandactivities/presentations/timeline/expref/oregtral/.

Library of Congress. "World Digital Library." Accessed August 13, 2018. https://www.wdl.org/.

Locke, Brandon T. "Digital Humanities Pedagogy as Essential Liberal Education: A Framework for Curriculum Development." *Digital Humanities Quarterly* 11, no. 3 (October 2, 2017). http://www.digitalhumanities.org/dhq/vol/11/3/000303/000303.html.

Loucadellis, Jonathan, and Graeme Glebe. "About—Digital History Project Proposal." Accessed August 27, 2018. https://dhprojectproposal.wordpress.com/about/.

Luxembourg Centre for Contemporary and Digital History. "A Series of Lessons on Digital Source Criticism." Accessed October 1, 2019. https://ranke2.uni.lu/.

Luxembourg Centre for Contemporary and Digital History. "Why Digital Source Criticism? About the Platform." Accessed October 1, 2019. https://ranke2.uni.lu/about-platform/.

Mallick, Samip. "First Days Project." Accessed January 2, 2019. https://www.firstdaysproject.org.

Marr, Bernard. "How Much Data Do We Create Every Day? The Mind-Blowing Stats Everyone Should Read." *Forbes*. Accessed October 10, 2018. https://www.forbes.com/sites/bernardmarr/2018/05/21/how-much-data-do-we-create-every-day-the-mind-blowing-stats-everyone-should-read/.

Marsh, Allison C. "Omeka in the Classroom: The Challenges of Teaching Material Culture in a Digital World." *Literary and Linguistic Computing* 28, no. 2 (June 1, 2013): 279–82. https://doi.org/10.1093/llc/fqs068.

Mason, Austin, and Susannah Ottaway. "Twine Storyboards." *Bringing the Past to Virtual Life* (course website). Accessed January 17, 2016. https://blogs.carleton.edu/hist235/twine-storyboards/.

Mason, Betsy. "The Underappreciated Man behind the 'Best Graphic Ever Produced.'" *National Geographic*, March 16, 2017. https://www.nationalgeographic.com/culture/article/charles-minard-cartography-infographics-history.

Matthews-Jones, Lucinda. "Assessing Creatively, or Why I've Embraced the #unessay." September 11, 2019. https://lucindamatthewsjones.com/2019/09/11/assessing-creatively-or-why-ive-embraced-the-unessay/.

Mauro, Aaron, Daniel Powell, Sarah Potvin, Jacob Heil, Eric Dye, Bridget Jenkins, and Dene Grigar. "Towards a Seamful Design of Networked Knowledge: Practical Pedagogies in Collaborative Teams." *Digital Humanities Quarterly* 11, no. 3

(October 2, 2017). http://www.digitalhumanities.org/dhq/vol/11/3/000322/000322.html.

McCall, Jeremiah. "Teaching History with Digital Historical Games: An Introduction to the Field and Best Practices." *Simulation and Gaming* 47, no. 4 (August 1, 2016): 517–42. https://doi.org/10.1177/1046878116646693.

McClurken, Jeffrey. "Digital History Reviews." Accessed July 12, 2019. https://jah.oah.org/submit/digital-history-reviews/.

McClurken, Jeffrey. "Syllabus: Digital History HIST 471C3." 2008. http://digitalhistory.umwblogs.org/syllabus/.

McClurken, Jeffrey. "Teaching with Omeka." *Chronicle of Higher Education* (ProfHacker Blog), August 9, 2010. http://chronicle.com/blogs/profhacker/teaching-with-omeka/26078.

McDaniel, Caleb, Alyssa Anderson, Franco Bettati, Aaron Braunstein, Daniel Burns, Clare Jansen, and Kaitlyn Sisk. "Digital History Methods." Accessed August 20, 2018. http://ricedh.github.io/#our-data.

McDuffie, Allyson. "High School Mashup: Digital History Class." *Sketchup* (blog), January 11, 2011. https://sketchupdate.blogspot.com/2011/01/high-school-mashup-digital-history.html?m=1.

McKittrick, Katherine. "Mathematics Black Life." *Black Scholar* 44, no. 2 (2014): 16–28.

Milligan, Ian. "Network Analysis Fundamentals." In Shawn Graham, Ian Milligan, and Scott Weingart, *Exploring Big Historical Data: The Historian's Macroscope*. 2016. http://web.archive.org/web/20200618171130/http://www.themacroscope.org/?page_id=584.

Milligan, Ian. "Networks Analysis." In Shawn Graham, Ian Milligan, and Scott Weingart, *Exploring Big Historical Data: The Historian's Macroscope*. 2016. http://web.archive.org/web/20200618171130/http://www.themacroscope.org/?page_id=584.

Milligan, Ian, Shawn Graham, and Scott Weingart. "Making Your Data Legible: A Basic Introduction to Visualizations." In Shawn Graham, Ian Milligan, and Scott Weingart, *Exploring Big Historical Data: The Historian's Macroscope*. 2016. http://web.archive.org/web/20200618171130/http://www.themacroscope.org/?page_id=584.

Moravec, Michelle. "How Digitized* Changed Historical Research." *Medium* (blog), January 24, 2017. https://medium.com/on-archivy/how-digitized-changed-historical-research-d77c78540878.

Morris, James Harry. "Historical Storytelling with Twine." *Digital Orientalist* (blog), May 27, 2019. https://digitalorientalist.com/2019/05/27/historical-storytelling-with-twine/.

Murray, Padmini Ray. "Bringing Up the Bodies." In *Bodies of Information: Intersectional Feminism and the Digital Humanities*, edited by Elizabeth Losh and Jacqueline Wernimont, 185–200. Minneapolis: University of Minnesota Press, 2018.

Nakamura, Lisa. *Digitizing Race: Visual Cultures of the Internet*. Minneapolis: University of Minnesota Press, 2008.

Nakamura, Lisa, and Peter A. Chow-White. "Introduction—Race and Digital Technology: Code, the Color Line, and the Information Society." In *Race after the Internet*, edited by Lisa Nakamura and Peter Chow-White, 7–24. New York: Routledge, 2013.

Nakamura, Lisa, and Peter A. Chow-White, eds. *Race after the Internet*. New York: Routledge, 2013.

National Archives and Records Administration. "Digitization at the National Archives." June 26, 2017. https://www.archives.gov/digitization.

National Archives UK. "What Discoveries Have You Made in the Archives?" YouTube, November 14, 2013. https://www.youtube.com/watch?v=h92aWHUsVrk.

National Archives UK. "What Would the World Look Like without Archives?" YouTube, November 14, 2013. https://www.youtube.com/watch?v=Rbs5UnzDQdY.

Noble, Safiya Umoja. *Algorithms of Oppression: How Search Engines Reinforce Racism*. New York: New York University Press, 2018.

Noordegraaf, Julia, Loes Opgenhaffen, and Norbert Bakker. "Cinema Parisien 3D: 3D Visualisation as a Tool for the History of Cinemagoing." *Alphaville*, no. 11 (2016): 45–61. http://www.alphavillejournal.com/Issue11/HTML/ArticleNoordegraaf_OpgenhaffenandBakker.html.

O'Donnell, Daniel. "The Unessay." Accessed October 16, 2014. http://people.uleth.ca/~daniel.odonnell/Teaching/the-unessay.

Onishi, Norimitsu. "Yokosuka Journal; Ripples from Perry's Ships Are Still Felt in Japan." *New York Times*, August 11, 2003. https://www.nytimes.com/2003/08/11/world/yokosuka-journal-ripples-from-perry-s-ships-are-still-felt-in-japan.html.

Onuoha, Mimi. "On Missing Data Sets." 2019. https://github.com/MimiOnuoha/missing-datasets.

Osterberg, Gayle. "Update on the Twitter Archive at the Library of Congress," *Library of Congress Blog*, December 26, 2017. https://blogs.loc.gov/loc/2017/12/update-on-the-twitter-archive-at-the-library-of-congress-2/.

Owens, Trevor. "The Crowd and The Library." May 20, 2012. http://www.trevorowens.org/2012/05/the-crowd-and-the-library/.

Owens, Trevor. "Digital Sources and Digital Archives: The Evidentiary Basis of Digital History (Draft)." December 5, 2015. http://www.trevorowens.org/2015/12/digital-sources-digital-archives-the-evidentiary-basis-of-digital-history-draft/.

Owens, Trevor. "2019 (Spring) Digital History Methods AMU—Digital History Methods." Accessed May 16, 2019. http://www.dighist.org/syllabi/syllabus-2019-amu-digital-history/.

Owens, Trevor. "What Do You Mean by Archive? Genres of Usage for Digital Preservers." February 27, 2014. //blogs.loc.gov/thesignal/2014/02/what-do-you-mean-by-archive-genres-of-usage-for-digital-preservers/.

Padilla, Thomas. "Getting Started with OpenRefine." June 30, 2015. http://thomaspadilla.org/dataprep.

Paju, Petri, Mila Oiva, and Mats Fridlund. "Digital and Distant Histories: Emergent Approaches within the New Digital History." In *Digital Histories: Emergent Approaches within the New Digital History*, edited by Mats Fridlund, Mila Oiva, and Petri Paju, 3–18. Helsinki: Helsinki University Press, 2020. https://doi.org/10.2307/j.ctv1c9hpt8.6.

Parr, Jessica. "Reflecting on Digital History." *Junto* (blog), January 26, 2017. https://earlyamericanists.com/2017/01/26/reflecting-on-digital-history/.

Paul, Richard, and Linda Elder. *Critical Thinking Competency Standards*. Tomales, CA: Foundation for Critical Thinking, 2005. http://www.criticalthinking.org/resources/PDF/CT-competencies%202005.pdf.

Perry, James. "Geo-Locating Census Micro-Data." *Current Research in Digital History* 1 (2018). https://doi.org/10.31835/crdh.2018.05.

Phillips, Murray G. "Wikipedia and History: A Worthwhile Partnership in the Digital Era?" *Rethinking History* 20, no. 4 (2016): 523–43.

Picard, Danielle, and Derek Bruff. "Digital Timelines." Vanderbilt University Center for Teaching and Learning, April 20, 2016. https://wpo.vanderbilt.edu/cft/guides-sub-pages/digital-timelines/.

Poole, Alex. "The Strange Career of Jim Crow Archives: Race, Space, and History in the Mid-Twentieth-Century American South." *American Archivist* 77, no. 1 (April 1, 2014): 23–63. https://doi.org/10.17723/aarc.77.1.g621m3701g821442.

Posner, Miriam. "Final Project—Introduction to Digital Humanities." Accessed August 23, 2018. http://miriamposner.com/classes/dh101f17/assignments/final-project/.

Posner, Miriam. "Humanities Data: A Necessary Contradiction." Accessed June 7, 2020. http://miriamposner.com/blog/humanities-data-a-necessary-contradiction/.

Posner, Miriam. "Introduction to Digital Humanities—DH101, Fall 2017." Accessed August 20, 2018. http://miriamposner.com/classes/dh101f17/.

Potter, Leah. "Creating Digital History." Fall 2017. https://s18798.pcdn.co/archivesandpublichistory/wp-content/uploads/sites/5465/2018/06/Fall-17-Creating-DH-Potter.pdf.

Preist, Chris, Daniel Schien, and Paul Shabajee. "Evaluating Sustainable Interaction Design of Digital Services: The Case of YouTube." In *Proceedings of the 2019 CHI Conference on Human Factors in Computing Systems*, paper no. 397, 1–12. New York: Association for Computing Machinery, 2019. https://doi.org/10.1145/3290605.3300627.

Prensky, Marc. "Digital Natives, Digital Immigrants." Accessed August 24, 2018. https://www.marcprensky.com/writing/Prensky%20-%20Digital%20Natives,%20Digital%20Immigrants%20-%20Part1.pdf.

Prescott, Andrew, and Lorna Hughes. "Why Do We Digitize? The Case for Slow Digitization." *Archive Journal*. Accessed July 11, 2019. http://www.archivejournal.net/?p=7962.

Presner, Todd. "The Ethics of the Algorithm: Close and Distant Listening to the Shoah Foundation Visual History Archive." In *Probing the Ethics of Holocaust Culture*, edited by Claudio Fogu, Wulf Kansteiner, and Todd Presner, 175–202. Cambridge, MA: Harvard University Press, 2016.

Purcell, Sarah J. "Visualizing Data (Excel PivotTables and Tableau)—Fall 2019: Digital History at Grinnell College." Accessed June 28, 2020. https://his100.sarahjpurcell.sites.grinnell.edu/fall-2019/tutorials/data-analysis-and-visualization/visualizing-data/.

Putnam, Lara. "The Transnational and the Text-Searchable: Digitized Sources and the Shadows They Cast." *American Historical Review* 121, no. 2 (April 1, 2016): 377–402. https://doi.org/10.1093/ahr/121.2.377.

Rawson, Katie, and Trevor Muñoz. "Against Cleaning." *Curating Menus* (blog), July 6, 2016. http://www.curatingmenus.org/articles/against-cleaning/.

Rehr, Jean-Paul. "Re-mapping the 'Great Inquisition' of 1245–46: The Case of Mas-Saintes-Puelles and Saint-Martin-Lalande." *Open Library of Humanities* 5, no. 1 (April 16, 2019): 28. https://doi.org/10.16995/olh.414.

Rettberg, Jill Walker. "Situated Data Analysis: A New Method for Analysing Encoded Power Relationships in Social Media Platforms and Apps." *Humanities and Social Sciences Communications* 7, no. 1 (June 17, 2020): 1–13. https://doi.org/10.1057/s41599-020-0495-3.

R Foundation. "R: What Is R?" Accessed July 6, 2020. https://www.r-project.org/.

Ridge, Mia. *Crowdsourcing Our Cultural Heritage*. New York: Routledge, 2017.

Ridge, Mia. "New Challenges in Digital History: Sharing Women's History on Wikipedia." 2013. http://repository.brynmawr.edu/greenfield_conference/papers/Saturday/37?utm_source=repository.brynmawr.edu%2Fgreenfield_conference%2Fpapers%2Fsaturday%2F37&utm_medium=PDF&utm_campaign=PDFCoverPages.

Risam, Roopika. "Decolonizing the Digital Humanities in Theory and Practice." May 2018. https://digitalcommons.salemstate.edu/cgi/viewcontent.cgi?article=1006&context=english_facpub.

Risam, Roopika. "'It's Data, Not Reality': On Situated Data with Jill Walker Rettberg." *Medium* (blog), June 29, 2020. https://medium.com/nightingale/its-data-not-reality-on-situated-data-with-jill-walker-rettberg-d27c71b0b451.

Risam, Roopika. *New Digital Worlds: Postcolonial Digital Humanities in Theory, Praxis, and Pedagogy*. Evanston, IL: Northwestern University Press, 2018.

Robertson, Stephen. "CHNM's Histories: Collaboration in Digital History." October 14, 2014. http://drstephenrobertson.com/blog-post/chnms-histories-collaboration-in-digital-history/.

Romano, Renee C., and Claire Bond Potter, eds. *Historians on "Hamilton": How a Blockbuster Musical Is Restaging America's Past*. New Brunswick, NJ: Rutgers University Press, 2018.

Rose, Colin. "HIST2P26: Intro to Digital History." Accessed September 17, 2019. https://colinrose.ca/teaching/hist2p26/.

Rosenzweig, Roy. "Can History Be Open Source? Wikipedia and the Future of the Past." *Journal of American History* 93, no. 1 (2006): 117–46.

Rosenzweig, Roy. "Scarcity or Abundance? Preserving the Past in a Digital Era." *American Historical Review* 108, no. 3 (June 1, 2003): 735–62. https://doi.org/10.1086/ahr/108.3.735.

Rosenzweig, Roy, and David Thelen. *The Presence of the Past: Popular Uses of History in American Life*. New York: Columbia University Press, 2000.

Rosinblum, John. "Teaching with Digital Archives." *Perspectives on History: The Newsmagazine of the American Historical Association*, November 2017. https://www.historians.org/publications-and-directories/perspectives-on-history/november-2017/teaching-with-digital-archives.

Rutner, Jennifer, and Roger Schonfeld. "Supporting the Changing Research Practices of Historians." *Ithaka S+R*, August 11, 2015. https://doi.org/10.18665/sr.22532.

Rybas, Natalia, and Radhika Gajjala. "Developing Cyberethnographic Research Methods for Understanding Digitally Mediated Identities." *Forum Qualitative Sozialforschung / Forum: Qualitative Social Research* 8, no. 3 (2007). https://www.qualitative-research.net/index.php/fqs/article/view/282.

Saeki, Chizuru. "The Perry Centennial of 1953 in Okinawa: U.S. Cultural Policy in Cold War Okinawa." *Journal of International and Area Studies* 19, no. 2 (2012): 13–27.

Salmi, Hannu. *What Is Digital History?* Cambridge: Polity Books, 2020.

Sandberg, Michael. "DataViz as History: When Napoleon Ventured East—Revising Minard's Map." *Michael Sandberg's Data Visualization Blog*, December 27, 2017. https://datavizblog.com/2017/12/27/dataviz-as-history-when-napoleon-ventured-east/.

Sanderson, Eric, Kim Fisher, Markley Boyer, Amanda Huron, and Danielle LaBruna. "The Welikia Project." Digital project. 2008. https://welikia.org/about/overview/.

Sassoon, Joanna. "Photographic Materiality in the Age of Digital Reproduction." *LASIE: Library Automated Systems Information Exchange* 29, no. 4 (1998): 5–15. https://search.informit.com.au/documentSummary;dn=753187057136599;res=IELHSS.

Saya. "First History Harvest: Teachers Share Their Prized Artifacts." *The International*. International School of the Sacred Heart, Tokyo, January 2014.

Scheinfeldt, Tom. "Stuff Digital Humanists Like: Defining Digital Humanities by Its Values." *Found History* (blog), December 2, 2010. http://foundhistory.org/2010/12/stuff-digital-humanists-like/.

Schmidt, Benjamin M. "Digital History 7370." 2017. http://benschmidt.org/dighist17/syllabus__syllabus.html#overview.

Schmidt, Benjamin M. "Sapping Attention: Reading Digital Sources: A Case Study in Ship's Logs." *Sapping Attention* (blog), November 15, 2012. http://sappingattention.blogspot.com/2012/11/reading-digital-sources-case-study-in.html.

Schmidt, Benjamin M. "Words Alone: Dismantling Topic Models in the Humanities." *Journal of Digital Humanities* 2, no. 1 (Winter 2012). http://journalofdigitalhumanities.org/2-1/words-alone-by-benjamin-m-schmidt/.

Schnapp, Jeffrey, Todd Presner, Peter Lunenfeld, and Johanna Drucker. "A Digital Humanities Manifesto." Accessed September 5, 2018. http://manifesto.humanities.ucla.edu/.

Scholars' Lab at the University of Virginia. "Praxis Program Charters—The Praxis Program." Accessed September 5, 2018. https://praxis.scholarslab.org/charter/.

Schulten, Susan. "Capturing the Past through Maps." In *Mapping the Nation: History and Cartography in Nineteenth-Century America*, 41–76. Chicago: University of Chicago Press, 2012.

Schwartz, Michelle, and Constance Crompton. "Remaking History: Lesbian Feminist Historical Methods in the Digital Humanities." In *Bodies of Information: Intersectional Feminism and the Digital Humanities*, edited by Elizabeth Losh and Jacqueline Wernimont, 131–56. Minneapolis: University of Minnesota Press, 2018.

Seefeldt, Douglas, and William G. Thomas. "What Is Digital History?" *Perspectives on History: The Newsmagazine of the American Historical Association*, May 1, 2009. https://www.historians.org/publications-and-directories/perspectives-on-history/may-2009/what-is-digital-history.

Seligman, Amanda. "Teaching Wikipedia without Apologies." In *Writing History in the Digital Age*, edited by Kristen Nawrotzki and Jack Dougherty, 121–30. Ann Arbor: University of Michigan Press, 2013. https://quod.lib.umich.edu/d/dh/12230987.0001.001/1:6/—writing-history-in-the-digital-age?g=dculture;rgn=div1;view=fulltext;xc=1.

Sherratt, Tim. "Exposing the Archives of White Australia." Accessed July 12, 2019. https://vimeo.com/60639104.

Sherratt, Tim. "It's All about the Stuff: Collections, Interfaces, Power, and People." *Journal of Digital Humanities*, March 9, 2012. http://journalofdigitalhumanities.org/1-1/its-all-about-the-stuff-by-tim-sherratt/.

Shrout, Anelise Hanson. "Data Cultures." Accessed June 23, 2020. https://docs.google.com/document/d/1DSB20K-GTPMcQkqoPG5d8JZYyOMU51vrbiUmxqI15PA/edit.

"SIUE's 'Madison Historical' Brings Digital History to High School Classroom." *EdGlenToday.Com*. Accessed September 5, 2018. http://www.edglentoday.com/articles/details/siues-madison-historical-brings-digital-history-to-high-school-classroom-28788.cfm.

Smith, Carl. "Can You Do Serious History on the Web?" *Perspectives on History: The Newsmagazine of the American Historical Association*, February 1, 1998. https://www.historians.org/publications-and-directories/perspectives-on-history/february-1998/can-you-do-serious-history-on-the-web.

Smith, Linda Tuhiwai. *Decolonizing Methodologies: Research and Indigenous Peoples*. London: Zed, 2013.

Smithsonian Institute 3D Digitization. "Apollo 11 CM." Accessed October 16, 2019. https://3d.si.edu/apollo11cm.

Soozandehfar, Seyyed Mohammad Ali, and Mohammad Reza Adeli. "A Critical Appraisal of Bloom's Taxonomy." *American Research Journal of English and Literature* 2 (2016). https://www.arjonline.org/papers/arjel/v2-i1/14.pdf.

Spiro, Lisa. "'This Is Why We Fight': Defining the Values of the Digital Humanities." In *Debates in the Digital Humanities*, edited by Matthew K. Gold, 16–36. Minneapolis: University of Minnesota Press, 2012. http://dhdebates.gc.cuny.edu/debates/text/13.

Spiro, Lisa, and Members of the Digital Humanities Education Group. "Digital Humanities Education." Accessed June 15, 2020. https://www.zotero.org/groups/25016/digital_humanities_education?

Stephens, Robert, and Josh Thumma. "Faculty-Undergraduate Collaboration in Digital History at a Public Research University." *History Teacher* 38, no. 4 (2005): 525–42. https://doi.org/10.2307/30036719.

Sternfeld, Joshua. "Historical Understanding in the Quantum Age." *Journal of Digital Humanities* 3, no. 2 (August 25, 2014). http://journalofdigitalhumanities.org/3-2/historical-understanding-in-the-quantum-age/.

Stoler, Ann Laura. *Along the Archival Grain: Epistemic Anxieties and Colonial Common Sense*. Princeton, NJ: Princeton University Press.

Swain, Larry. "Past, Present, and Future of Digital Medievalism." *Literature Compass* 9, no. 12 (December 1, 2012): 923–32. https://doi.org/10.1111/lic3.12011.

Szabo, Victoria. "Knowledge in 3D: How 3D Data Visualization Is Reshaping Our World." *Items* (blog). Accessed June 28, 2020. https://items.ssrc.org/parameters/knowledge-in-3d-how-3d-data-visualization-is-reshaping-our-world/.

Tabak, Edin. "A Hybrid Model for Managing DH Projects." *Digital Humanities Quarterly* 11, no. 1 (January 10, 2017). http://digitalhumanities.org:8081/dhq/vol/11/1/000284/000284.html.

Templeton, Clay, Travis Brown, Sayan Battacharyya, and Jordan Boyd-Graber. "Mining the Dispatch under Supervision: Using Casualty Counts to Guide Topics from the Richmond *Daily Dispatch* Corpus." Chicago Colloquium on Digital Humanities and Computer Science, 2011.

Theibault, John. "Visualizations and Historical Arguments." In *Writing History in the Digital Age*, edited by Kristen Nawrotzki and Jack Dougherty, 173–85. Ann Arbor: University of Michigan Press, 2013. https://quod.lib.umich.edu/d/dh/12230987.0001.001/1:8/—writing-history-in-the-digital-age?g=dculture;rgn=div1;view=fulltext;xc=1.

Theimer, Kate. "Archives in Context and as Context." *Journal of Digital Humanities* 1, no. 2 (June 26, 2012). http://journalofdigitalhumanities.org/1-2/archives-in-context-and-as-context-by-kate-theimer/.

Theimer, Kate. "A Distinction Worth Exploring: 'Archives' and 'Digital Historical Representations.'" *Journal of Digital Humanities* 3, no. 2 (August 4, 2014). http://journalofdigitalhumanities.org/3-2/a-distinction-worth-exploring-archives-and-digital-historical-representations/.

Thompson, Tyechia Lynn. "Baldwin's Paris." Accessed October 14, 2018. https://www.google.com/maps/d/viewer?mid=1RZRF9kyQy9woabmAeQIYECnLuaI.

Tracy, Dan. "LibGuides: Scalar: An Introduction: Home." Accessed June 29, 2020. http://guides.library.illinois.edu/c.php?g=348220&p=2348685.

Trivellato, Francesca. "Is There a Future for Italian Microhistory in the Age of Global History?" *California Italian Studies* 2, no. 1 (2011). https://escholarship.org/uc/item/0z94n9hq.

Trouillot, Michel-Rolph. *Silencing the Past: Power and the Production of History*. Boston: Beacon, 1995.

Tufte, Edward R. *The Visual Display of Quantitative Information*. Cheshire, CT: Graphics Press, 1983.

Turkel, William J. "How To." February 26, 2011. https://williamjturkel.net/how-to/.

Underwood, Ted. "Theorizing Research Practices We Forgot to Theorize Twenty Years Ago." *Representations* 127, no. 1 (August 1, 2014): 64–72. https://doi.org/10.1525/rep.2014.127.1.64.

United Nations High Commissioner for Refugees. "Figures at a Glance." Accessed July 9, 2019. https://www.unhcr.org/figures-at-a-glance.html.

Vaidhyanathan, Siva. *The Googlization of Everything (and Why We Should Worry)*. Berkeley: University of California Press, 2012.

van Hooland, Seth, Ruben Verborgh, and Max De Wilde. "Cleaning Data with OpenRefine." *Programming Historian*, August 5, 2013. http://programminghistorian.org/lessons/cleaning-data-with-openrefine.html.

van Strien, Daniel. "An Introduction to Version Control Using GitHub Desktop." *Programming Historian*, June 17, 2016. https://programminghistorian.org/en/lessons/getting-started-with-github-desktop.

Walsh, Brandon. "Editing Audio with Audacity." *Programming Historian*, August 5, 2016. https://programminghistorian.org/en/lessons/editing-audio-with-audacity.

Weatherhead East Asian Institute. "Asia for Educators." 2002. http://afe.easia.columbia.edu/.

WebAIM at Utah State University. WAVE Web Accessibility Evaluation Tool. Accessed July 6, 2020. https://wave.webaim.org/.

Weingart, Scott. "Demystifying Networks." *Scottbot Irregular* (blog), December 14, 2011. http://www.scottbot.net/HIAL/?p=6279.

Weingart, Scott, Shawn Graham, and Ian Milligan. "Principles of Information Visualization." In Shawn Graham, Ian Milligan, and Scott Weingart, *Exploring Big Historical Data: The Historian's Macroscope*. 2016. http://web.archive.org/web/20200618171130/http://www.themacroscope.org/?page_id=584.

Whisnant, Anne Mitchell. "Blue Ridge Parkway." Accessed August 23, 2018. https://docsouth.unc.edu/blueridgeparkway/about/about_project/acknowledgements/.

Whisnant, Anne Mitchell. "Names in Brick and Stone: Histories from UNC's Built Landscape | History/American Studies 671: Introduction to Public History, UNC–Chapel Hill." Accessed August 23, 2018. http://unchistory.web.unc.edu/.

Wieck, Lindsey Passenger. "Tutorial—Gathering and Curating Data." 2016. http://lindseywieck.org/fall_2016_sf/gatheringdatatutorial.html.

Williams, George. "Disability, Universal Design, and the Digital Humanities." In *Debates in the Digital Humanities*, edited by Matthew K. Gold, 202–12.

Minneapolis: University of Minnesota Press, 2012. http://dhdebates.gc.cuny.edu/debates/text/44.

Wingo, Rebecca. "Cincinnati's West End." Accessed September 16, 2019. https://rebeccawingo.com/courses/hist2098/.

Winterer, Caroline. "Where Is America in the Republic of Letters?" *Modern Intellectual History* 9, no. 3 (November 2012): 597–623. https://doi.org/10.1017/S1479244312000212.

Wolff, Robert. "The Historian's Craft, Popular Memory, and Wikipedia." In *Writing History in the Digital Age*, edited by Kristen Nawrotzki and Jack Dougherty, 64–74. Ann Arbor: University of Michigan Press, 2013.

Wolfram, Stephen. "What Is a Computational Essay?" Accessed September 14, 2018. https://writings.stephenwolfram.com/2017/11/what-is-a-computational-essay/.

Index

ABBYY FineReader, 100, 179
accessibility, 125–26
active learning, 45
"Against Cleaning" (Rawson and Muñoz), 28–29
aggregators, 87, 179
Ajapaik, 165, 179
Alexander, Bryan, 153
algorithms, 44–45, 179
Alliance for Networking Visual Culture, 157
Ambaras, David R., 154–57
American Social History Project, 4
Ancestry.com, 168
Ancient Lives, 165, 179
AnnoTate, 165, 179
annotation: of analog documents, 87–88; Hypothes.is, 91, 94; Scalar, 93*f*. *See also* source criticism
Anzaldúa, Gloria, 176
ArcGIS, 56, 179
ArcGIS StoryMaps, 159, 179
"Archive(s) Is a Foreign Country, The" (Cook), 132–33
archives, exhibits, and collections, digital: audience and, 139–40; community-based archives and digitization, 143–47; course planning, 140–43; definitions, 133, 183, 184; as digital historical representations, 133–34; Documenting Ferguson and DocNow, 144–45; historical thinking, relating to, 132–33, 146; history-visit-in-a-box, 131; LGBTQ history projects, 146; personal digital archiving, 131–32; physical archives, understanding, 130–31; Real Face of White Australia/National Archives of Australia exercise, 134–39, 135*f*, 137*f*; Revealing la Révolution, 129–30; speculative design exercise, 146–47; standards, 133–34
Arnold, Taylor, 79, 111–12
Assassin's Creed, 160
Atlanta Rail Corridor Archive, 140, 180
Audacity, 152, 180
audience: accessibility and, 125–26; archives and, 139–40; importance of, 8; storytelling and, 161–62; visualization and, 124–26
audio analysis, 180
augmented reality, 173, 180
authority, false or transferable, 64–65
Aydelotte, William O., 4
Ayers, Edward, 4

Bagnall, Kate, 134, 139
Baldwin, James, 122
Bartel, Nick, 118
Bates College history project, 23, 36–37
beginning-intermediate-advanced structure, 37–38, 173–74
Belanger, Elizabeth, 153–54
Ben Franklin's World podcast, 150, 162, 180
beta-tester, 180
bias: in datasets, 28–31; historical thinking and, 5–9. *See also* ethics
Bibliothèque Municipale de Toulouse, MS 609, 108–9
big data, 98, 180
Black Ships & Samurai website, 180
Blades, Rob, 77
Bloom's Revised Taxonomy for Learning, Teaching, and Assessing, 35, 180
Bodies and Structures, 154–57, 155*f*, 162, 180
Bonnett, John, 124
born-digital materials: as data, 21–22; defined, 90, 180, 201n2; loss in, 90–91; in personal digital archives, 131
Brennan, Sheila, 3
Brown, Vincent, 119–22
Bush, Erin, 59–60

Cabaret Commons, 146, 181
Call of Duty: World at War, 160
"Can You Do Serious History on the Web?" (Smith), 139
"Capturing the Past through Maps" (Schulten), 118–19
cárdenas, micha, 176
Cascading Style Sheets (CSS): beginning courses and, 174; CSS3, 119; defined, 181; digital literacy and, 41; Scalar and, 158; TimelineJS and, 40
census rolls as dataset, 26, 31
Center for Digital Storytelling, 153
Center for the History of Print and Digital Culture, 80
Century America, 62, 181
Citizen Archivist Dashboard, 165, 181
Civilization, 160
Clark, Emily Suzanne, 53–54
Clio, 56, 181
close listening, 181
close reading, 102, 108, 181
close viewing, 181
code, defined, 181
code repositories, 27, 77, 79, 181
collaboration: Africa and, 6; curricular arcs and, 173–74; disconnection, bridging, 7; Discover Indiana, 142–43; documentaries and, 154; ethics of student work and labor and, 65–66; learning outcomes and, 45–47; Omeka and, 142. *See also* community partnerships; crowdsourcing
Colony in Crisis, A, 129–30, 181
Colored Conventions, 165, 166*f*, 167, 181–82
command line, 104–5, 182
comma-separated value files, 24, 26–27, 182
community-based archives, 143–47, 182
community partnerships, 63, 176
computational analysis, 41, 182
Computational Historical Thinking (Mullen), 48, 182
Connected Histories, 182
content management systems (CMS), 73, 182. *See also* Mukurtu; Omeka; WordPress

Cook, Terry, 132–33
Cordell, Ryan, 54
Corlett-Rivera, Kelsey, 129–30
corpora, 79, 97–98, 103–5, 182
corpus analysis, 98, 182
counterdata, 30–31, 182
course evaluations, 50–52
Covart, Liz, 150–51
COVID-19, 20–21
Cowan, T. L., 146
Creative Commons, 158, 182
critique proficiency, 41–42
crowdsourcing, 163–70, 183
Crymble, Adam, 74–75
CSS. *See* Cascading Style Sheets
culminating digital projects, 61–65
Curatescape, 142
curricular arcs, 171–76. *See also* multi-course digital projects
Curti, Merle, 4

Dale, Elizabeth, 107
Dame-Grift, Avery, 146
data and datasets: assembling datasets for classroom use, 31–32; assembly and curation, 24–28, 25*f*; biases and ethics, 28–31; counterdata, 30–31; COVID-19 example, 20–21; data aggregation, 183; data curation, 27–28, 183; data feminism, 28–29; data literacy, 41, 183; data mining, 183; data privacy, 63; data standardization, 26, 29, 183; defined, 183; humanist scholarship, complexity, and situatedness, 22–23; identification and transformation, 23–24; missing datasets, data saturation, and quality, 29–30; multiclass, 173; qualitative data, 20, 194; quantitative data, 20, 114, 194; research data, 27, 195; as research publication, 32–33; source criticism, 86–87; structured and unstructured data, 20, 197, 199; tabular data, 26, 197; text analysis and quality data, 109; time-series data, 112
database, defined, 183
Data Curation Guide, 27, 183
decision making, methods and, 76
dendrograms, 112
Denial, Cate, 54–55
DH Box, 78, 183
digital assets: annotation of, 157; crowdsourcing, 169; defined, 183; embedding, 159; source criticism and, 94; TimelineJS and, 40; transforming formats, 133–34
digital divide and digital insecurity, 7–8
digital documentary editions, 92, 184. *See also* SourceLab
digital exhibits and collections. *See* archives, exhibits, and collections, digital
digital historical representations, 133–34, 184. *See also* archives, exhibits, and collections, digital
digital history: definitions of, 2–4, 184; review of, 44–45
Digital History Reviews criteria, 41–42
digital humanities. *See* humanities, digital
Digital Humanities Manifesto 2.0 (Schnapp), 46, 184
Digital Karnak, 123–24, 184
digital literacy, 41, 184
Digital Mappa, 80, 184
Digital National Security Archive (DNSA), 99–100
digital object identifier (DOI), 184
Digital Panopticon, 184–85

Digital Public Library of America (DPLA), 87, 185
digital repositories, defined, 185. *See also* archives, exhibits, and collections, digital; code repositories
digital reproduction, defined, 185
digital source criticism. *See* source criticism
digital surrogates: Colored Conventions and, 166*f*; as data, 21; defined, 92, 185; digitization workflow and, 88–89; downloading, 27–28; Real Face of White Australia and, 137–38, 137*f*; SourceLab and, 92
digitization: community-based, 143–46; defined, 185; three-dimensional, 198; workflow of, 88–89
D'Ignazio, Catherine, 28, 30
dimensions and measures, 117
directory structures, 49, 185
Discover Indiana, 142–43, 185
distant listening, 185
distant reading, 100–101, 185
distant viewing, 100–101, 185
Distant Viewing Toolkit, 79, 185
"Distinction Worth Exploring, A" (Theimer), 133
DIYHistory (University of Iowa), 165, 185
Dize, Nathan, 129
documentaries, 153–54
Documenting Ferguson, 144, 186
Documenting the American South, 29, 186
Documenting the Now (DocNow), 144–45, 186
Dolan-Mescal, Alexandra, 145
drafts and revision, 42–45
Dublin Core, 61–62, 141, 186
Du Bois, W. E. B, 55
DuckDuckGo, 186
dynamic visualization, 116, 186

Engerman, Stanley, 4
Estonian Photographic Heritage Society, 165
ethics: crowdsourcing and, 168; datasets and, 28–31; digital tools as sites of resistance, 176; of student work and labor, 65–66. *See also* bias
ethnography, digital, 73, 184
Europeana Network Association, 122, 186
Europeana 1914–1918, 186
Ewing, E. Thomas, 115–16
Exploring Big Data: The Historian's Macroscope (Graham, Milligan, and Weingart), 106–7, 113, 187

Facebook, 5, 20, 23, 125, 186
faceting, 116
"facts and FACTS" (Garvey), 29
"Faculty-Undergraduate Collaboration in Digital History at a Public Research University" (Stephens and Thumma), 45–46
failure, fear of, 67–69
FamilySearch, 169
Favro, Diane, 123
feminism, 5, 28–29, 136, 146
fictionalized history, 149–50
Flanders, Julia, 27
Fleisher, Jack, 115
Flickr, 40, 58, 186
fluency principle, 9
Fogel, Robert, 4
Franks, Bobby, 60*f*
frequency analysis, 98–99, 103, 186
Fridlund, Mats, 2

Friedman, Matthew, 160
FromthePage, 165, 186

Gale Cengage, 27
game design, 159–61, 187
Garvey, Ellen Gruber, 29
geographic information systems, 187. *See also* ArcGIS
geography, influence of, 117–18. *See also* maps and mapping
Gephi, 187
Gernes, Todd, 153–54
Getty Museum, 168
Git, defined, 187
GitHub, 27, 77–78, 78*f*, 187
GitHub Pages, 187
Glebe, Graeme, 152–53
global positioning system (GPS), 5
Google, 135, 187
Google Docs, 105
Google Earth, 187
Google Lit Trips, 122–23, 187
Google Maps, 56, 59, 187
Google MyMap, 58
Graham, Shawn, 77–79, 106–7
grant proposals, 140
graphing, hierarchical, 112
Great War Archive (Oxford), 165, 187
guided study, 26
Guldi, Jo, 2–3

Ha, Jae, 115
Hadjikyriacou, Antonis, 92, 122
Hamilton (Miranda), 149–50
Hammel, Joey, 115
Han, Shin-Kap, 107
Haraway, Donna, 22, 176
harm assessments, 147
Hart, Jennifer, 6
hashtags, 68, 187
Heppler, Jason, 107
Hicks, Mar, 136
high-performance computing, 2, 187
histograms, 112
Historian's Macroscope (Graham, Milligan, and Weingart), 106–7, 113, 187
historical thinking: archives and, 132–33, 146; *Computational Historical Thinking* (Mullen), 48, 182; curricular arcs and, 175; digital history, biases, and, 5–9; storytelling and, 162
History Harvest, 131–32, 188
History Matters, 4
HistoryPin, 58, 188
History Twitter, 54
history-visit-in-a-box, 131
Hollerith Machines, 4, 188
Homicide in Chicago 1870–1930, 59, 188
humanities, digital: core values, 46; defined, 184; digital history and, 3, 46; *Digital Humanities Manifesto 2.0* (Schnapp), 46, 184; professional associations, 50; "A Student Collaborators' Bill of Rights" and, 66; unessays and, 54
Humanities Intensive Learning and Teaching Institute (HILT), 171–72, 175, 188
hyperlinking, 116
Hypertext Markup Language (HTML), 41, 79–80, 158, 174, 188
Hypertext Markup Language (HTML) 5, 119, 188
Hypothes.is, 91, 94, 188

image analysis, 79, 188. *See also* visualization
immersive experiences, 112, 188

independent study, 174–75
influence mapping, 101, 188
information literacy, 41, 188
Instagram, 20, 61, 125, 189
interactive visualization, 116, 189
interfaces, 136–39, 189
Internet Archive, 158, 189. *See also* Wayback Machine
Invisible Australians, 134, 189
IPython, 78–79, 189
"It's All about the Stuff" (Sherrat), 138

JavaScript, 40, 174, 189
JavaScript Object Notation (JSON) data format, 40, 189
Jekyll, 189
Johnson, Jessica Marie, 121
Jones, Christopher, 53
Journal of American History, 41
JSTOR, 27
Jupyter notebook, 77, 189
Justice, Austin R., 93*f*

Kaufman, Micki, 99–101
Kheraj, Sean, 152–53
Klein, Lauren F., 28, 30
Knight Lab, 59. *See also* TimelineJS
Koeser, Rebecca Sutton, 102
Kramer, Michael J., 139

Lab for the Education and Advancement in Digital Research (LEADR), Michigan State University, 40–41
Langer, Adina, 140
Lawrence, Adrea, 164
Leaflet, 119, 174, 189
Learning Lab (Smithsonian), 87
learning management software (LMS), 91
learning outcomes: Bates College example, 36–37; beginning-intermediate-advanced structure, 37–38; Bloom's Taxonomy, 35; collaboration, 45–47; computational digital history methods, 48; course evaluations and, 50–52; course syllabi and student expectations, 48–50; critique proficiency, 41–42; customized, 45; digital history reviews, 44–45; drafts and revisions, 42–45; history, method, technology formula, 36–41; peer review, 42–44
Leon, Sharon, 105
Leopold, Nathan, Jr., 60*f*
LexisNexis, 27
LGBTQ+, defined, 189
Liberated Africans, 189
Library of Congress, US: Oregon Trail collection, 160; Personal Digital Archiving site, 131–32; Twitter Archive, 145
Lincoln Logarithms (Emory University Digital Scholarship Commons), 98, 98*f*
linguistic analysis, 102
link rot, 190
Liverpool as a Trading Port website, 190
Locating London's Past, 190
Loeb, Richard, 60*f*
London Lives, 1690–1800, 190
Lorde, Audre, 176
Loucadellis, Jonathan, 152–53
Lowe, Brian, 39
Lowe, Charles, 98
Luxembourg Centre for Contemporary and Digital History (C^2DH), 89

MacLeod, Maureen, 55
macro-history, 190

Madison Historical, 190
Magazine of Early America, 107
MALLET, 78–79, 104, 190
"Manifesto for the Digital Humanities," 46
Mapping Ararat—An Imaginary Jewish Homelands, defined, 190
Mappingthenation.com, 119, 190
Mapping the Republic of Letters, 107, 190
maps and mapping, 114–15, 118–23, 120*f*
Markowitz, Eliz, 153
markup, 165, 191
Mason, Austin, 161
"Mathematics Black Life" (McKittrick), 23–24
Matthews-Jones, Lucinda, 55
McCall, Jeremiah, 159–60
McClurken, Jeffrey, 41–42, 62–63
McDaniel, Caleb, 103, 105–6
McDonald, Kate, 154–57
McKittrick, Katherine, 23–24
McLeod, Dayna, 146
McNeill Center for Early American Studies, 107
measures and dimensions, 117
mediation, layers of, 103
metadata: creation of, 92, 131, 165; defined, 191; Documenting Ferguson, 144; Omeka and, 141–42; peer review and, 42–43; Photogrammar and, 111; Ranke.2 and, 90; standards and, 133–34, 144
methods: analog origins, 71–73; decision-making process, 76; defined, 72; depth of methodological knowledge, 80–81; exposition of, 72; micro-projects and analog vs. digital methods, 58; research notebooks, 76–79; templates, 79–80; *TPH* tutorials, 73–76; trends, 81
micro-history, 191
micro-projects, digital, 55–61
Migration Heritage Center of New South Wales, 134
Milligan, Ian, 106–7
Minard, Charles Joseph, 114–15
Mining the *Dispatch*, 101–2, 104, 191
Miranda, Lin-Manuel, 149
mobile applications, 58, 119, 142, 191
Molvig, Ole, 38–39
Moravec, Michelle, 136
Morris, James Harry, 160–61
Mukurtu, 56, 145–46, 191
Mullen, Lincoln A., 48
multicourse digital projects, 62–63, 66, 140–41. *See also* curricular arcs
multimodal and motivocal storytelling, 154–58, 191
Muñoz, Trevor, 27, 28–29
Murray, Padmini Ray, 143
musicology, digital, 151, 184

named entity recognition (NER), 104–6, 191
National Archives, US, 165
National Archives and Records Administration (NARA), 168–69
National Archives of Australia, 134–38
National Archives UK video series, 130
National Recording Preservation Board, 151
Natural Language Toolkit, 79, 191
Nelson, Robert K., 101–2
network analysis, 106–9, 112, 191
networking, professional, 50
networks, defined, 191
1911 Triangle Factory Fire project, 59, 191
node visualizations, 112
Noe, Kenneth, 101

nonlinearity, 121
nonlinear storytelling, 154–58
North American Slave Narratives collection (Documenting the American South), 29
notebooks, research, 76–79

OCRopus, 100, 191
O'Donnell, Daniel, 54
Oiva, Mila, 2
Old Bailey Proceedings Online, 192
Old Weather, 165–67, 192
Omeka: archives and, 140–42, 146; culminating digital projects and, 61–62; defined, 192; micro-projects and, 58; Mukurtu compared to, 146; research notebooks and, 78–79; Scripto and, 167–68
Omeka+Curatescape, 65–66, 142
Omohundro Institute of Early American History and Culture, 150–51
Onuoha, Mimi, 29–30
Open Archival Information System (OAIS), 192
Open Archival Information System (OAIS) reference model, 133
open educational resources, 73, 192
OpenGIS, 173
OpenRefine, 26, 192
optical character recognition (OCR), 100, 192
oral history, 73, 192
Oral History in the Digital Age (Michigan State), 73; defined, 192
ORBIS: The Stanford Geospatial Network Model of the Roman World, 192
Oregon Trail game, 160
"Other Ride of Paul Revere, The" (Han), 107
Ottaway, Susannah, 161
Owens, Trevor, 58, 90–91, 133
Owsley, Frank, 4
Owsley, Harriet, 4

Paju, Petri, 2
Palladio, 107, 192
Papers of the War Department Project, 167, 192–93
Parr, Jessica, 140–41
partnerships. *See* collaboration; community partnerships
Pearson, Ellen Holmes, 62–63
peer review: collegial, 51–52; among students, 42–44, 91–92, 141–42
Peihuo, Cai, 157
Pelagios Network, 122, 193
personal digital archiving, 131–32, 193
Personal Histories (Holocaust Memorial Museum), 193
phone directory project, 24–26, 25*f*
Photogrammar, 111–12, 193
photogrammetry, 112, 193
platform: defined, 193; platform studies, 193
Play the Past, 2, 193
podcasts, 150–53, 193
Policía Nacional de Guatemala / Guatemalan National Police Historical Archive, 144, 193
Portal to Texas History, 106, 194
Posner, Miriam, 22, 26
Potter, Leah, 41
probability analysis, 194
probability theory, 74–75
Programming Historian (*PH*), 73–76, 174, 194
Prospect, 194
Puar, Jasbir, 176

public history, digital: Atlanta Rail Corridor Archive, 140; caution with, 64; culminating projects, 61–62; Discover Indiana, 142–43; grant proposals, 140; history of, 4; National Council on Public History, 50
Purcell, Sarah J., 117
Putnam, Lara, 121
Python, 78*f*, 79, 104, 194

QGIS, 194
qualitative data, 20; defined, 194
qualitative history, defined, 194
Quality Matters (QM), 51, 194
Quantifying Kissinger, 99–100, 194
quantitative data, 20, 114, 194
quantitative history, 194
Queer Digital History Project, 146, 194

R (programming language), 48, 56, 195
Rainbow History Project, 146, 195
Randolph, John, 92
Ranke.2, 89–90, 195
Rault, Jasmine, 146
Rawson, Katie, 28–29
Real Face of White Australia, 44, 134, 135*f*, 137–39, 137*f*, 195
Reclaim Hosting, 59, 195
Recogito, 92–94, 122, 195
Recogito2, 195
regression analysis, 74–75, 195
regular expressions, 104, 195
Rehr, Jean-Paul, 108–9
repositories, defined, 195. *See also* archives, exhibits, and collections, digital; code repositories
research data. *See* data and datasets
research life cycle, 195
research notebooks, 76–79
Rettberg, Jill Walker, 22
Revealing la Révolution, 129–30
Risam, Roopika, 86
Rose, S. Colin, 124
Rosenzweig Center for History and New Media, 89
RStudio, 78–79, 195
Rubin, Anne Sarah, 4

Salmi, Hanna, 2
Scalar: annotation, 93*f*; defined, 196; peer-review checklists, 43; storytelling, 157–59; templates, 79–80; version updates and, 67
scatter-plot matrices, 112
Scheinfeldt, Tom, 46
Schmidt, Benjamin M., 28, 103
Schulten, Susan, 118–19
Sci2 tool, 107, 196
scripting, 105
Scripto, 167–68, 196
secondary sources, 41, 57, 94–95
Segrada, 107, 196
Seligman, Amanda, 164
sentiment mapping, 101, 196
Sherratt, Tim, 44, 134, 138–39
Shrout, Anelise H., 23, 36–37
SIMILE, 56
simulation, 123
situatedness, 22
SketchUp, 196
Slave Revolt in Jamaica, 1760–1761, 119–20, 120*f*, 196
Smith, Carl, 139
Smith, Linda Tuhiwai, 7
Smithsonian Institution, 87, 165
SnapChat, 125, 196
Social Humans (SH) Labels, 145, 196

social media: community-based archives and, 144–45; datasets and, 20–21, 86; ethical concerns, 5; as historical network, 107; micro-projects and, 61; optional assignments, 44; personal digital archives and, 131–32; seeking help via, 50; TimelineJS and, 40; visualizations on, 113. *See also specific platforms*
software, defined, 196
sonification studies, 151, 196
sound. *See* podcasts
SoundCloud, 40, 196
source criticism: analog document annotation, 87–88; definitions, 185, 196; digital aggregators and, 87; digitization workflow, 88–89; Hypothes.is, 91, 94; loss in born-digital sources, 90–91; peer review, 91–92; personal data tracking assignment, 86–87; Ranke.2, 89–90; secondary sources, 94–95; as starting point, 85–86; Tropy, 89; visual materials and Recogito, 92–94, 93*f*
SourceLab, 92, 196–97
sources as data. *See* data and datasets
spatial history, 38, 122, 154–59, 197
speculative design, 146–47
Spiro, Lisa, 46
Stanford Named Entity Recognizer, 105, 197
Stasiek, Artur, 93*f*
static visualization, 116, 197
Stein, Chris, 153
Stephens, Robert, 45–46, 130
StoryMapJS, 59, 197
storytelling: audience and, 161–62; Bodies and Structures, 154–57, 155*f*; defined, 185; documentaries, 153–54; fictionalized history, 149–50; gaming, 159–61; multimodal, multivocal, and nonlinear, 154–58; peer-review checklists, 43; podcasts, 150–53; Scalar, 157–59; Twine, 160–61; WordPress, Twitter, and ArcGIS, 159
Strong, Kimberly R., 60*f*
structured data, 20, 197
struggling students, 68–69
"Student Collaborators' Bill of Rights, A," 66, 197
student expectations, 48–50
"Stuff Digital Humanists Like" (Scheinfeldt), 46
syllabi, 48–50, 69–70, 207n19
Szabo, Victoria, 123

Tableau Public, 117, 174, 197
tabular data, 26, 197
TAPoR3, 116–17, 197
"Teaching History with Digital Historical Games" (McCall), 160
templates, digital, 79–80
Tesseract, 100, 197
text analysis: about, 97; corpus analysis, 98; defined, 97, 198; distance reading, 100–101; frequency analysis, 98–99, 103; hard sciences and, 109–10; Mining the *Dispatch* (Nelson), 101–2, 104; named entity recognition (NER), 104–6; optical character recognition (OCR), 100; Quantifying Kissinger (Kaufman), 99–100; topic modeling, 102–3
text encoding, 49, 198
Theibault, John, 114–15
Theimer, Kate, 133
"This Is Why We Fight" (Spiro), 46
Thomas, William G., III, 4
Thompson, Tyechia, 122

three-dimensional digitization, 198
three-dimensional visualization, 123–24, 198
Thumma, Josh, 45–46, 130
Tiki-Toki, 38–39, *39f*, 43, 198
Tilton, Lauren, 79, 111–12
TimelineJS (Knight Lab), 40, 43, 56, 59, 198
timeline technology, 38–40, *39f*
time-series data, 112
tools, defined, 198
topic modeling, 102–3, 198
Torget, Andrew, 4, 103, 105–6
Traditional Knowledge Labels, 145, 198
Transcribe Bentham, 165, 198
transcription: accessibility and, 125–26; crowdsourcing and, 165–69; defined, 198; OCR, 100
tree diagrams, 112
Tropy, 89, 198
Trove, 87, 198
Trusted Repository Archiving Checklist (TRAC), 133, 198
Tufte, Edward, 114
Tumblr, 61, 199
tutorials: Audacity, 152; in group, 69; *TPH*, 73–76, 174; version updates and, 67
Twine, 160–61, 199
Twitter: defined, 199; digital history review assignments, 44; Library of Congress Twitter Archive, 145; storytelling, 159; students on, 125; Twitterstorians, 150

unessays, 53–55
uniform resource locator (URL), 199
unstructured data, 20, 199
Upadhyay, Archana, *93f*

Valley of the Shadow, 4, 199
version updates, 66–67
Virtual Angkor, 124, 199
Virtual Paul's Cross, 199
virtual reality, 123, 199
visualization: about, 112; analog-digital relationship, 114; audience, accessibility, and, 124–26; bad visualizations and redesign exercise, 113–14; communication and interpretation, 115–17; defined, 112, 199; density and transparency, 114; dynamic, interactive, and static, 116, 186, 189, 197; limitations, 121–22; maps and mapping, 114–15, 118–23, *120f*; Photogrammar, 111–12; Tableau, 117; three-dimensional, 123–24
visual materials: dataset limitations, 48; Scalar and, 158; source criticism with, 92–94, *93f*
Voyant Tools, 98, 173, 199
VSim, 123–24, 199

Wakelet, 61, 199
Walden, Katherine, 117
Walsh, Brandon, 152
Wayback Machine, 91. *See also* Internet Archive
Waze, 163
Web Accessibility Evaluation Tool (WAVE), 126
website, defined, 199
Weingart, Scott, 106–7
Wexler, Laura, 111–12
"What Do You Mean by Archive?" (Owens), 133
White, Pliny, 98
Who Built America? (Clark and Hewitt; Rosenzweig and Lichtenstein), 200

Wieck, Lindsey Passenger, 24–26
Wikipedia, 125, 163–64, 200
Wingo, Rebecca, 61–62
Winterer, Caroline, 107
WordPress: culminating digital projects and, 62; defined, 200; Mukurtu compared to, 146; one infrastructure across courses, 66; storytelling, 159; templates, 79–80
"Words Alone" (Schmidt), 103
workbenches, 80
World Wide Web Consortium standards, 126

Yang, Timothy, 156, 157
YouTube, 40, 124, 157–58, 200

Zotero, 49–50, 200